PARROTT • CARLINI • ANGULO

SABAN'S

GO GO POWER RANGERS

VOLUME FOUR

BOOM!
STUDIOS

SABAN'S GO GO

SERIES DESIGNER
MICHELLE ANKLEY

COLLECTION DESIGNER
CHELSEA ROBERTS

ASSISTANT EDITOR
GWEN WALLER

EDITOR
DAFNA PLEBAN

SENIOR VICE PRESIDENT, POWER RANGERS FRANCHISE DEVELOPMENT & PRODUCTION
BRIAN CASENTINI

HASBRO STORY TEAM
MELISSA FLORES, JASON BISCHOFF, PAUL STRICKLAND, ED LANE, BETH ARTALE, AND MICHAEL KELLY

SABAN'S GO GO POWER RANGERS Volume Four, July 2019. Published by BOOM! Studios, a division of Boom Entertainment, Inc. Power Rangers and related characters are trademarks of SCG Power Rangers LLC and are used with permission. ™ and © 2019 SCG Power Rangers LLC and Hasbro. All Rights Reserved. Used Under Authorization. Originally published in single magazine form as SABAN'S GO GO POWER RANGERS No. 13-16. ™ & © 2019 SCG Power Rangers LLC and Hasbro. All Rights Reserved. BOOM! Studios™ and the BOOM! Studios logo are trademarks of Boom Entertainment, Inc., registered in various countries and categories. All characters, events, and institutions depicted herein are fictional. Any similarity between any of the names, characters, persons, events, and/or institutions in this publication to actual names, characters, and persons, whether living or dead, events, and/or institutions is unintended and purely coincidental. BOOM! Studios does not read or accept unsolicited submissions of ideas, stories, or artwork.

For information regarding the CPSIA on this printed material, call (203) 595-3636 and provide reference #RICH - 844877.

BOOM! Studios, 5670 Wilshire Boulevard, Suite 400, Los Angeles, CA 90036-5679. Printed in USA. First Printing.

ISBN: 978-1-68415-368-8, eISBN: 978-1-64144-351-7

Licensed by:

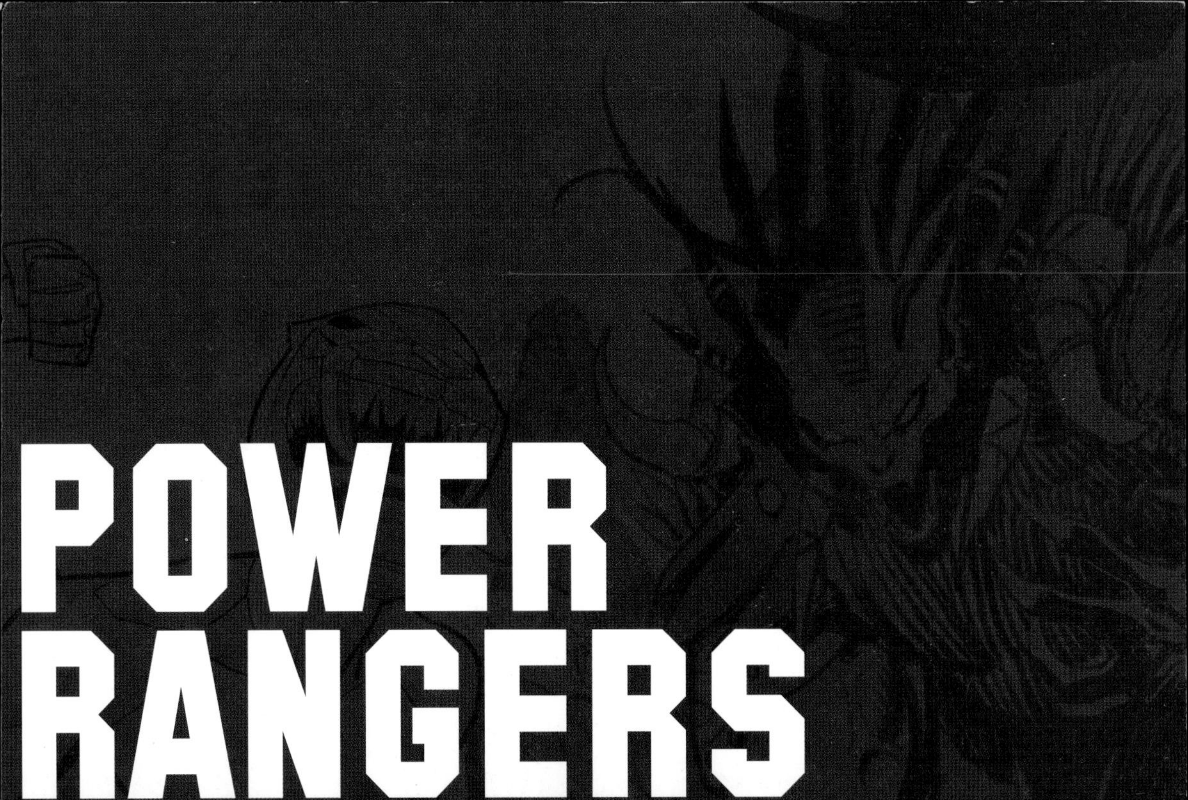

POWER RANGERS

THIRTEEN

DAN MORA | ISSUE THIRTEEN MAIN COVER

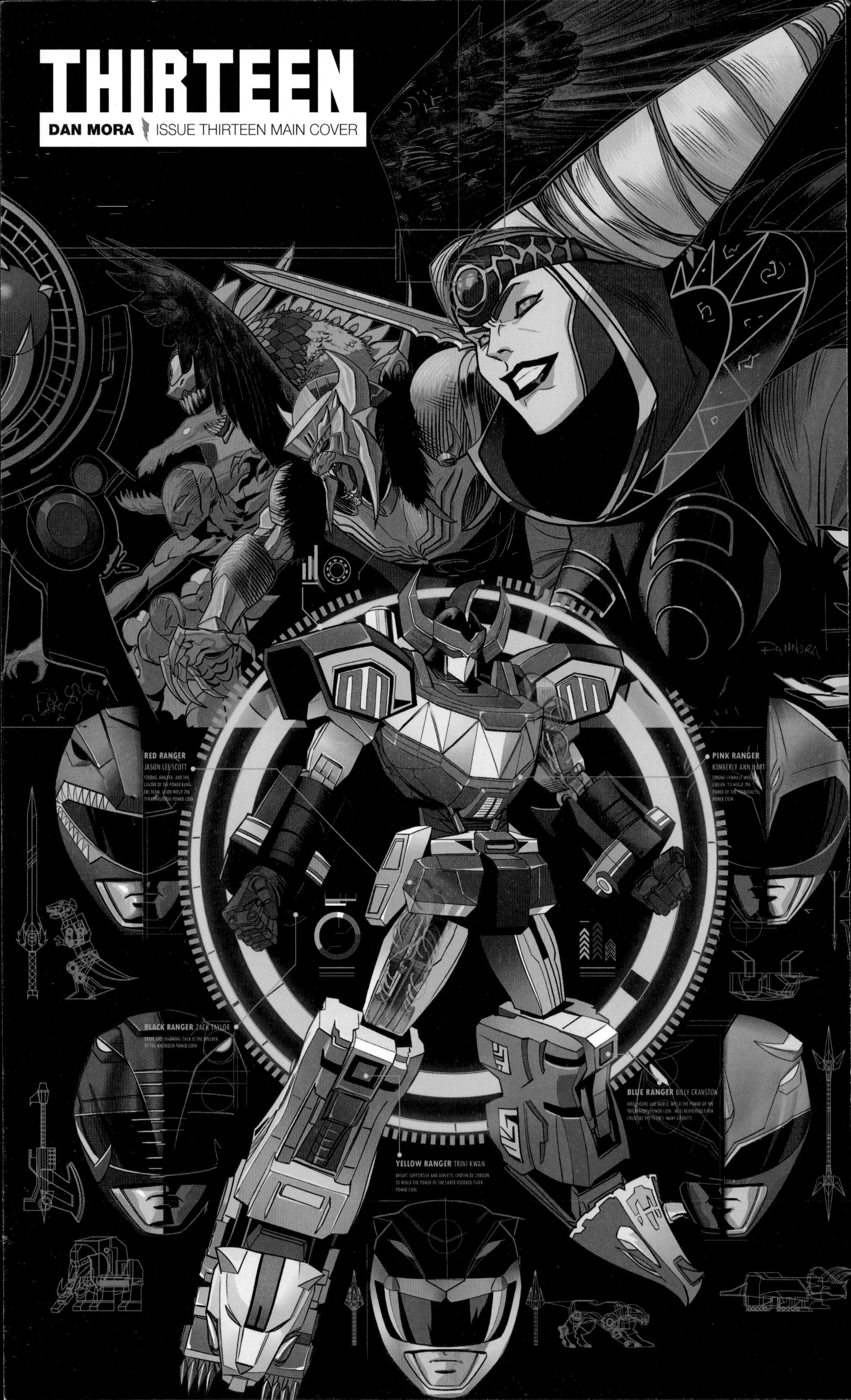

DANMORA
RED RANGER
JASON LEE SCOTT
STRONG, ATHLETIC AND THE LEADER OF THE POWER RANGERS TEAM, JASON WIELD THE TYRANNOSAURUS POWER COIN
PINK RANGER
KIMBERLY ANN HART
STRONG GYMNAST WHO CHOSEN TO WIELD THE
BLACK RANGER ZACK TAYLOR
BRAVE AND CHARMING, ZACK IS THE WIELDER OF THE MASTODON POWER COIN
BLUE RANGER BILLY CRANSTON
INTELLIGENT AND NOBLE, WIELD THE POWER OF THE
YELLOW RANGER TRINI KWAN
BRIGHT, SUPPORTIVE AND ATHLETIC CHOSEN BY ZORDON TO WIELD THE POWER OF THE SABER-TOOTHED TIGER POWER COIN

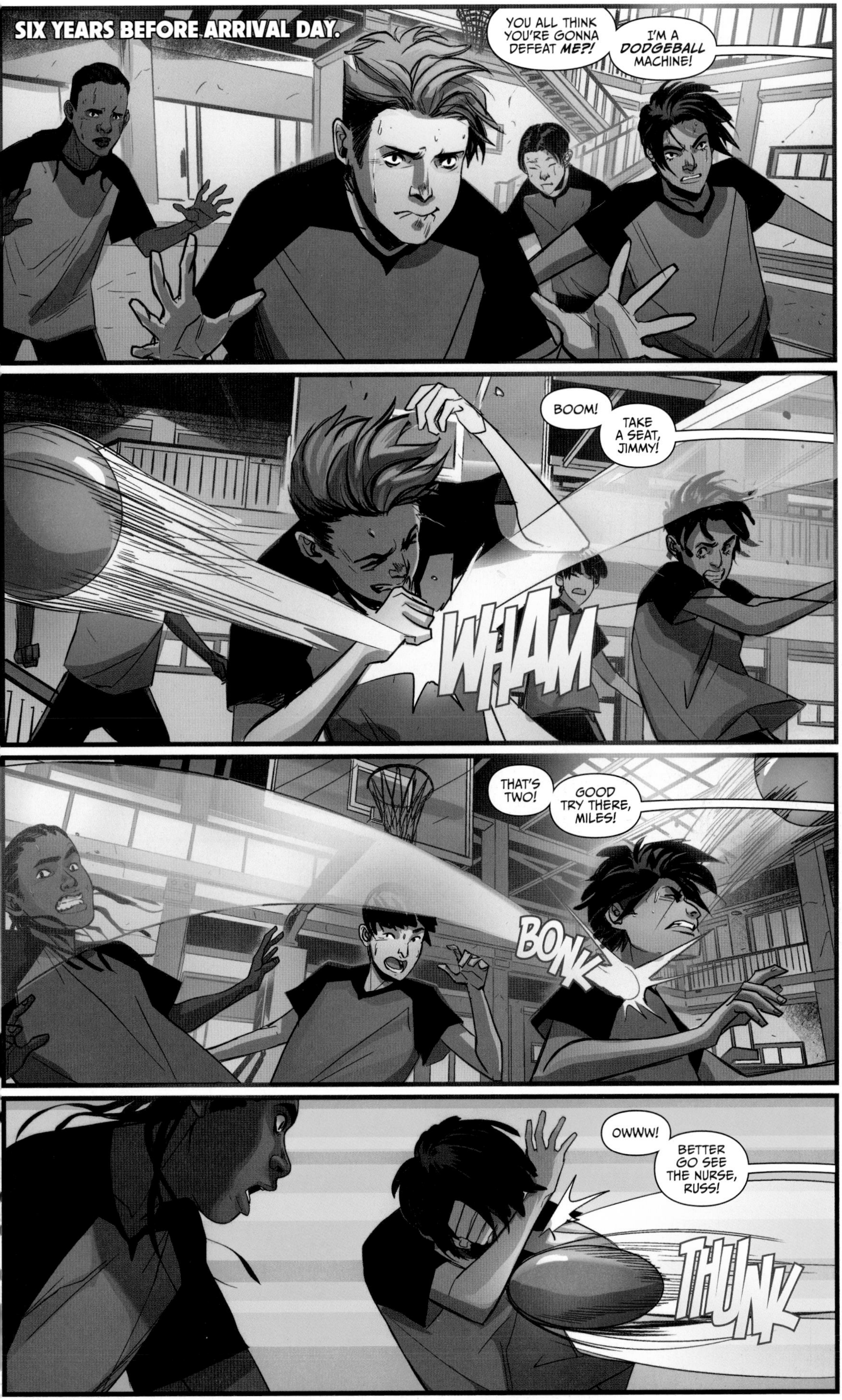
SIX YEARS BEFORE ARRIVAL DAY.
YOU ALL THINK YOU'RE GONNA DEFEAT *ME?!*
I'M A *DODGEBALL* MACHINE!
BOOM!
TAKE A SEAT, JIMMY!
WHAM
THAT'S TWO!
GOOD TRY THERE, MILES!
BONK
OWWW!
BETTER GO SEE THE NURSE, RUSS!
THUNK

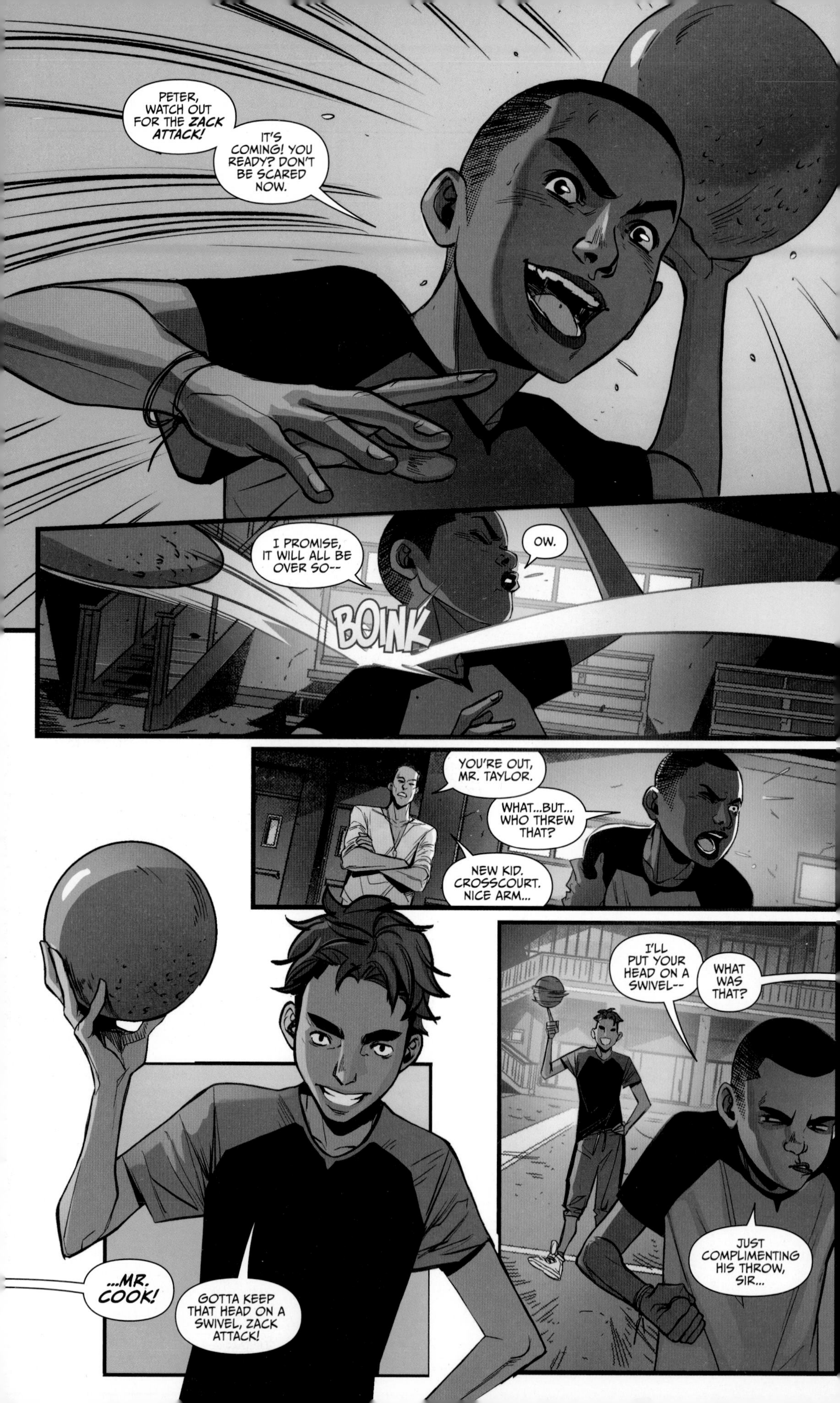

PETER, WATCH OUT FOR THE ZACK ATTACK!
IT'S COMING! YOU READY? DON'T BE SCARED NOW.
I PROMISE, IT WILL ALL BE OVER SO--
OW.
BOINK
YOU'RE OUT, MR. TAYLOR.
WHAT...BUT... WHO THREW THAT?
NEW KID. CROSSCOURT. NICE ARM...
...MR. COOK!
GOTTA KEEP THAT HEAD ON A SWIVEL, ZACK ATTACK!
I'LL PUT YOUR HEAD ON A SWIVEL--
WHAT WAS THAT?
JUST COMPLIMENTING HIS THROW, SIR...

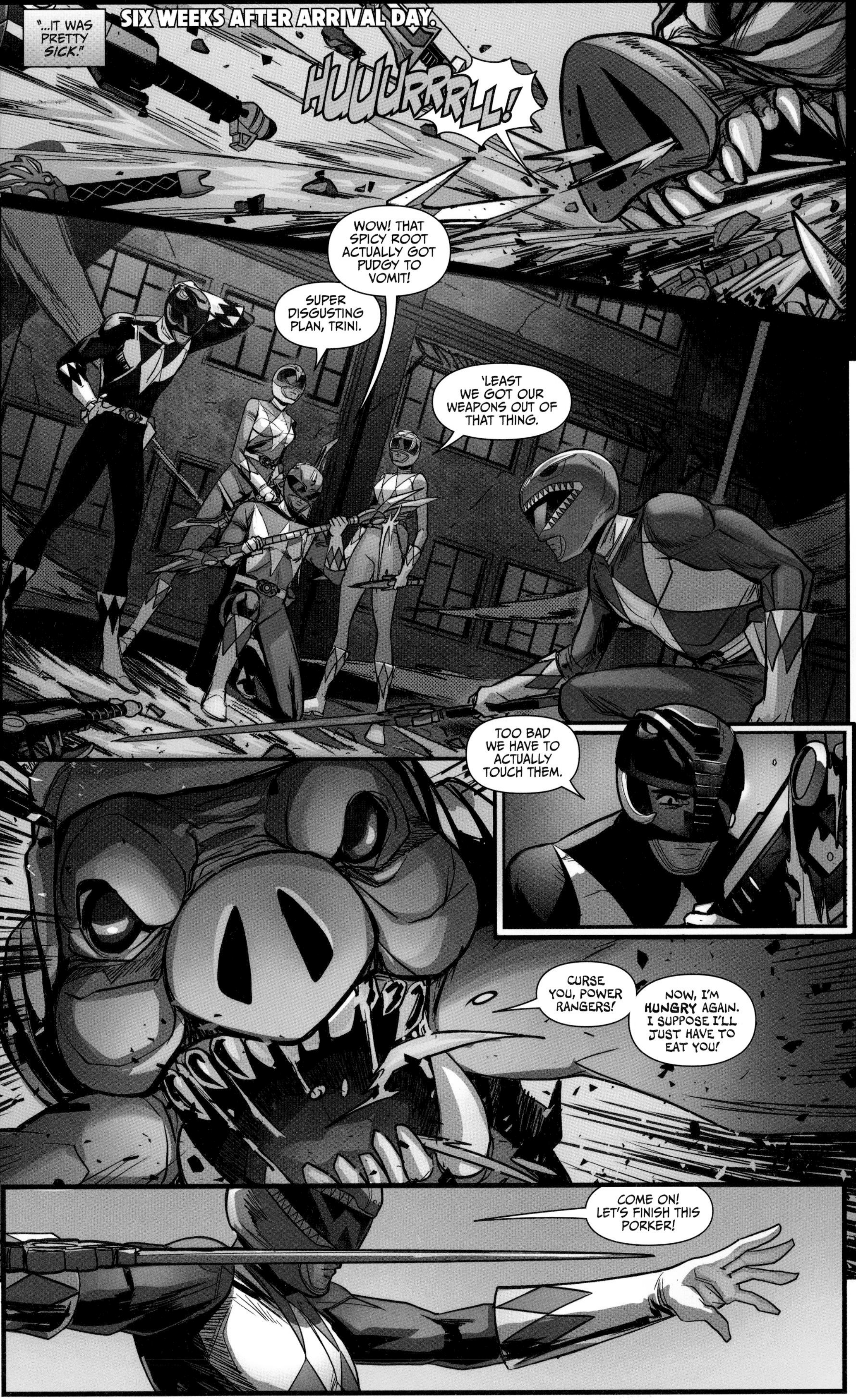
"...IT WAS PRETTY SICK."
SIX WEEKS AFTER ARRIVAL DAY.
HUUURRRLL!
WOW! THAT SPICY ROOT ACTUALLY GOT PUDGY TO VOMIT!
SUPER DISGUSTING PLAN, TRINI.
'LEAST WE GOT OUR WEAPONS OUT OF THAT THING.
TOO BAD WE HAVE TO ACTUALLY TOUCH THEM.
CURSE YOU, POWER RANGERS!
NOW, I'M HUNGRY AGAIN. I SUPPOSE I'LL JUST HAVE TO EAT YOU!
COME ON! LET'S FINISH THIS PORKER!

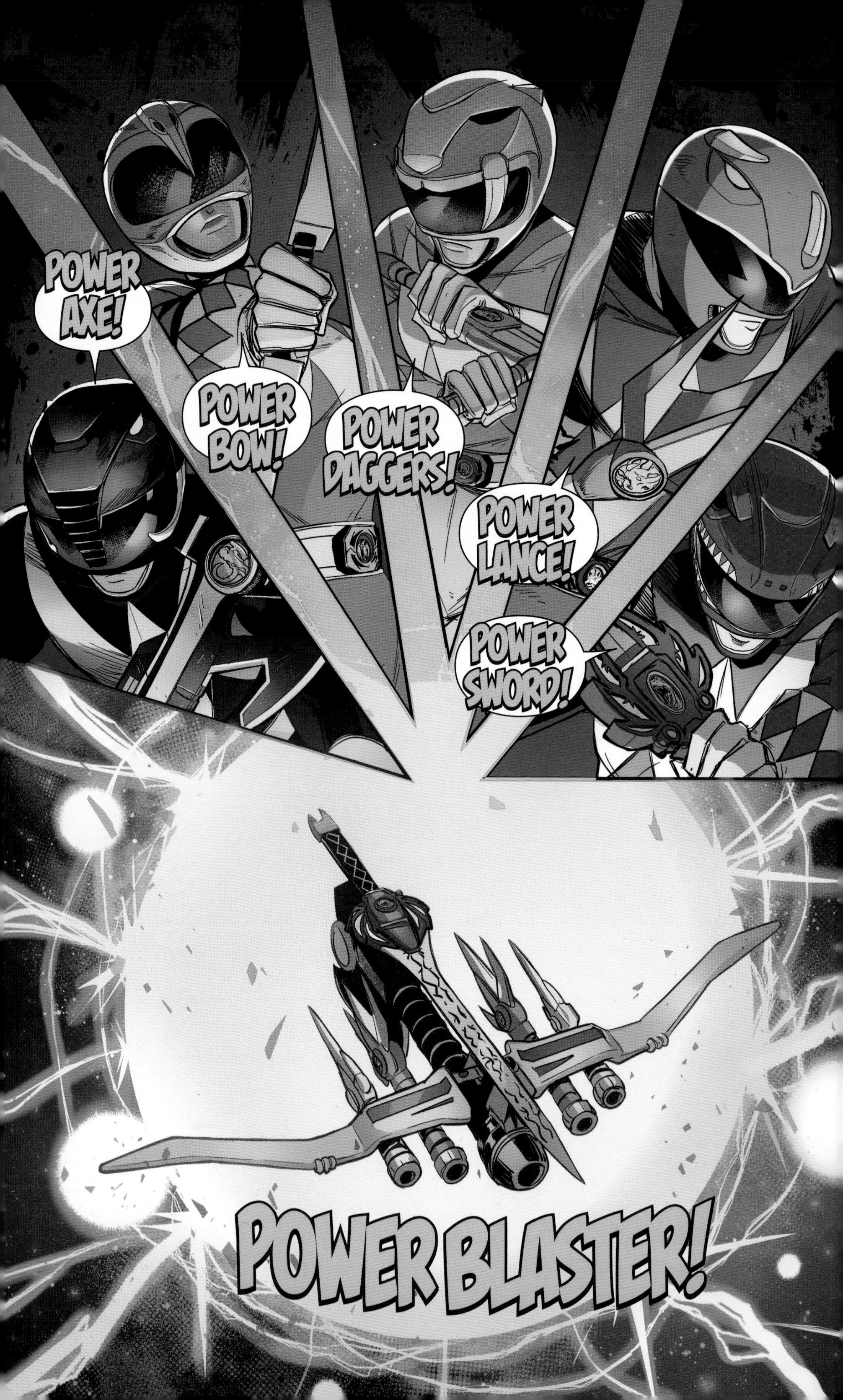

POWER AXE!
POWER BOW!
POWER DAGGERS!
POWER LANCE!
POWER SWORD!
POWER BLASTER!

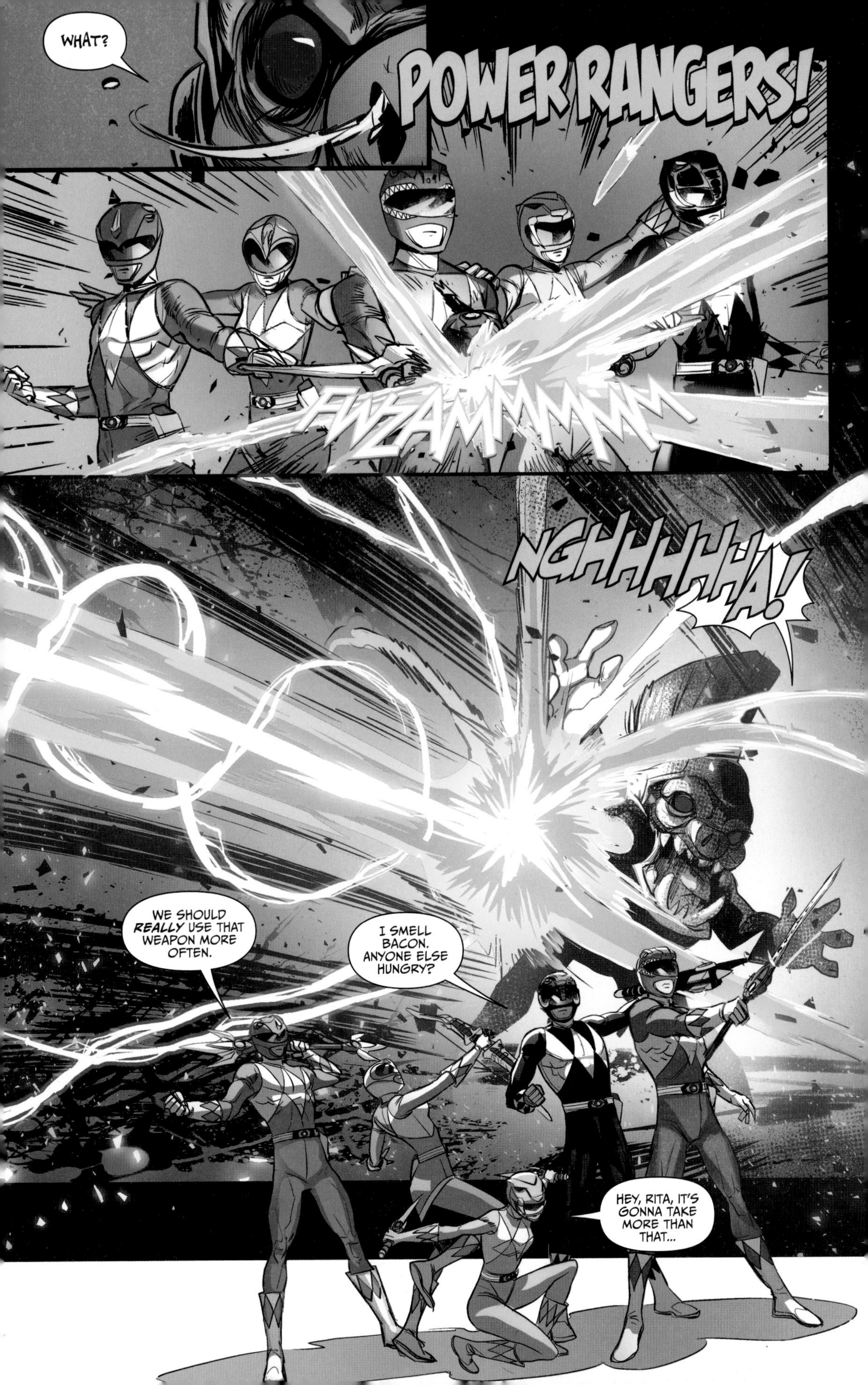
WHAT?
POWER RANGERS!
FWZAMMMMM
NGHHHHHA!
WE SHOULD REALLY USE THAT WEAPON MORE OFTEN.
I SMELL BACON. ANYONE ELSE HUNGRY?
HEY, RITA, IT'S GONNA TAKE MORE THAN THAT...

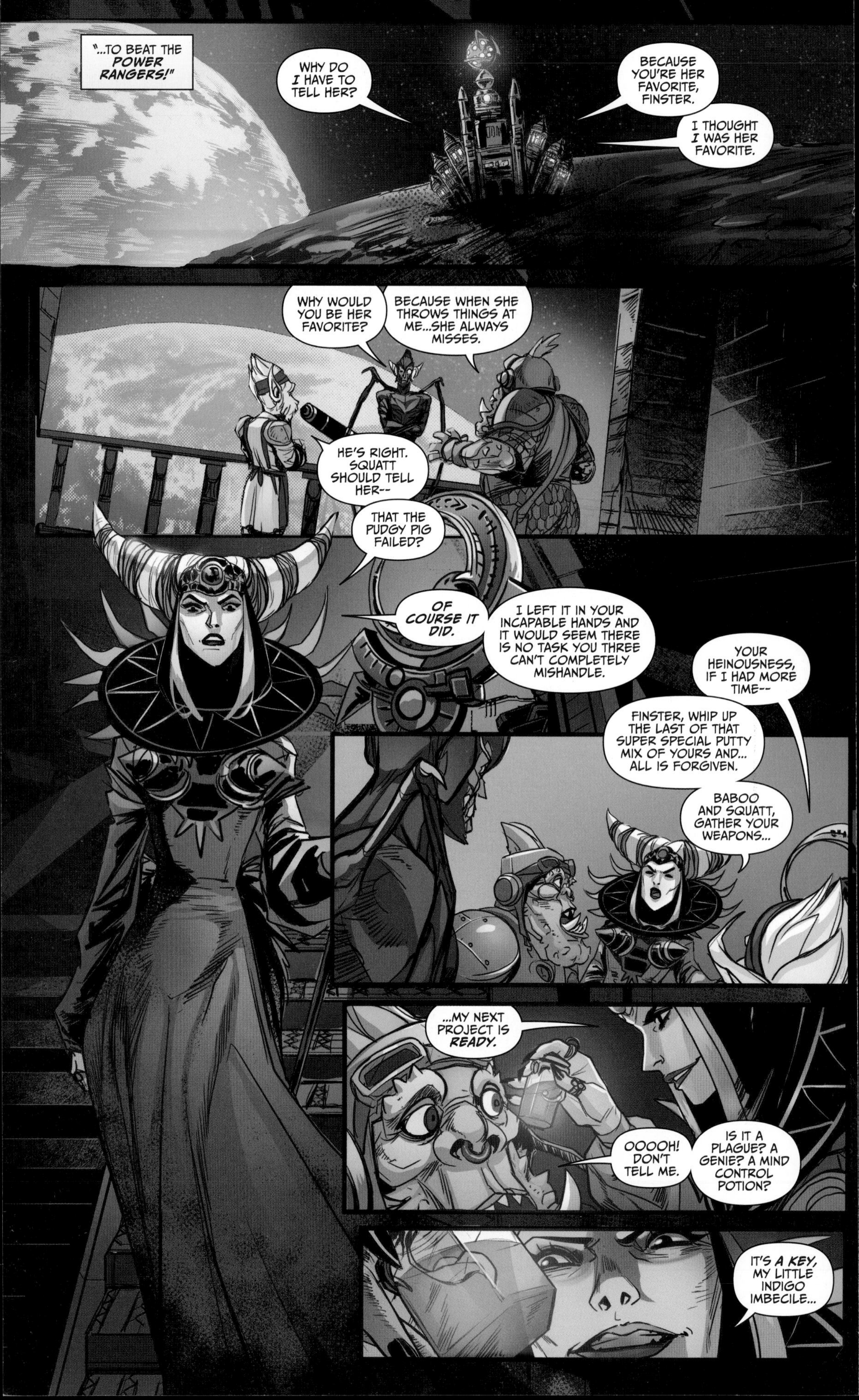
"...TO BEAT THE POWER RANGERS!"
WHY DO I HAVE TO TELL HER?
BECAUSE YOU'RE HER FAVORITE, FINSTER.
I THOUGHT I WAS HER FAVORITE.
WHY WOULD YOU BE HER FAVORITE?
BECAUSE WHEN SHE THROWS THINGS AT ME...SHE ALWAYS MISSES.
HE'S RIGHT. SQUATT SHOULD TELL HER--
THAT THE PUDGY PIG FAILED?
OF COURSE IT DID.
I LEFT IT IN YOUR INCAPABLE HANDS AND IT WOULD SEEM THERE IS NO TASK YOU THREE CAN'T COMPLETELY MISHANDLE.
YOUR HEINOUSNESS, IF I HAD MORE TIME--
FINSTER, WHIP UP THE LAST OF THAT SUPER SPECIAL PUTTY MIX OF YOURS AND... ALL IS FORGIVEN.
BABOO AND SQUATT, GATHER YOUR WEAPONS...
...MY NEXT PROJECT IS READY.
OOOOH! DON'T TELL ME.
IS IT A PLAGUE? A GENIE? A MIND CONTROL POTION?
IT'S A KEY, MY LITTLE INDIGO IMBECILE...

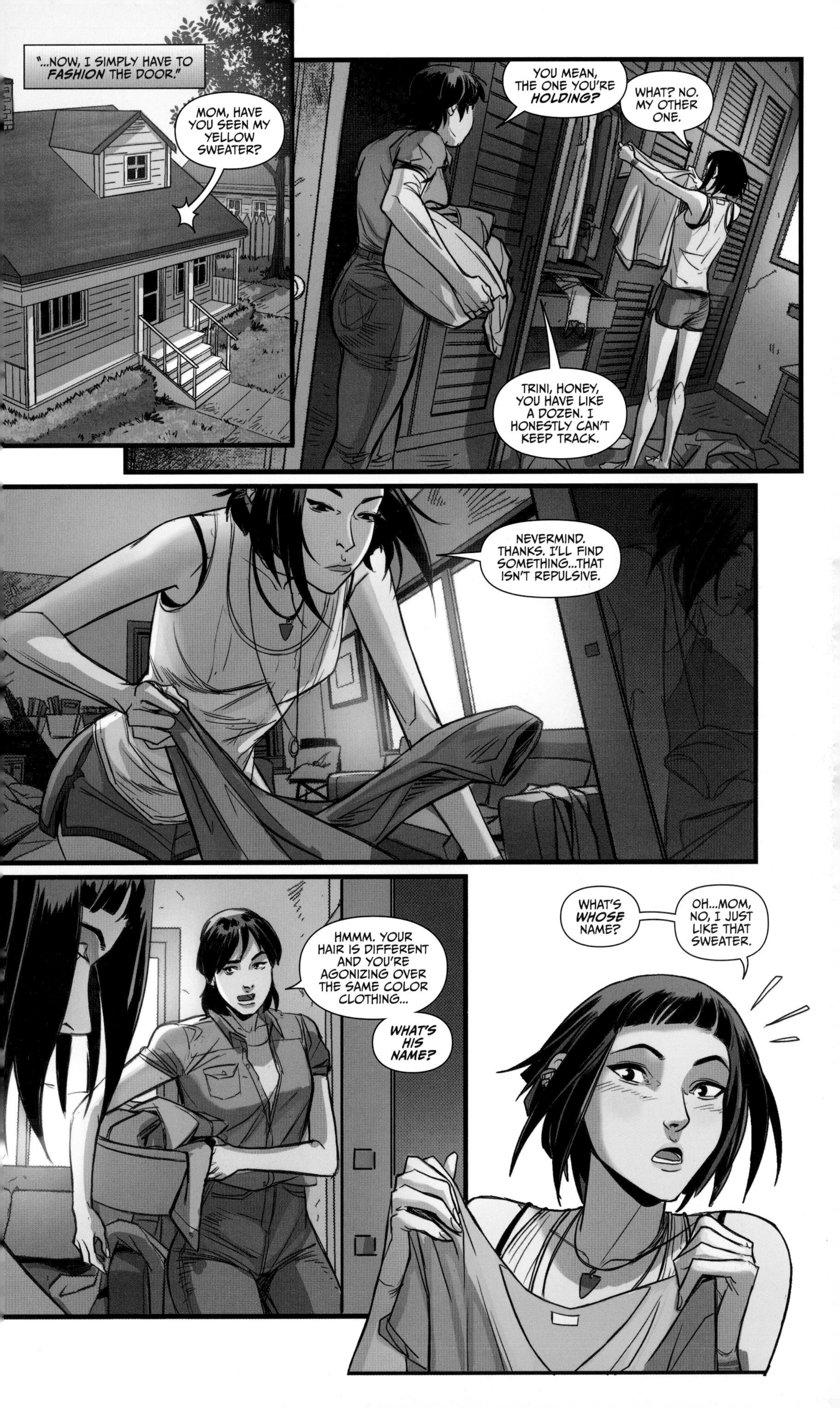
"...NOW, I SIMPLY HAVE TO *FASHION* THE DOOR."
MOM, HAVE YOU SEEN MY YELLOW SWEATER?
YOU MEAN, THE ONE YOU'RE *HOLDING?*
WHAT? NO. MY OTHER ONE.
TRINI, HONEY, YOU HAVE LIKE A DOZEN. I HONESTLY CAN'T KEEP TRACK.
NEVERMIND. THANKS. I'LL FIND SOMETHING...THAT ISN'T REPULSIVE.
HMMM. YOUR HAIR IS DIFFERENT AND YOU'RE AGONIZING OVER THE SAME COLOR CLOTHING...
WHAT'S HIS NAME?
WHAT'S *WHOSE* NAME?
OH...MOM, NO, I JUST LIKE THAT SWEATER.

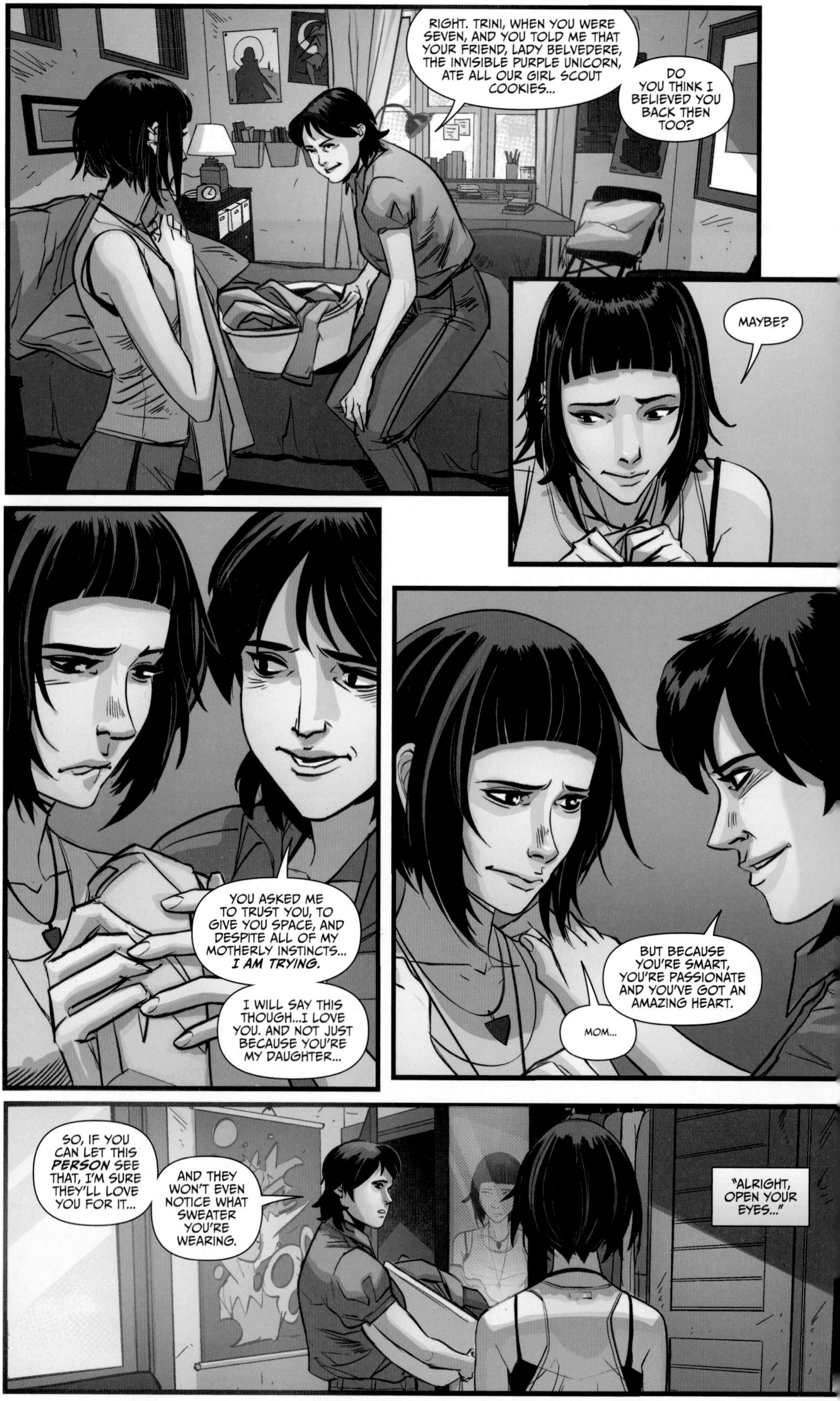
RIGHT. TRINI, WHEN YOU WERE SEVEN, AND YOU TOLD ME THAT YOUR FRIEND, LADY BELVEDERE, THE INVISIBLE PURPLE UNICORN, ATE ALL OUR GIRL SCOUT COOKIES...
DO YOU THINK I BELIEVED YOU BACK THEN TOO?
MAYBE?
YOU ASKED ME TO TRUST YOU, TO GIVE YOU SPACE, AND DESPITE ALL OF MY MOTHERLY INSTINCTS... *I AM TRYING.*
I WILL SAY THIS THOUGH...I LOVE YOU. AND NOT JUST BECAUSE YOU'RE MY DAUGHTER...
BUT BECAUSE YOU'RE SMART, YOU'RE PASSIONATE AND YOU'VE GOT AN AMAZING HEART.
MOM...
SO, IF YOU CAN LET THIS *PERSON* SEE THAT, I'M SURE THEY'LL LOVE YOU FOR IT...
AND THEY WON'T EVEN NOTICE WHAT SWEATER YOU'RE WEARING.
"ALRIGHT, OPEN YOUR EYES..."

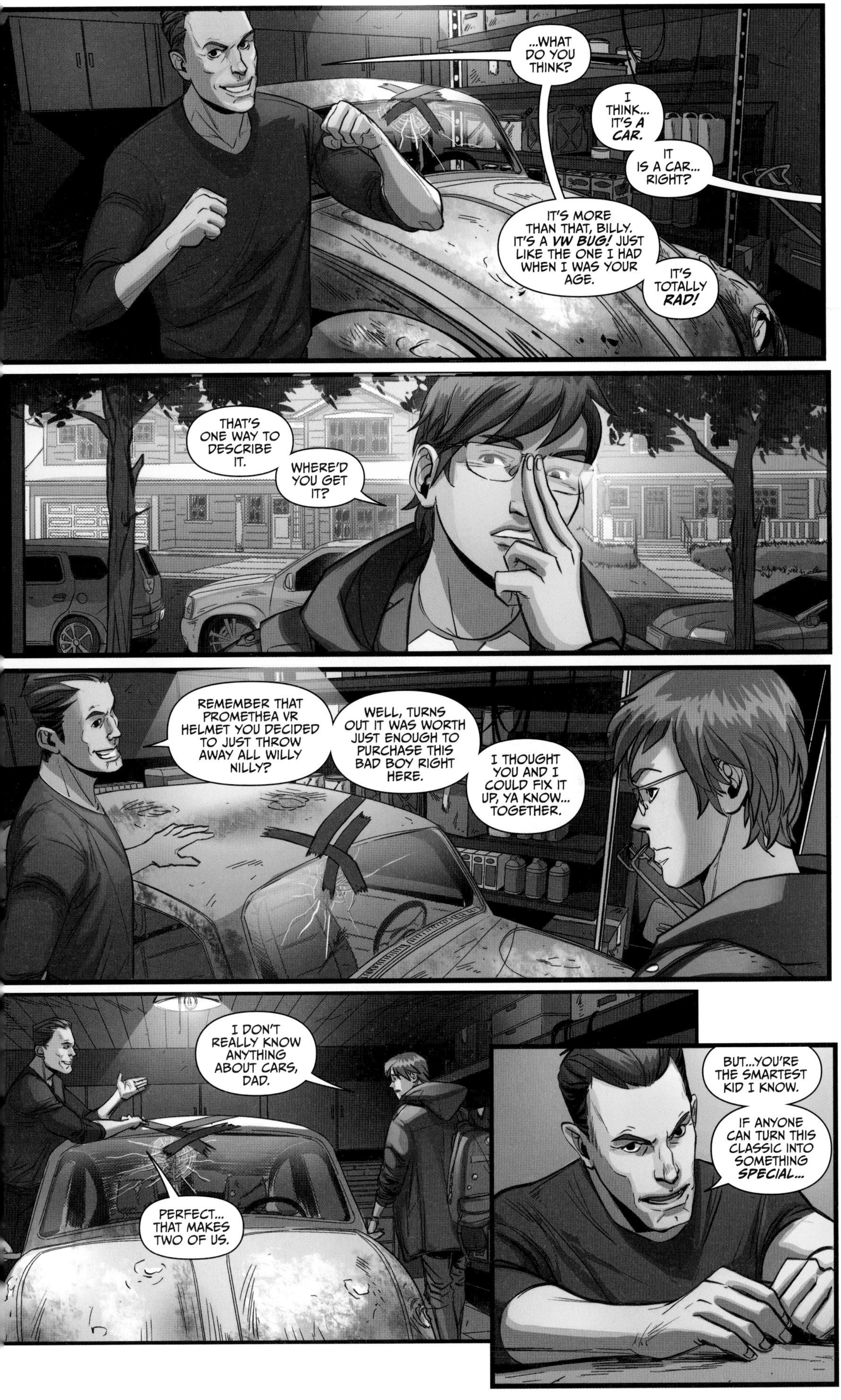
...WHAT DO YOU THINK?
I THINK... IT'S A CAR.
IT IS A CAR... RIGHT?
IT'S MORE THAN THAT, BILLY. IT'S A VW BUG! JUST LIKE THE ONE I HAD WHEN I WAS YOUR AGE.
IT'S TOTALLY RAD!
THAT'S ONE WAY TO DESCRIBE IT.
WHERE'D YOU GET IT?
REMEMBER THAT PROMETHEA VR HELMET YOU DECIDED TO JUST THROW AWAY ALL WILLY NILLY?
WELL, TURNS OUT IT WAS WORTH JUST ENOUGH TO PURCHASE THIS BAD BOY RIGHT HERE.
I THOUGHT YOU AND I COULD FIX IT UP, YA KNOW... TOGETHER.
I DON'T REALLY KNOW ANYTHING ABOUT CARS, DAD.
PERFECT... THAT MAKES TWO OF US.
BUT...YOU'RE THE SMARTEST KID I KNOW.
IF ANYONE CAN TURN THIS CLASSIC INTO SOMETHING SPECIAL...

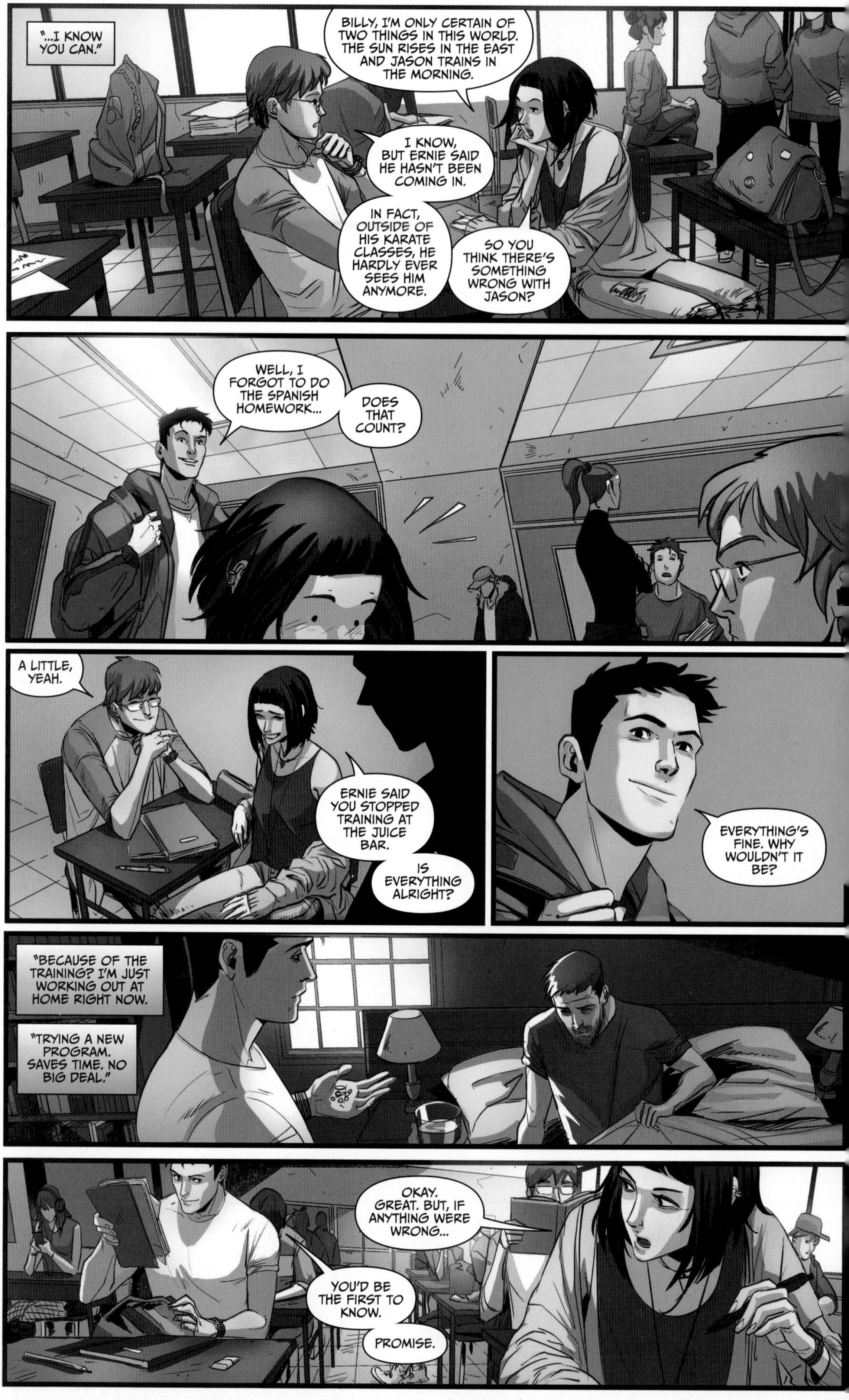
"...I KNOW YOU CAN."
BILLY, I'M ONLY CERTAIN OF TWO THINGS IN THIS WORLD. THE SUN RISES IN THE EAST AND JASON TRAINS IN THE MORNING.
I KNOW, BUT ERNIE SAID HE HASN'T BEEN COMING IN.
IN FACT, OUTSIDE OF HIS KARATE CLASSES, HE HARDLY EVER SEES HIM ANYMORE.
SO YOU THINK THERE'S SOMETHING WRONG WITH JASON?
WELL, I FORGOT TO DO THE SPANISH HOMEWORK...
DOES THAT COUNT?
A LITTLE, YEAH.
ERNIE SAID YOU STOPPED TRAINING AT THE JUICE BAR.
IS EVERYTHING ALRIGHT?
EVERYTHING'S FINE. WHY WOULDN'T IT BE?
"BECAUSE OF THE TRAINING? I'M JUST WORKING OUT AT HOME RIGHT NOW.
"TRYING A NEW PROGRAM. SAVES TIME. NO BIG DEAL."
OKAY. GREAT. BUT, IF ANYTHING WERE WRONG...
YOU'D BE THE FIRST TO KNOW.
PROMISE.

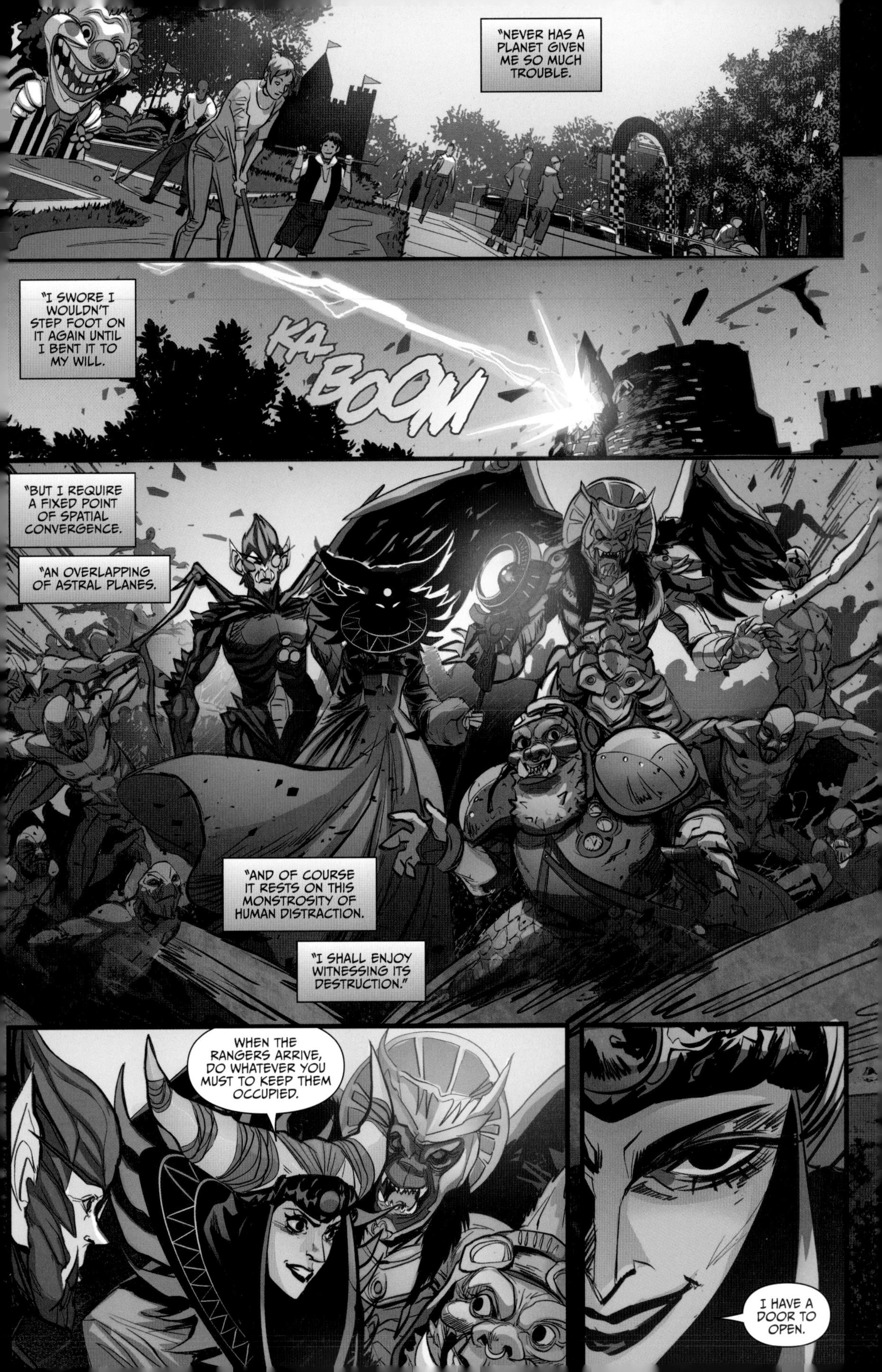
"NEVER HAS A PLANET GIVEN ME SO MUCH TROUBLE.
"I SWORE I WOULDN'T STEP FOOT ON IT AGAIN UNTIL I BENT IT TO MY WILL.
KA BOOM
"BUT I REQUIRE A FIXED POINT OF SPATIAL CONVERGENCE.
"AN OVERLAPPING OF ASTRAL PLANES.
"AND OF COURSE IT RESTS ON THIS MONSTROSITY OF HUMAN DISTRACTION.
"I SHALL ENJOY WITNESSING ITS DESTRUCTION."
WHEN THE RANGERS ARRIVE, DO WHATEVER YOU MUST TO KEEP THEM OCCUPIED.
I HAVE A DOOR TO OPEN.

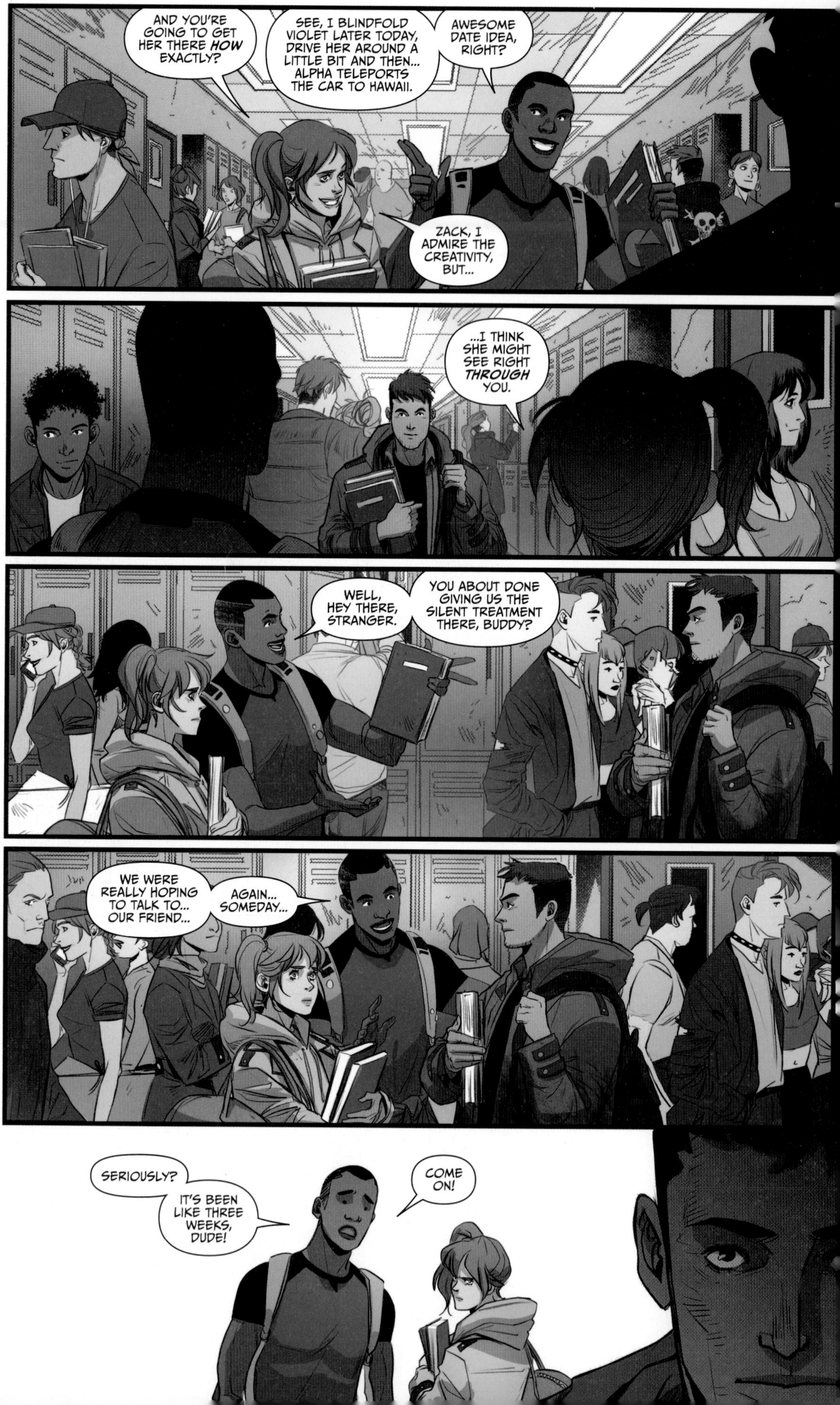
AND YOU'RE GOING TO GET HER THERE HOW EXACTLY?
SEE, I BLINDFOLD VIOLET LATER TODAY, DRIVE HER AROUND A LITTLE BIT AND THEN... ALPHA TELEPORTS THE CAR TO HAWAII.
AWESOME DATE IDEA, RIGHT?
ZACK, I ADMIRE THE CREATIVITY, BUT...
...I THINK SHE MIGHT SEE RIGHT THROUGH YOU.
WELL, HEY THERE, STRANGER.
YOU ABOUT DONE GIVING US THE SILENT TREATMENT THERE, BUDDY?
WE WERE REALLY HOPING TO TALK TO... OUR FRIEND...
AGAIN... SOMEDAY...
SERIOUSLY?
IT'S BEEN LIKE THREE WEEKS, DUDE!
COME ON!

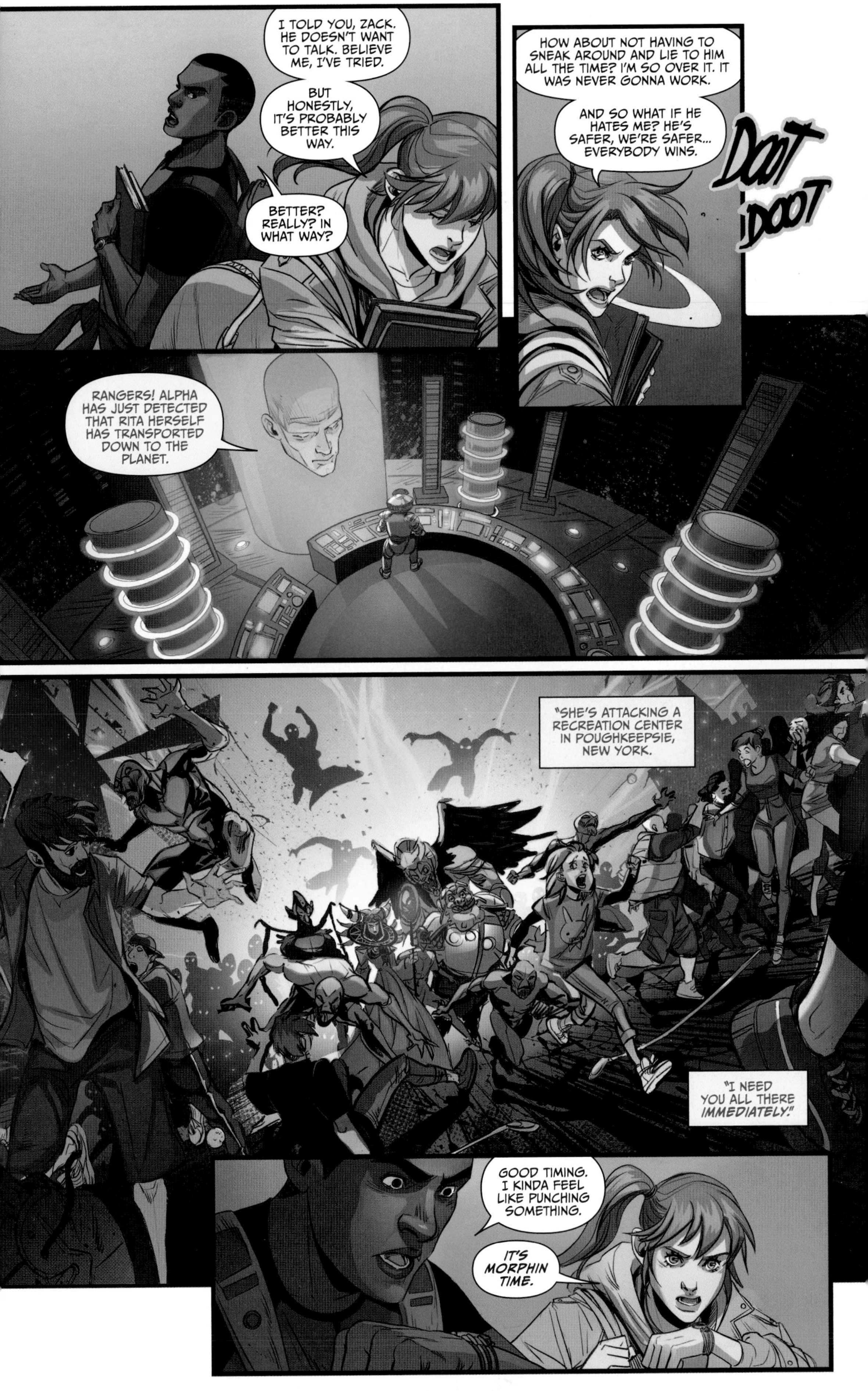
I TOLD YOU, ZACK. HE DOESN'T WANT TO TALK. BELIEVE ME, I'VE TRIED.
BUT HONESTLY, IT'S PROBABLY BETTER THIS WAY.
BETTER? REALLY? IN WHAT WAY?
HOW ABOUT NOT HAVING TO SNEAK AROUND AND LIE TO HIM ALL THE TIME? I'M SO OVER IT. IT WAS NEVER GONNA WORK.
AND SO WHAT IF HE HATES ME? HE'S SAFER, WE'RE SAFER... EVERYBODY WINS.
DOOT DOOT
RANGERS! ALPHA HAS JUST DETECTED THAT RITA HERSELF HAS TRANSPORTED DOWN TO THE PLANET.
"SHE'S ATTACKING A RECREATION CENTER IN POUGHKEEPSIE, NEW YORK.
"I NEED YOU ALL THERE *IMMEDIATELY*."
GOOD TIMING. I KINDA FEEL LIKE PUNCHING SOMETHING.
IT'S MORPHIN TIME.

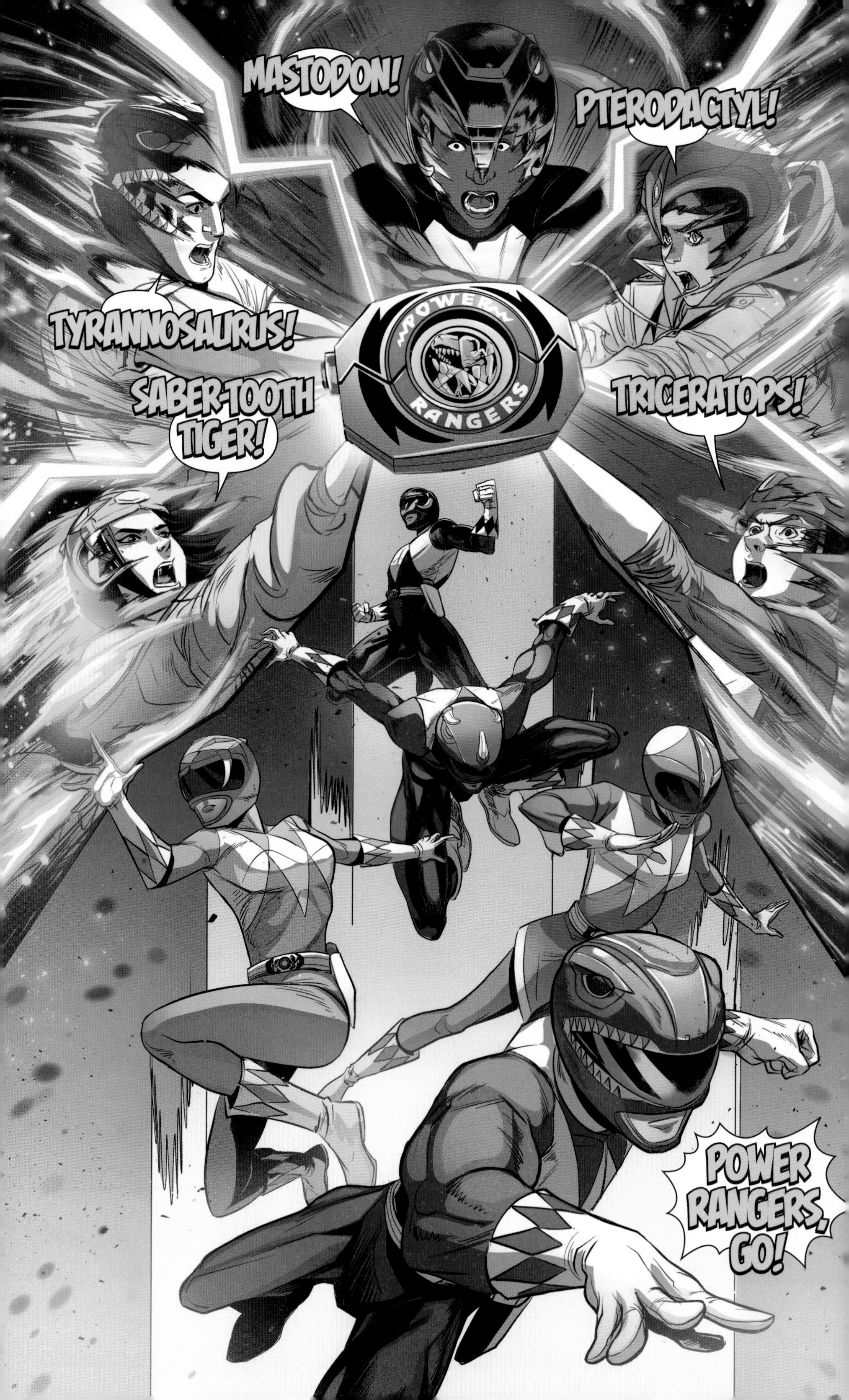
MASTODON!
PTERODACTYL!
TYRANNOSAURUS!
SABER-TOOTH TIGER!
TRICERATOPS!
POWER RANGERS, GO!

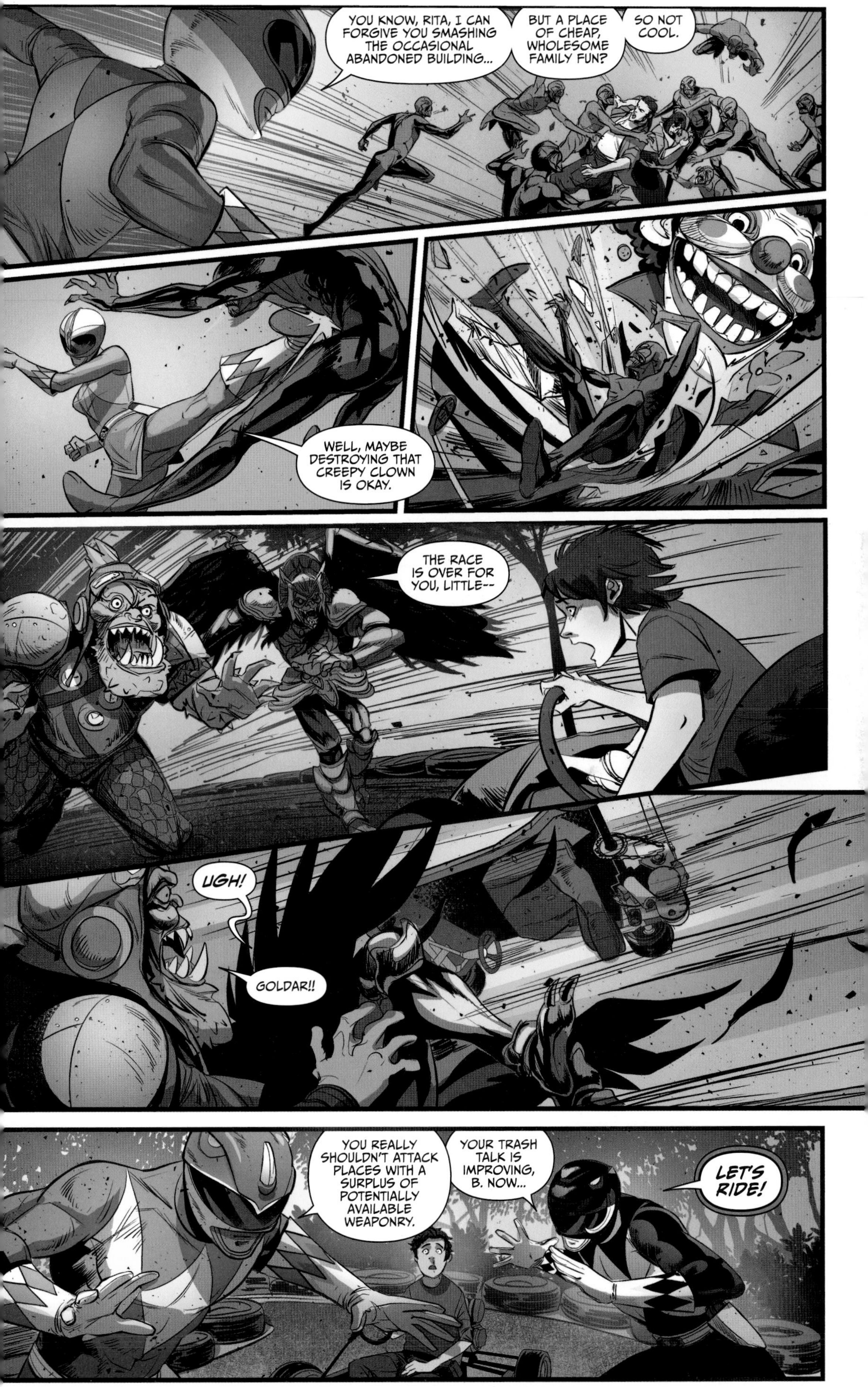
YOU KNOW, RITA, I CAN FORGIVE YOU SMASHING THE OCCASIONAL ABANDONED BUILDING...
BUT A PLACE OF CHEAP, WHOLESOME FAMILY FUN?
SO NOT COOL.
WELL, MAYBE DESTROYING THAT CREEPY CLOWN IS OKAY.
THE RACE IS OVER FOR YOU, LITTLE--
UGH!
GOLDAR!!
YOU REALLY SHOULDN'T ATTACK PLACES WITH A SURPLUS OF POTENTIALLY AVAILABLE WEAPONRY.
YOUR TRASH TALK IS IMPROVING, B. NOW...
LET'S RIDE!

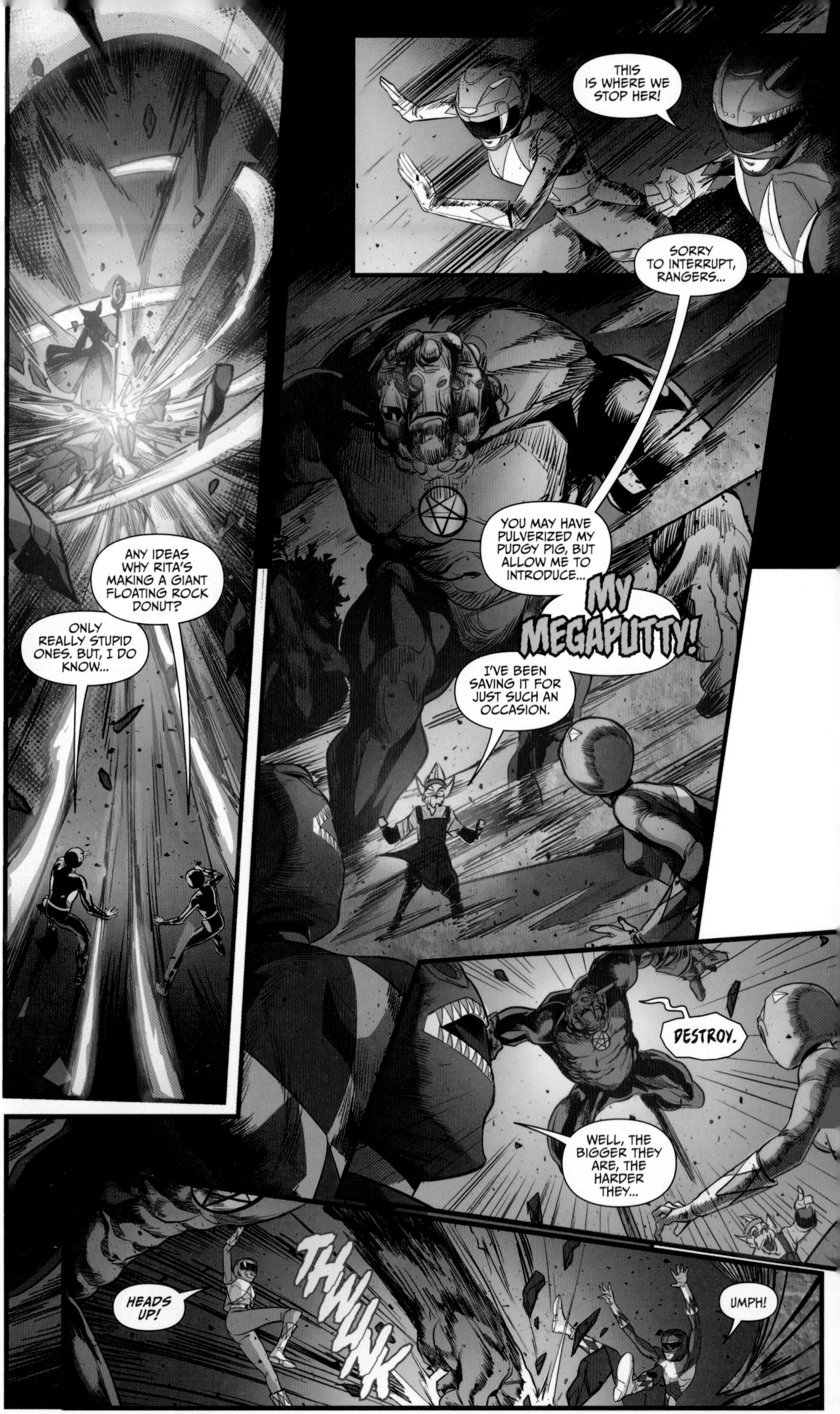

THIS IS WHERE WE STOP HER!
SORRY TO INTERRUPT, RANGERS...
YOU MAY HAVE PULVERIZED MY PUDGY PIG, BUT ALLOW ME TO INTRODUCE...
MY MEGAPUTTY!
I'VE BEEN SAVING IT FOR JUST SUCH AN OCCASION.
ANY IDEAS WHY RITA'S MAKING A GIANT FLOATING ROCK DONUT?
ONLY REALLY STUPID ONES. BUT, I DO KNOW...
DESTROY.
WELL, THE BIGGER THEY ARE, THE HARDER THEY...
HEADS UP!
THWUNK
UMPH!

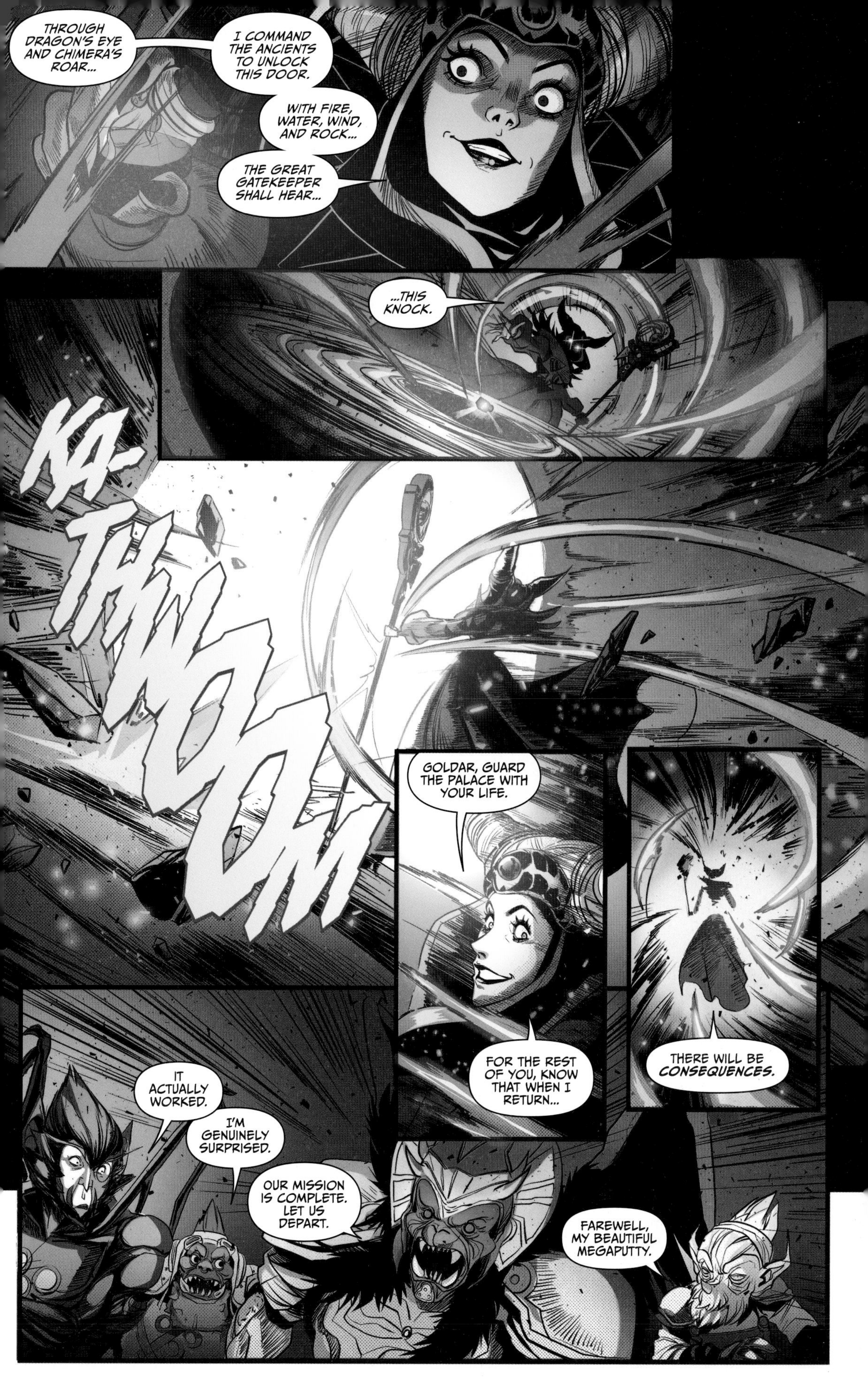
THROUGH DRAGON'S EYE AND CHIMERA'S ROAR...
I COMMAND THE ANCIENTS TO UNLOCK THIS DOOR.
WITH FIRE, WATER, WIND, AND ROCK...
THE GREAT GATEKEEPER SHALL HEAR...
...THIS KNOCK.
KA-THWOOM
GOLDAR, GUARD THE PALACE WITH YOUR LIFE.
FOR THE REST OF YOU, KNOW THAT WHEN I RETURN...
THERE WILL BE *CONSEQUENCES.*
IT ACTUALLY WORKED.
I'M GENUINELY SURPRISED.
OUR MISSION IS COMPLETE. LET US DEPART.
FAREWELL, MY BEAUTIFUL MEGAPUTTY.

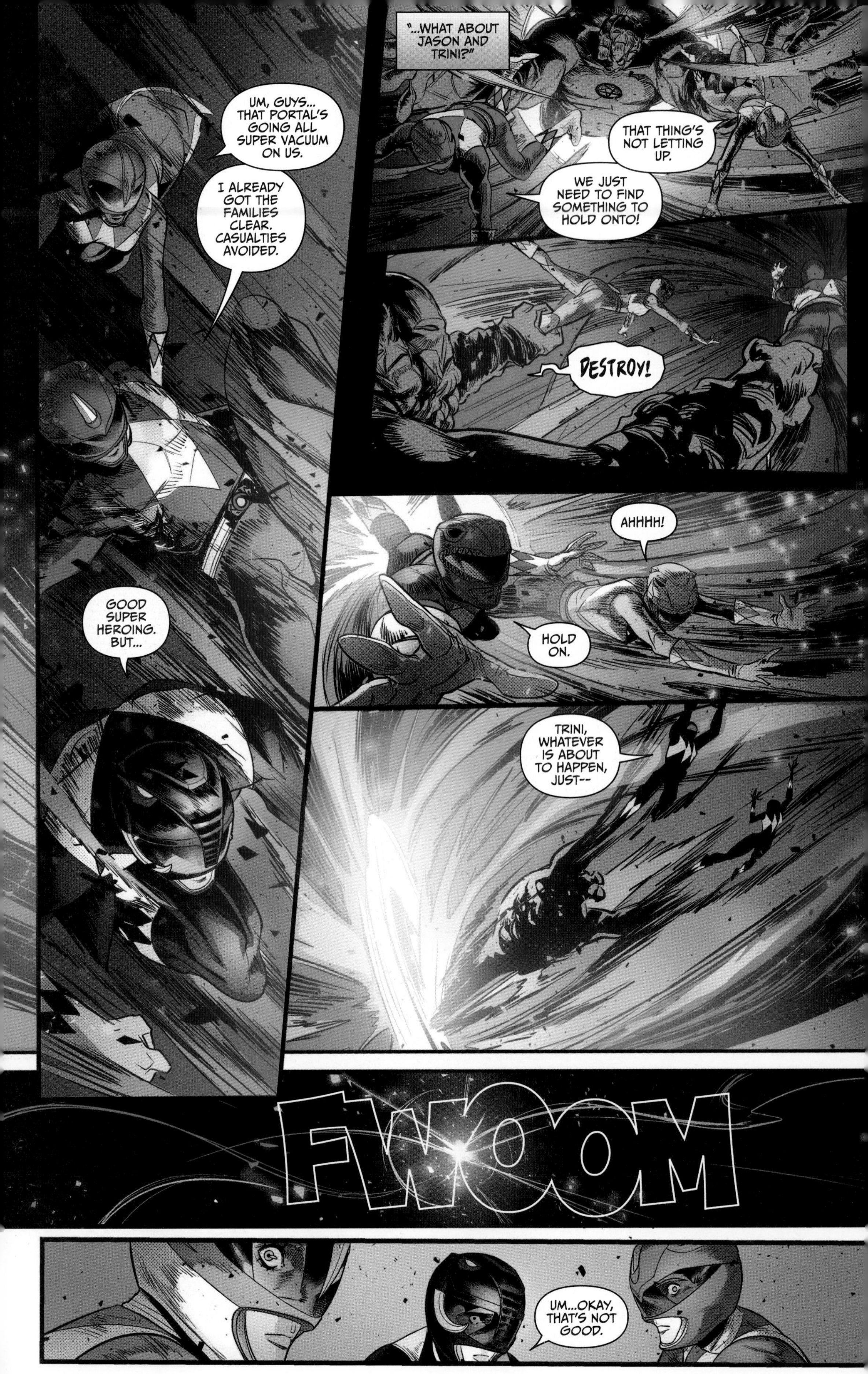
UM, GUYS... THAT PORTAL'S GOING ALL SUPER VACUUM ON US.
I ALREADY GOT THE FAMILIES CLEAR. CASUALTIES AVOIDED.
GOOD SUPER HEROING. BUT...
"...WHAT ABOUT JASON AND TRINI?"
THAT THING'S NOT LETTING UP.
WE JUST NEED TO FIND SOMETHING TO HOLD ONTO!
DESTROY!
AHHHH!
HOLD ON.
TRINI, WHATEVER IS ABOUT TO HAPPEN, JUST--
FWOOM
UM...OKAY, THAT'S NOT GOOD.

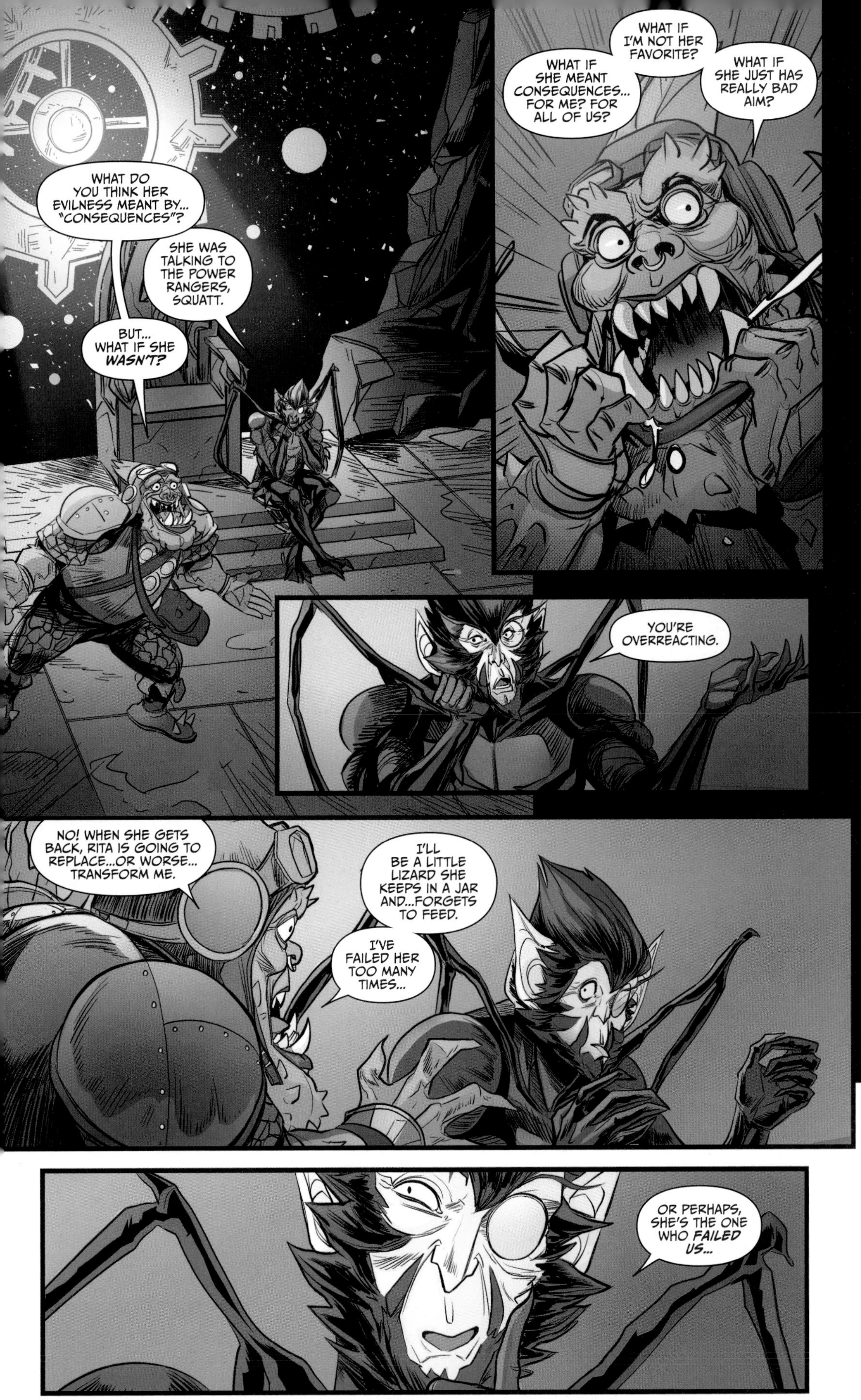
WHAT DO YOU THINK HER EVILNESS MEANT BY... "CONSEQUENCES"?
SHE WAS TALKING TO THE POWER RANGERS, SQUATT.
BUT... WHAT IF SHE *WASN'T?*
WHAT IF SHE MEANT CONSEQUENCES... FOR ME? FOR ALL OF US?
WHAT IF I'M NOT HER FAVORITE?
WHAT IF SHE JUST HAS REALLY BAD AIM?
YOU'RE OVERREACTING.
NO! WHEN SHE GETS BACK, RITA IS GOING TO REPLACE...OR WORSE... TRANSFORM ME.
I'LL BE A LITTLE LIZARD SHE KEEPS IN A JAR AND...FORGETS TO FEED.
I'VE FAILED HER TOO MANY TIMES...
OR PERHAPS, SHE'S THE ONE WHO *FAILED US...*

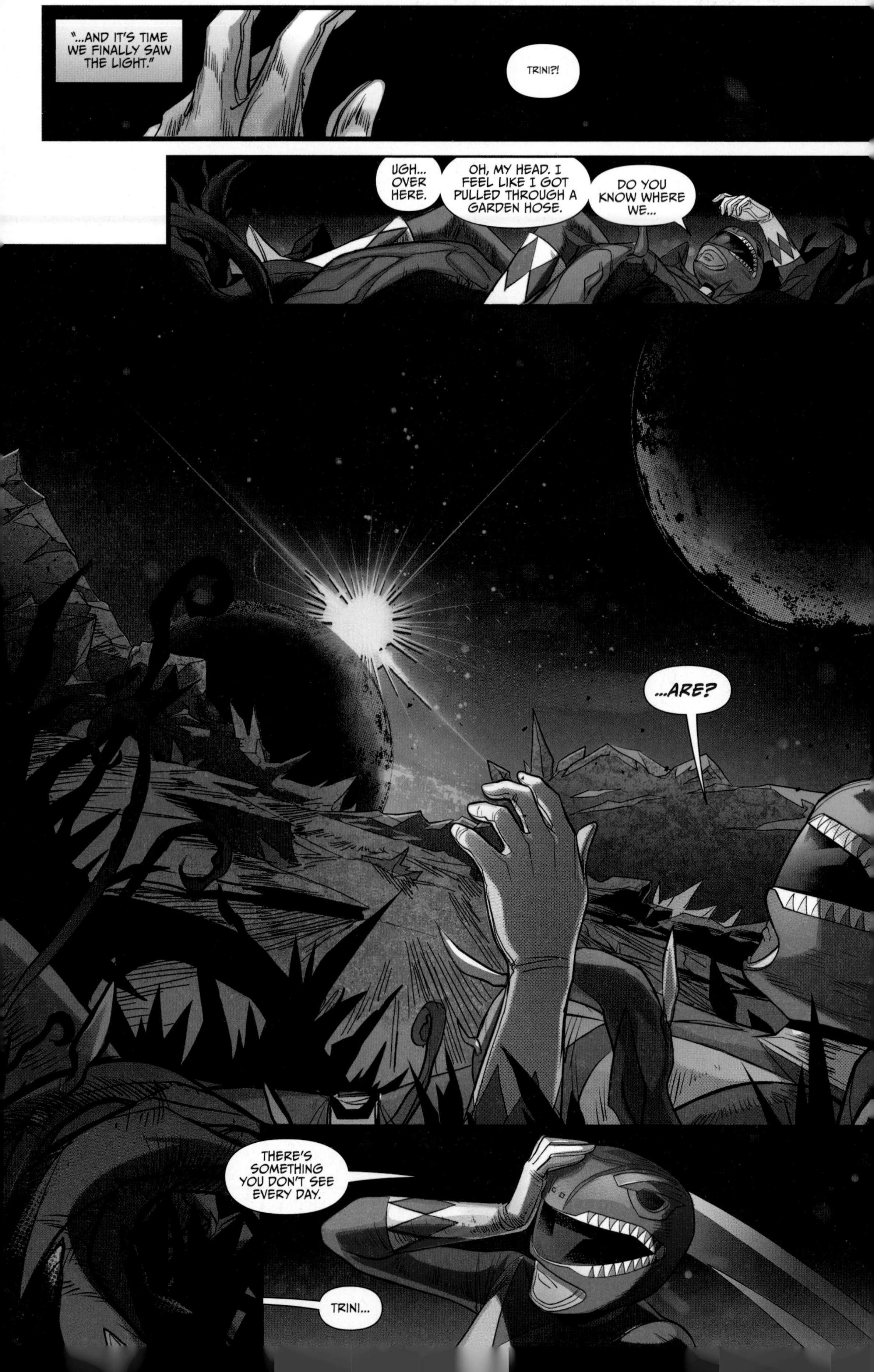
"...AND IT'S TIME WE FINALLY SAW THE LIGHT."
TRINI?!
UGH... OVER HERE.
OH, MY HEAD. I FEEL LIKE I GOT PULLED THROUGH A GARDEN HOSE.
DO YOU KNOW WHERE WE...
...ARE?
THERE'S SOMETHING YOU DON'T SEE EVERY DAY.
TRINI...

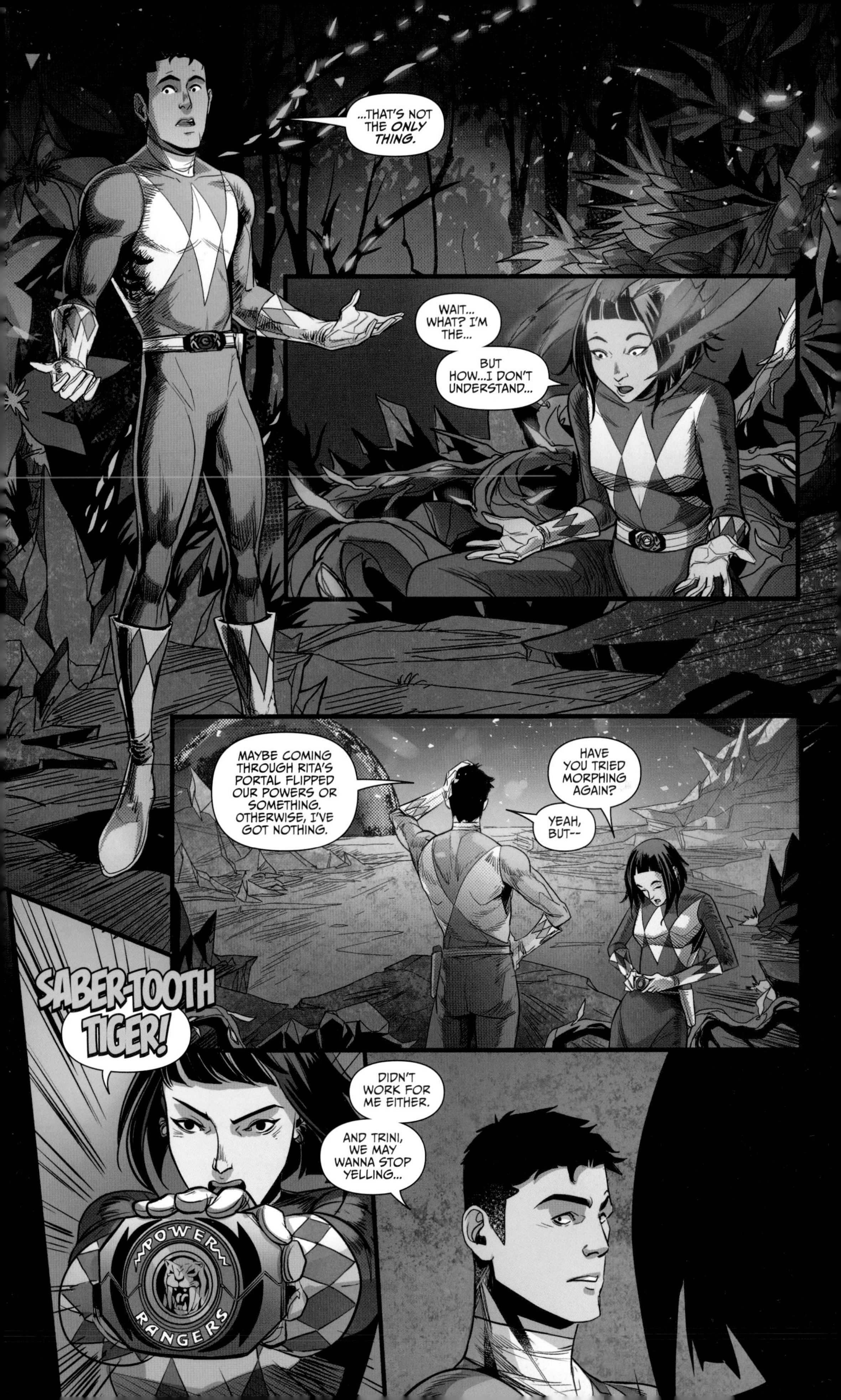
...THAT'S NOT THE *ONLY THING.*
WAIT... WHAT? I'M THE...
BUT HOW...I DON'T UNDERSTAND...
MAYBE COMING THROUGH RITA'S PORTAL FLIPPED OUR POWERS OR SOMETHING. OTHERWISE, I'VE GOT NOTHING.
HAVE YOU TRIED MORPHING AGAIN?
YEAH, BUT--
SABER-TOOTH TIGER!
POWER RANGERS
DIDN'T WORK FOR ME EITHER.
AND TRINI, WE MAY WANNA STOP YELLING...

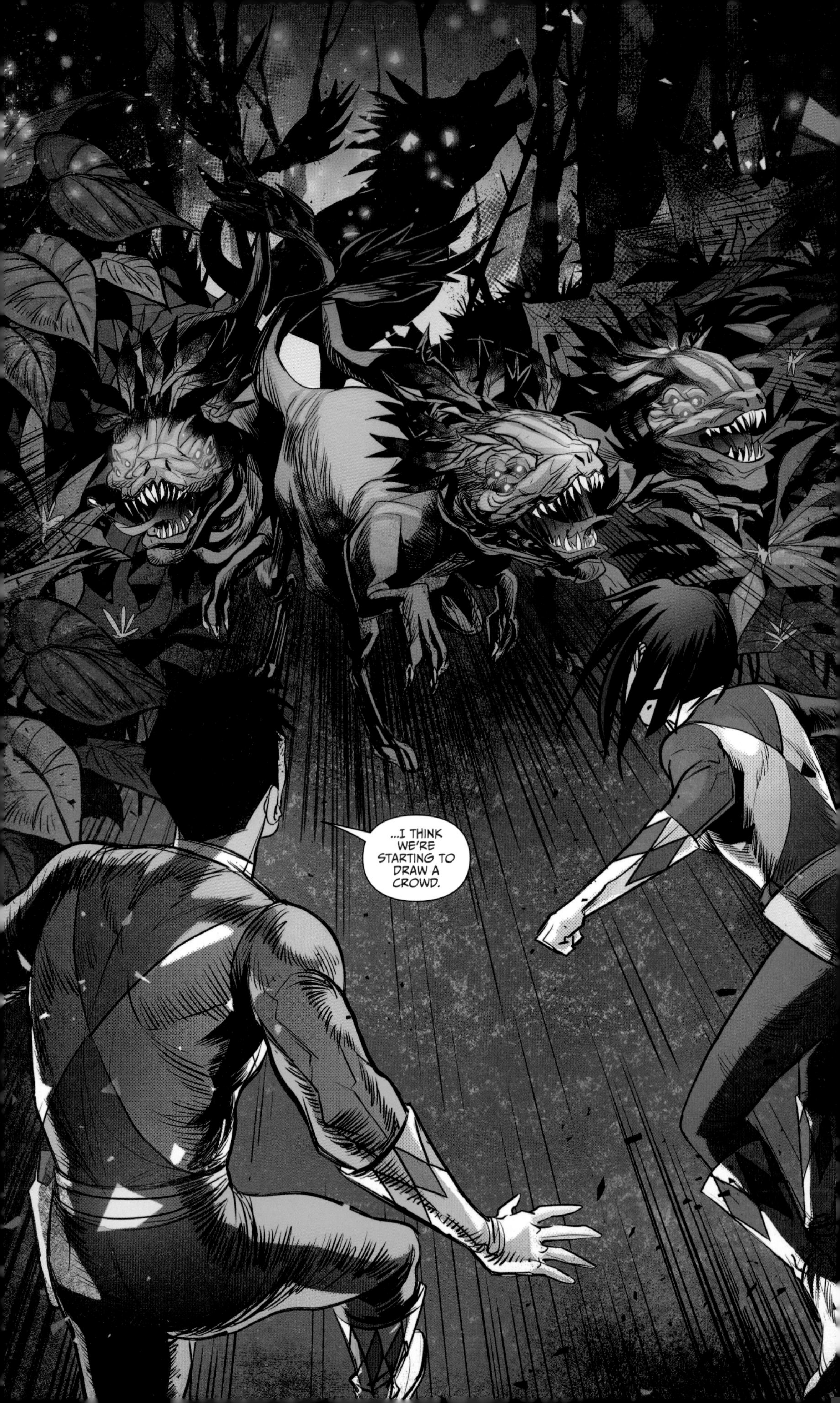
...I THINK WE'RE STARTING TO DRAW A CROWD.

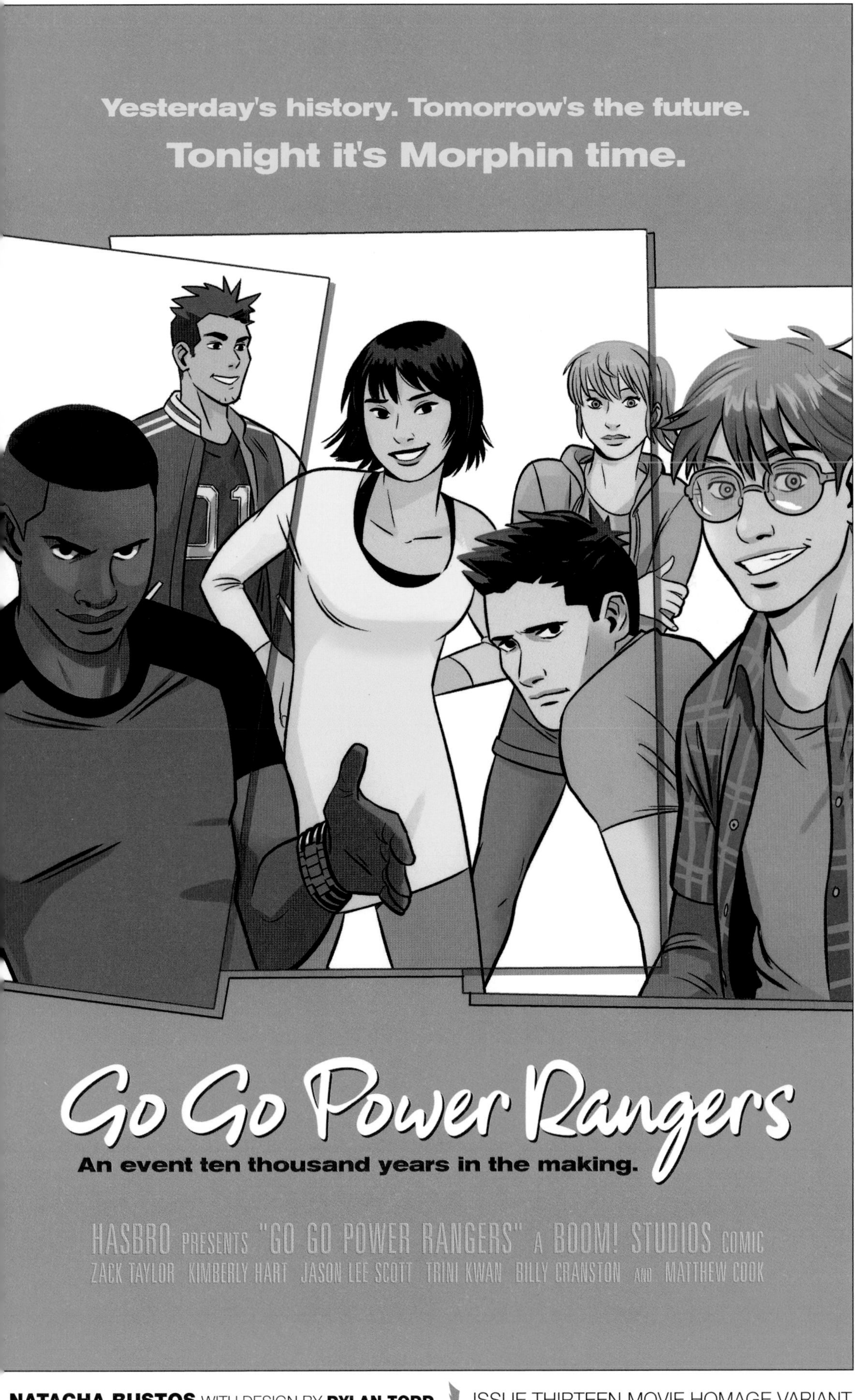
Yesterday's history. Tomorrow's the future.
Tonight it's Morphin time.
Go Go Power Rangers
An event ten thousand years in the making.
HASBRO PRESENTS "GO GO POWER RANGERS" A BOOM! STUDIOS COMIC
ZACK TAYLOR KIMBERLY HART JASON LEE SCOTT TRINI KWAN BILLY CRANSTON AND MATTHEW COOK

NATACHA BUSTOS WITH DESIGN BY **DYLAN TODD** ISSUE THIRTEEN MOVIE HOMAGE VARIANT

FOURTEEN

DAN MORA ISSUE FOURTEEN MAIN COVER

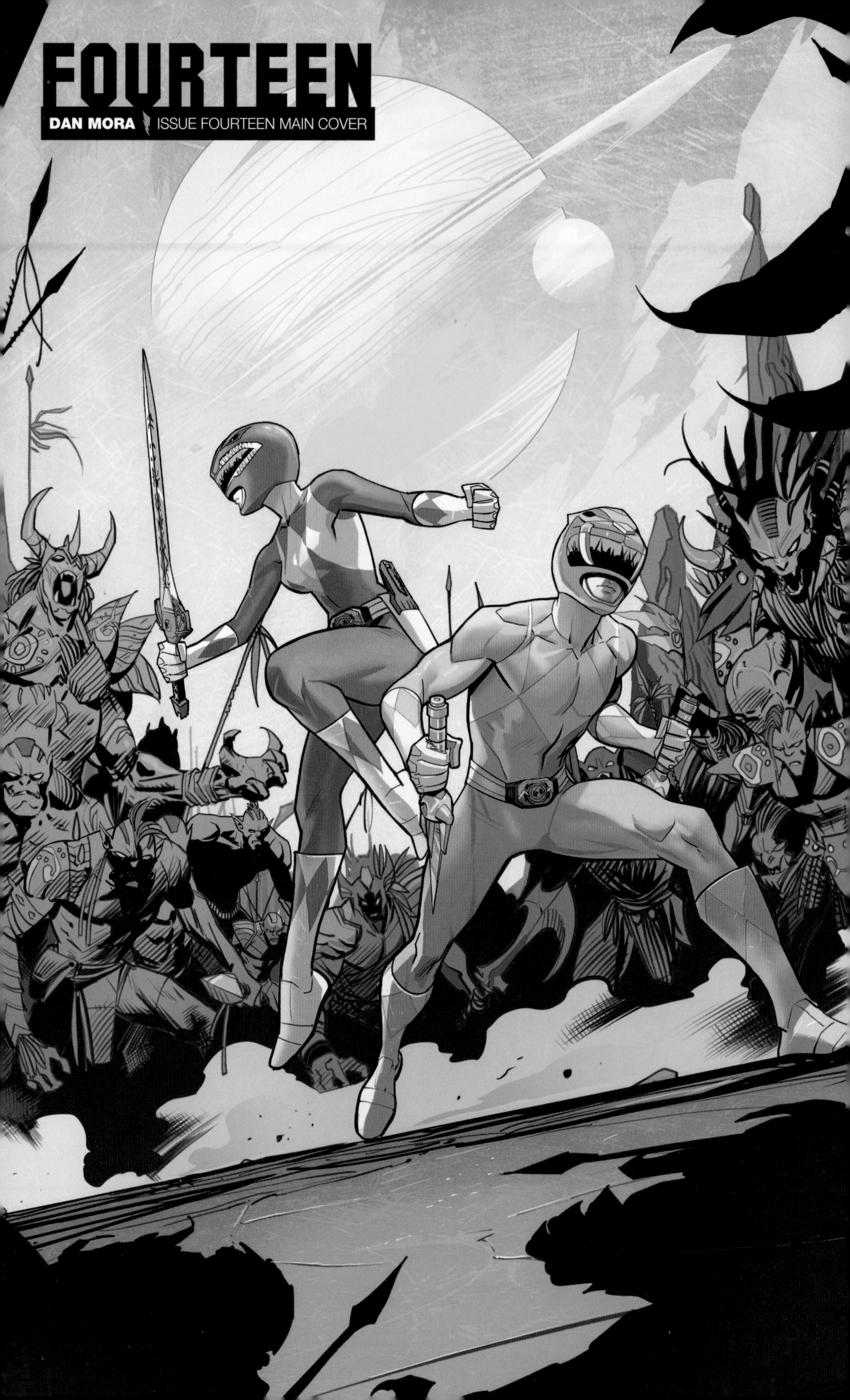

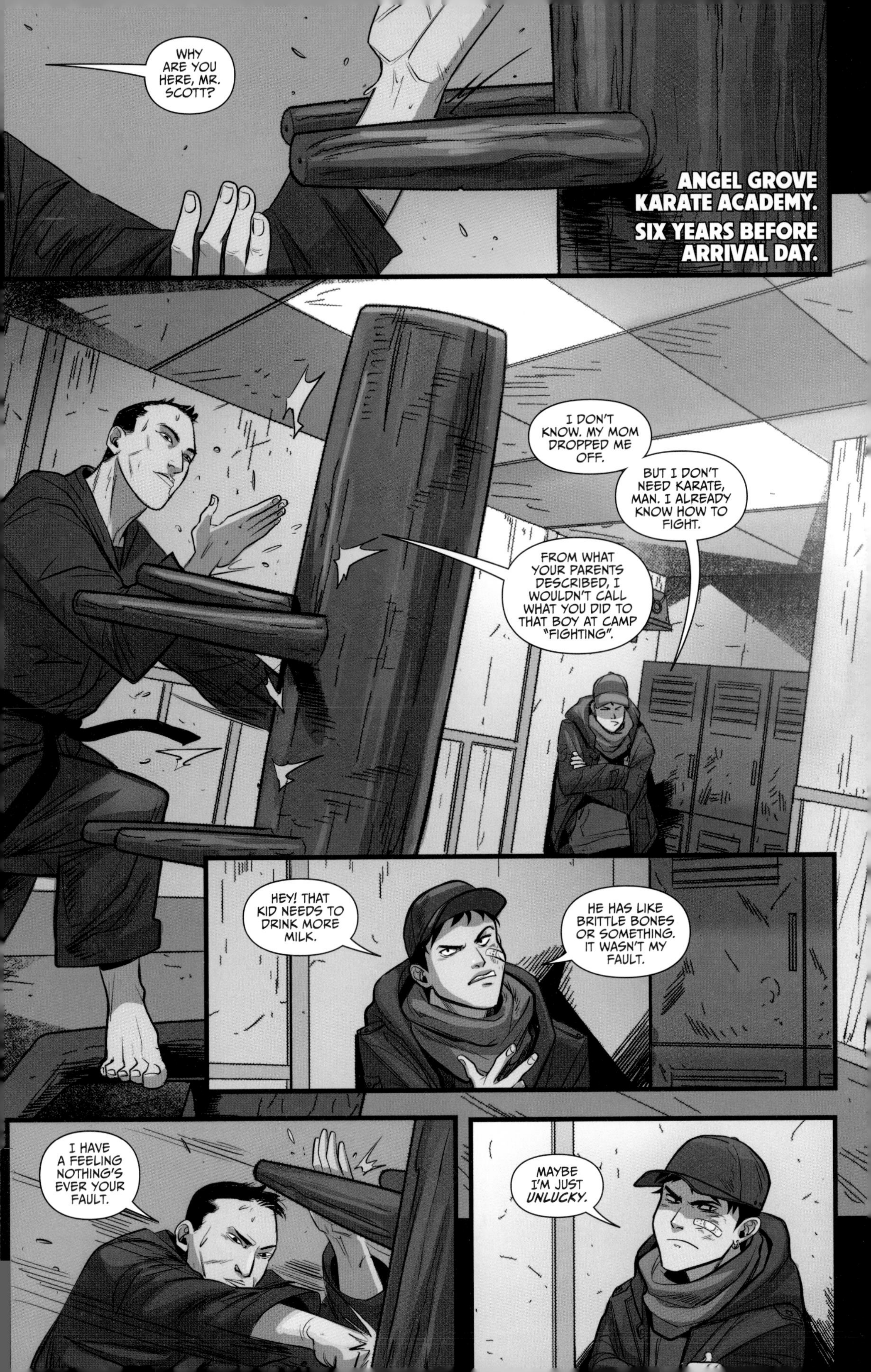
WHY ARE YOU HERE, MR. SCOTT?
ANGEL GROVE KARATE ACADEMY.
SIX YEARS BEFORE ARRIVAL DAY.
I DON'T KNOW. MY MOM DROPPED ME OFF.
BUT I DON'T NEED KARATE, MAN. I ALREADY KNOW HOW TO FIGHT.
FROM WHAT YOUR PARENTS DESCRIBED, I WOULDN'T CALL WHAT YOU DID TO THAT BOY AT CAMP "FIGHTING".
HEY! THAT KID NEEDS TO DRINK MORE MILK.
HE HAS LIKE BRITTLE BONES OR SOMETHING. IT WASN'T MY FAULT.
I HAVE A FEELING NOTHING'S EVER YOUR FAULT.
MAYBE I'M JUST *UNLUCKY.*

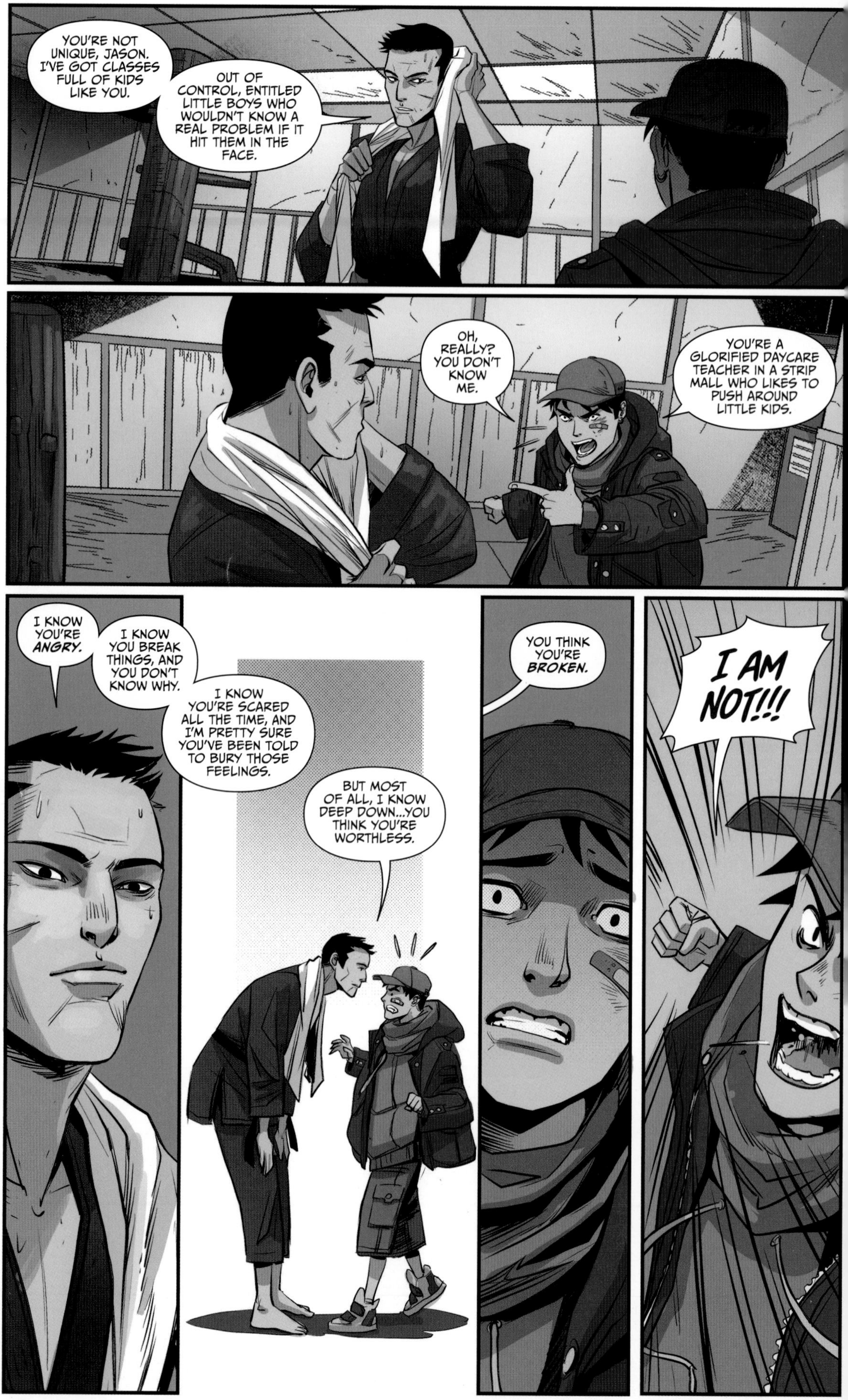
YOU'RE NOT UNIQUE, JASON. I'VE GOT CLASSES FULL OF KIDS LIKE YOU.
OUT OF CONTROL, ENTITLED LITTLE BOYS WHO WOULDN'T KNOW A REAL PROBLEM IF IT HIT THEM IN THE FACE.
OH, REALLY? YOU DON'T KNOW ME.
YOU'RE A GLORIFIED DAYCARE TEACHER IN A STRIP MALL WHO LIKES TO PUSH AROUND LITTLE KIDS.
I KNOW YOU'RE ANGRY.
I KNOW YOU BREAK THINGS, AND YOU DON'T KNOW WHY.
I KNOW YOU'RE SCARED ALL THE TIME, AND I'M PRETTY SURE YOU'VE BEEN TOLD TO BURY THOSE FEELINGS.
BUT MOST OF ALL, I KNOW DEEP DOWN...YOU THINK YOU'RE WORTHLESS.
YOU THINK YOU'RE BROKEN.
I AM NOT!!!

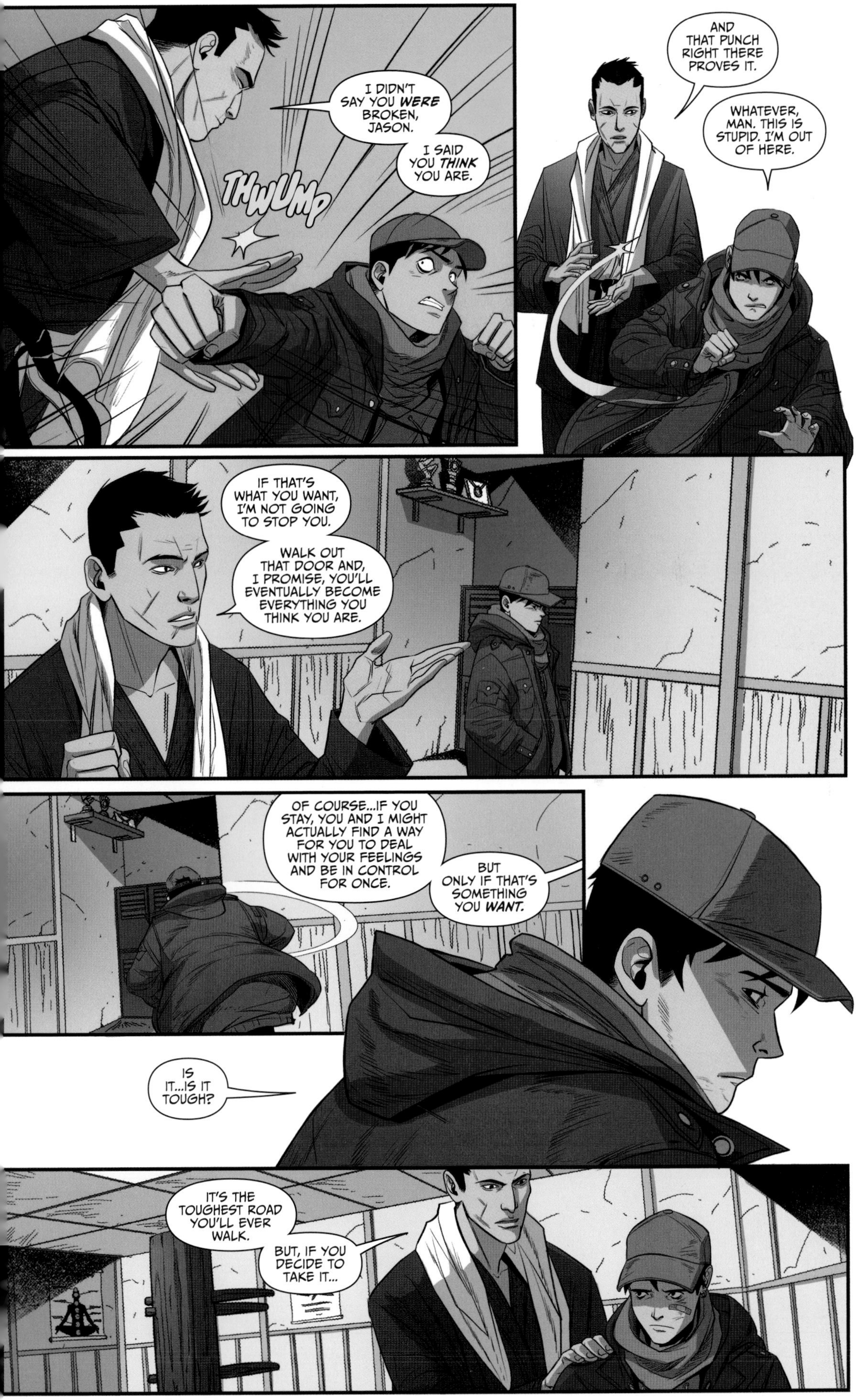
I DIDN'T SAY YOU WERE BROKEN, JASON.
I SAID YOU THINK YOU ARE.
THWUMP
AND THAT PUNCH RIGHT THERE PROVES IT.
WHATEVER, MAN. THIS IS STUPID. I'M OUT OF HERE.
IF THAT'S WHAT YOU WANT, I'M NOT GOING TO STOP YOU.
WALK OUT THAT DOOR AND, I PROMISE, YOU'LL EVENTUALLY BECOME EVERYTHING YOU THINK YOU ARE.
OF COURSE...IF YOU STAY, YOU AND I MIGHT ACTUALLY FIND A WAY FOR YOU TO DEAL WITH YOUR FEELINGS AND BE IN CONTROL FOR ONCE.
BUT ONLY IF THAT'S SOMETHING YOU WANT.
IS IT...IS IT TOUGH?
IT'S THE TOUGHEST ROAD YOU'LL EVER WALK.
BUT, IF YOU DECIDE TO TAKE IT...

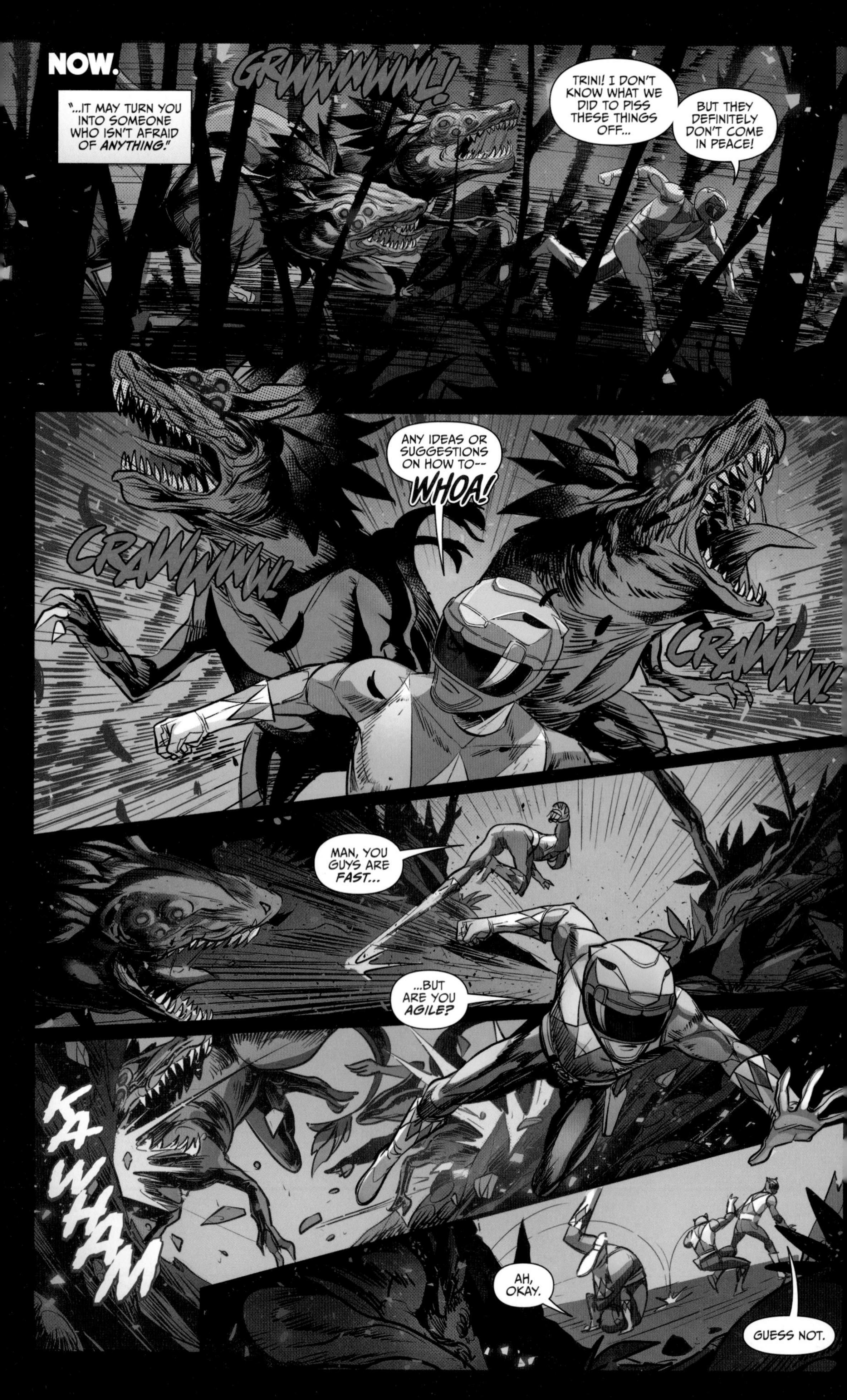
NOW.
GRAWWWWWL!
"...IT MAY TURN YOU INTO SOMEONE WHO ISN'T AFRAID OF ANYTHING."
TRINI! I DON'T KNOW WHAT WE DID TO PISS THESE THINGS OFF...
BUT THEY DEFINITELY DON'T COME IN PEACE!
ANY IDEAS OR SUGGESTIONS ON HOW TO-- WHOA!
CRAWWWW!
CRAWWW!
MAN, YOU GUYS ARE FAST...
...BUT ARE YOU AGILE?
KA-WHAM
AH, OKAY.
GUESS NOT.

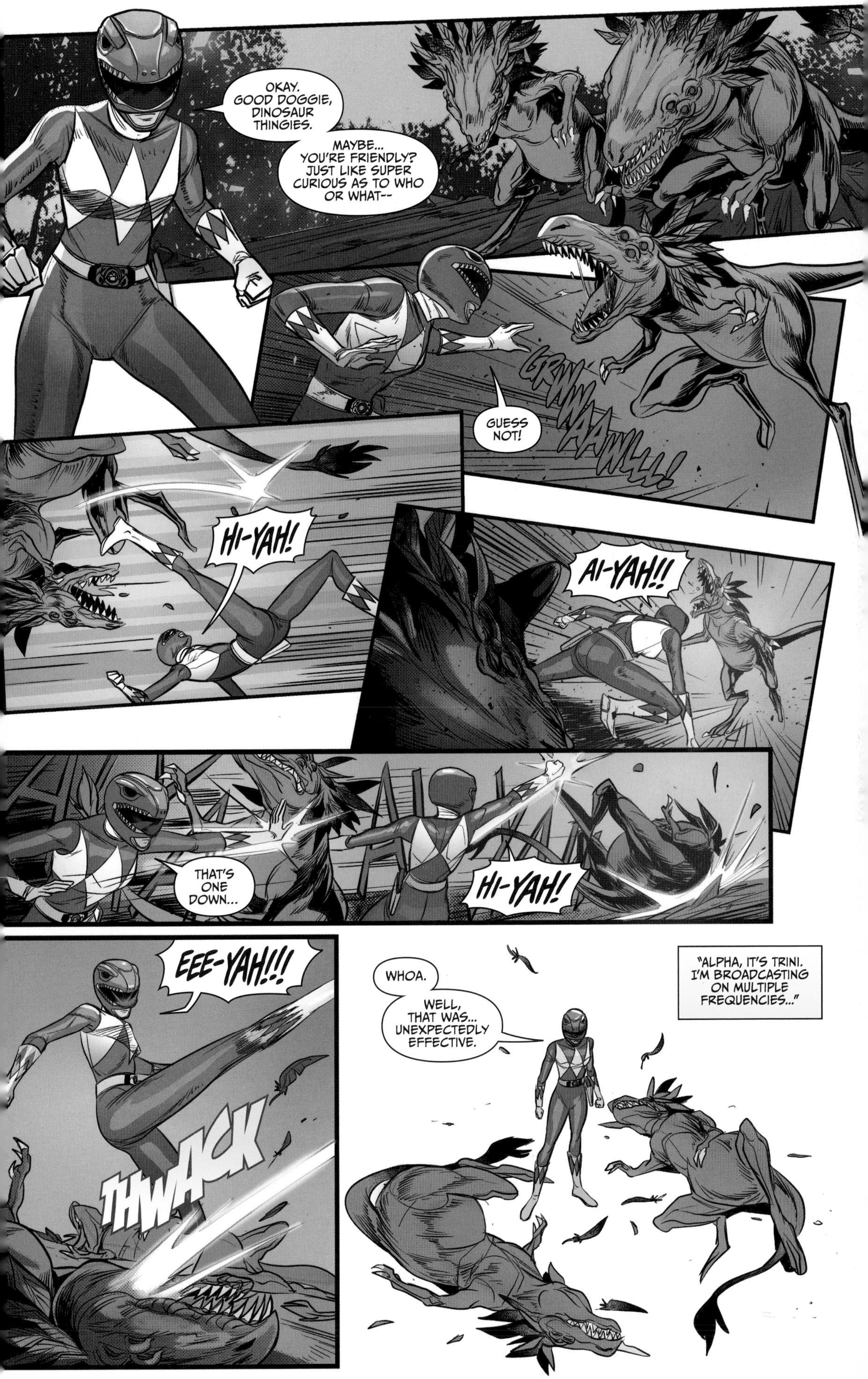
OKAY. GOOD DOGGIE, DINOSAUR THINGIES.
MAYBE... YOU'RE FRIENDLY? JUST LIKE SUPER CURIOUS AS TO WHO OR WHAT--
GRWWAAWLLL!
GUESS NOT!
HI-YAH!
AI-YAH!!
THAT'S ONE DOWN...
HI-YAH!
EEE-YAH!!!
THWACK
WHOA.
WELL, THAT WAS... UNEXPECTEDLY EFFECTIVE.
"ALPHA, IT'S TRINI. I'M BROADCASTING ON MULTIPLE FREQUENCIES..."

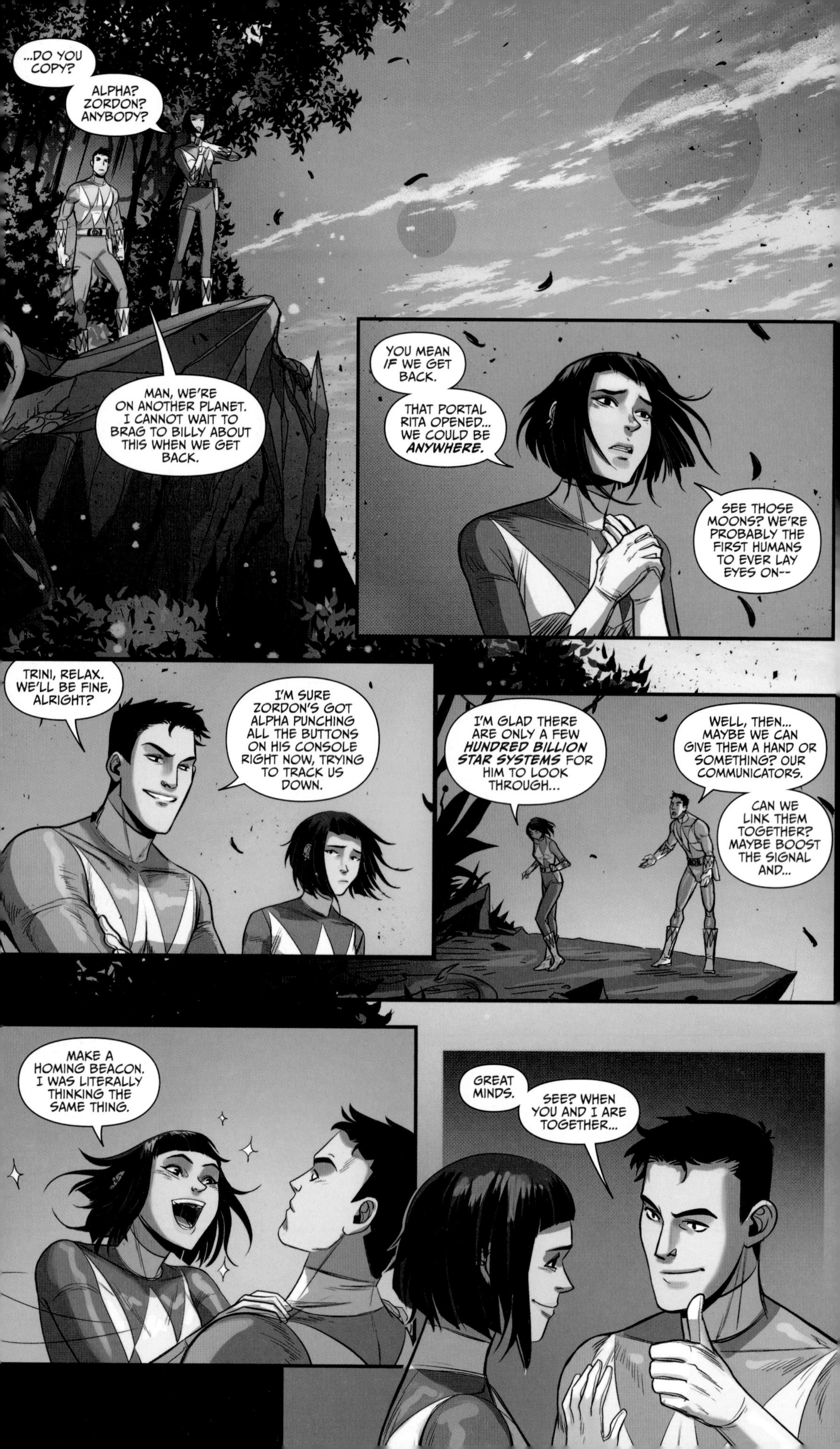
...DO YOU COPY?
ALPHA? ZORDON? ANYBODY?
MAN, WE'RE ON ANOTHER PLANET. I CANNOT WAIT TO BRAG TO BILLY ABOUT THIS WHEN WE GET BACK.
YOU MEAN *IF* WE GET BACK.
THAT PORTAL RITA OPENED... WE COULD BE ***ANYWHERE.***
SEE THOSE MOONS? WE'RE PROBABLY THE FIRST HUMANS TO EVER LAY EYES ON--
TRINI, RELAX. WE'LL BE FINE, ALRIGHT?
I'M SURE ZORDON'S GOT ALPHA PUNCHING ALL THE BUTTONS ON HIS CONSOLE RIGHT NOW, TRYING TO TRACK US DOWN.
I'M GLAD THERE ARE ONLY A FEW ***HUNDRED BILLION STAR SYSTEMS*** FOR HIM TO LOOK THROUGH...
WELL, THEN... MAYBE WE CAN GIVE THEM A HAND OR SOMETHING? OUR COMMUNICATORS.
CAN WE LINK THEM TOGETHER? MAYBE BOOST THE SIGNAL AND...
MAKE A HOMING BEACON. I WAS LITERALLY THINKING THE SAME THING.
GREAT MINDS.
SEE? WHEN YOU AND I ARE TOGETHER...

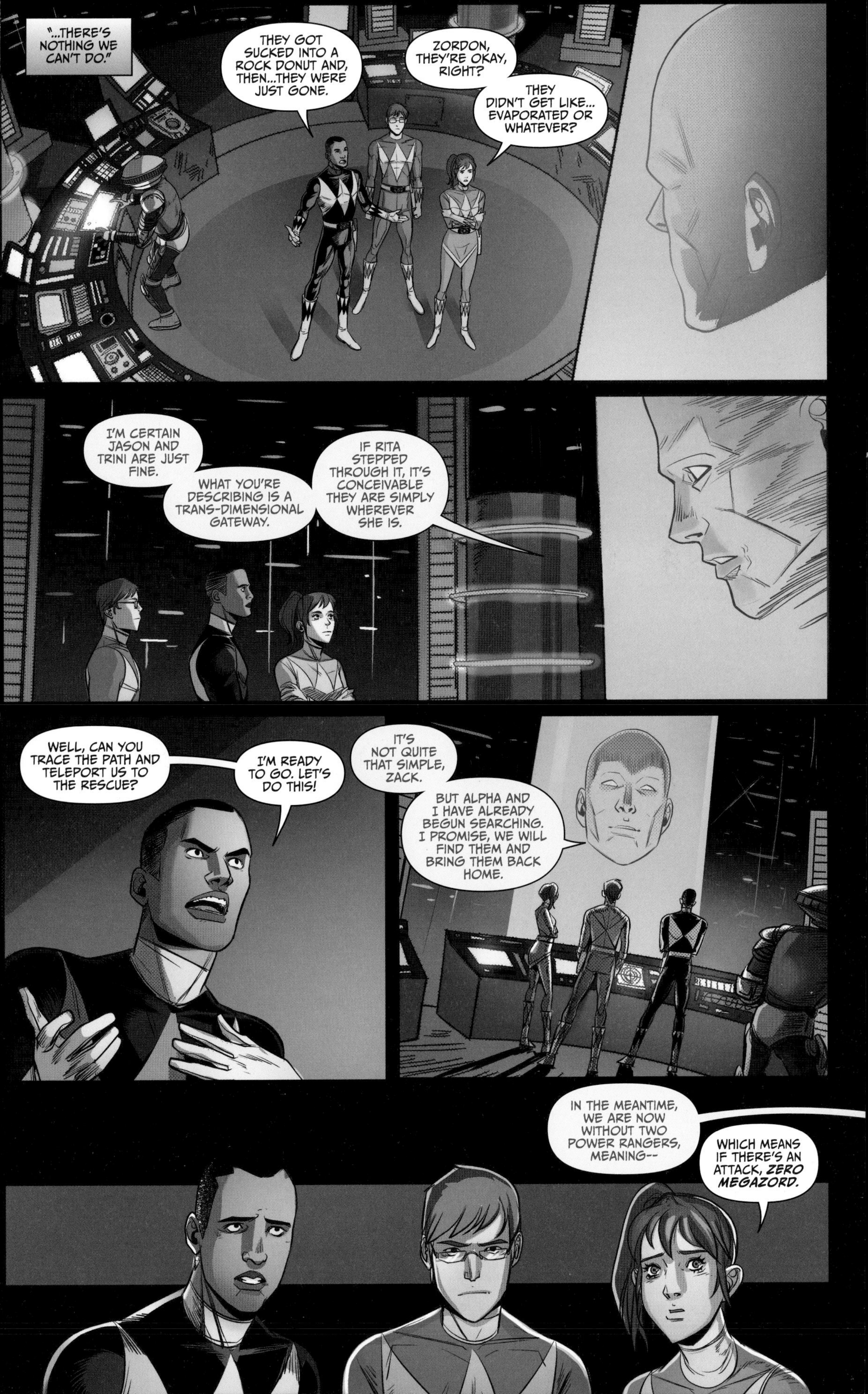
"...THERE'S NOTHING WE CAN'T DO."
THEY GOT SUCKED INTO A ROCK DONUT AND, THEN...THEY WERE JUST GONE.
ZORDON, THEY'RE OKAY, RIGHT?
THEY DIDN'T GET LIKE... EVAPORATED OR WHATEVER?
I'M CERTAIN JASON AND TRINI ARE JUST FINE.
WHAT YOU'RE DESCRIBING IS A TRANS-DIMENSIONAL GATEWAY.
IF RITA STEPPED THROUGH IT, IT'S CONCEIVABLE THEY ARE SIMPLY WHEREVER SHE IS.
WELL, CAN YOU TRACE THE PATH AND TELEPORT US TO THE RESCUE?
I'M READY TO GO. LET'S DO THIS!
IT'S NOT QUITE THAT SIMPLE, ZACK.
BUT ALPHA AND I HAVE ALREADY BEGUN SEARCHING. I PROMISE, WE WILL FIND THEM AND BRING THEM BACK HOME.
IN THE MEANTIME, WE ARE NOW WITHOUT TWO POWER RANGERS, MEANING--
WHICH MEANS IF THERE'S AN ATTACK, ZERO MEGAZORD.

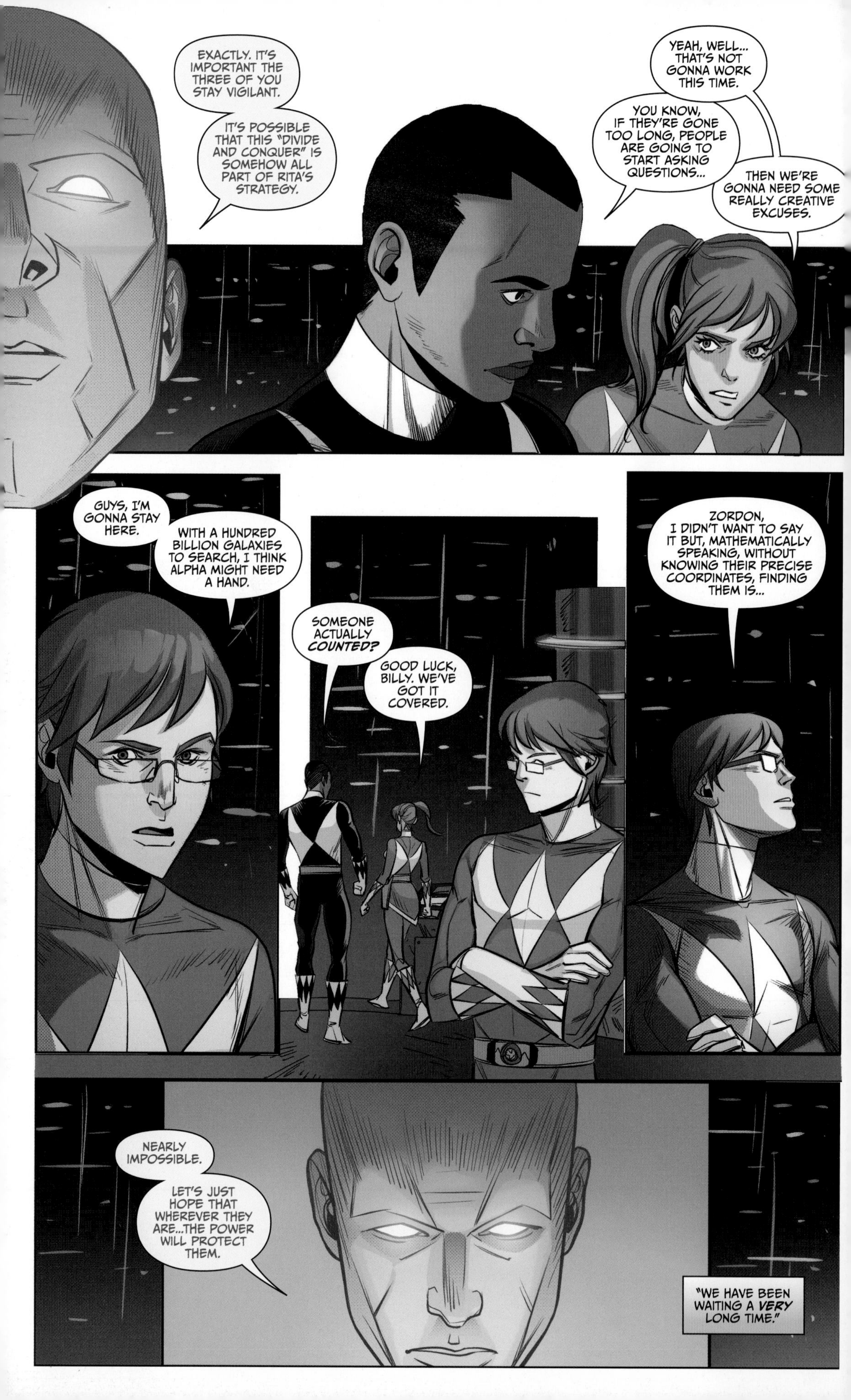
EXACTLY. IT'S IMPORTANT THE THREE OF YOU STAY VIGILANT.
IT'S POSSIBLE THAT THIS "DIVIDE AND CONQUER" IS SOMEHOW ALL PART OF RITA'S STRATEGY.
YOU KNOW, IF THEY'RE GONE TOO LONG, PEOPLE ARE GOING TO START ASKING QUESTIONS...
YEAH, WELL... THAT'S NOT GONNA WORK THIS TIME.
THEN WE'RE GONNA NEED SOME REALLY CREATIVE EXCUSES.
GUYS, I'M GONNA STAY HERE.
WITH A HUNDRED BILLION GALAXIES TO SEARCH, I THINK ALPHA MIGHT NEED A HAND.
SOMEONE ACTUALLY *COUNTED?*
GOOD LUCK, BILLY. WE'VE GOT IT COVERED.
ZORDON, I DIDN'T WANT TO SAY IT BUT, MATHEMATICALLY SPEAKING, WITHOUT KNOWING THEIR PRECISE COORDINATES, FINDING THEM IS...
NEARLY IMPOSSIBLE.
LET'S JUST HOPE THAT WHEREVER THEY ARE...THE POWER WILL PROTECT THEM.
"WE HAVE BEEN WAITING A *VERY* LONG TIME."

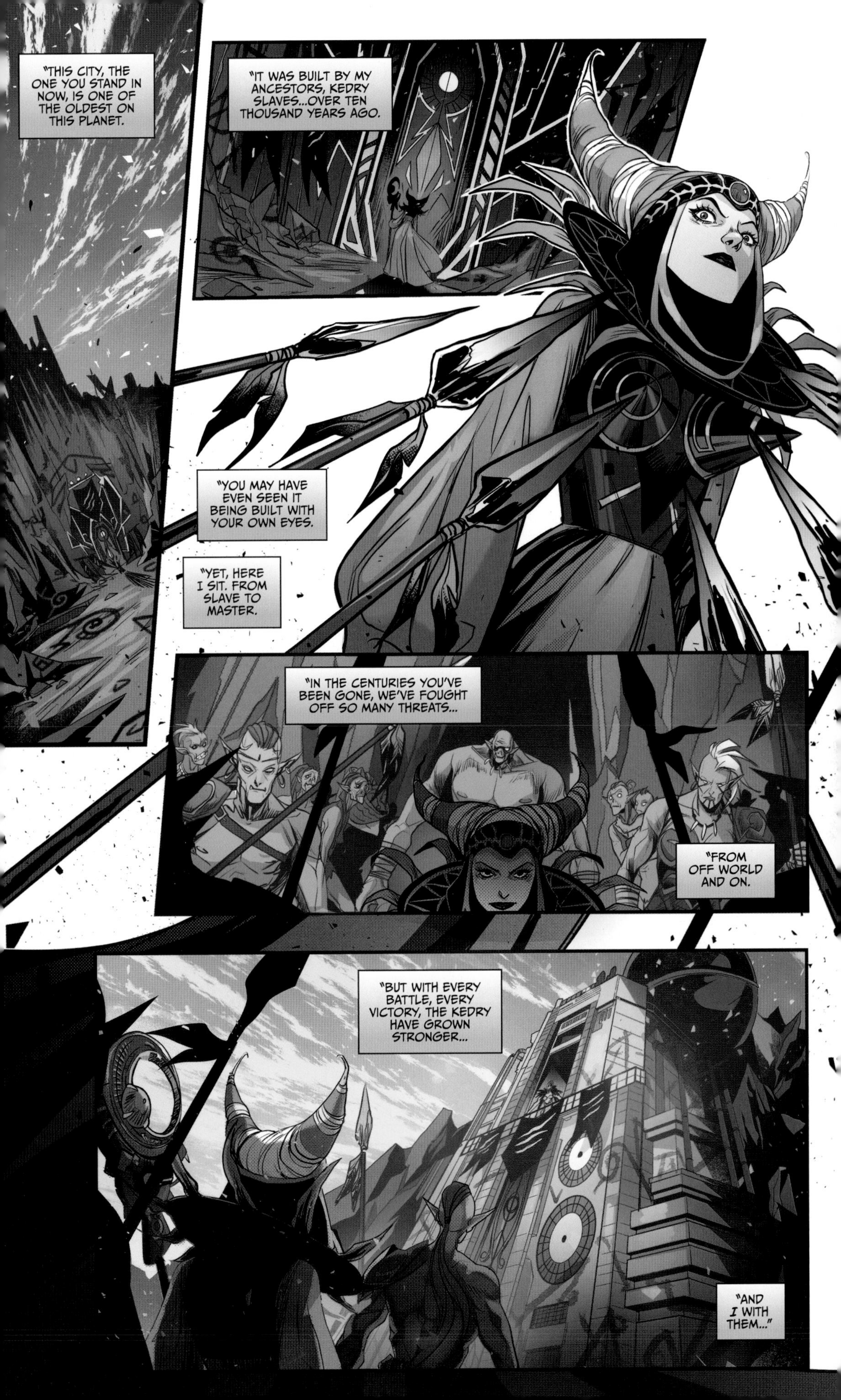
"THIS CITY, THE ONE YOU STAND IN NOW, IS ONE OF THE OLDEST ON THIS PLANET.
"IT WAS BUILT BY MY ANCESTORS, KEDRY SLAVES...OVER TEN THOUSAND YEARS AGO.
"YOU MAY HAVE EVEN SEEN IT BEING BUILT WITH YOUR OWN EYES.
"YET, HERE I SIT. FROM SLAVE TO MASTER.
"IN THE CENTURIES YOU'VE BEEN GONE, WE'VE FOUGHT OFF SO MANY THREATS...
"FROM OFF WORLD AND ON.
"BUT WITH EVERY BATTLE, EVERY VICTORY, THE KEDRY HAVE GROWN STRONGER...
"AND I WITH THEM..."

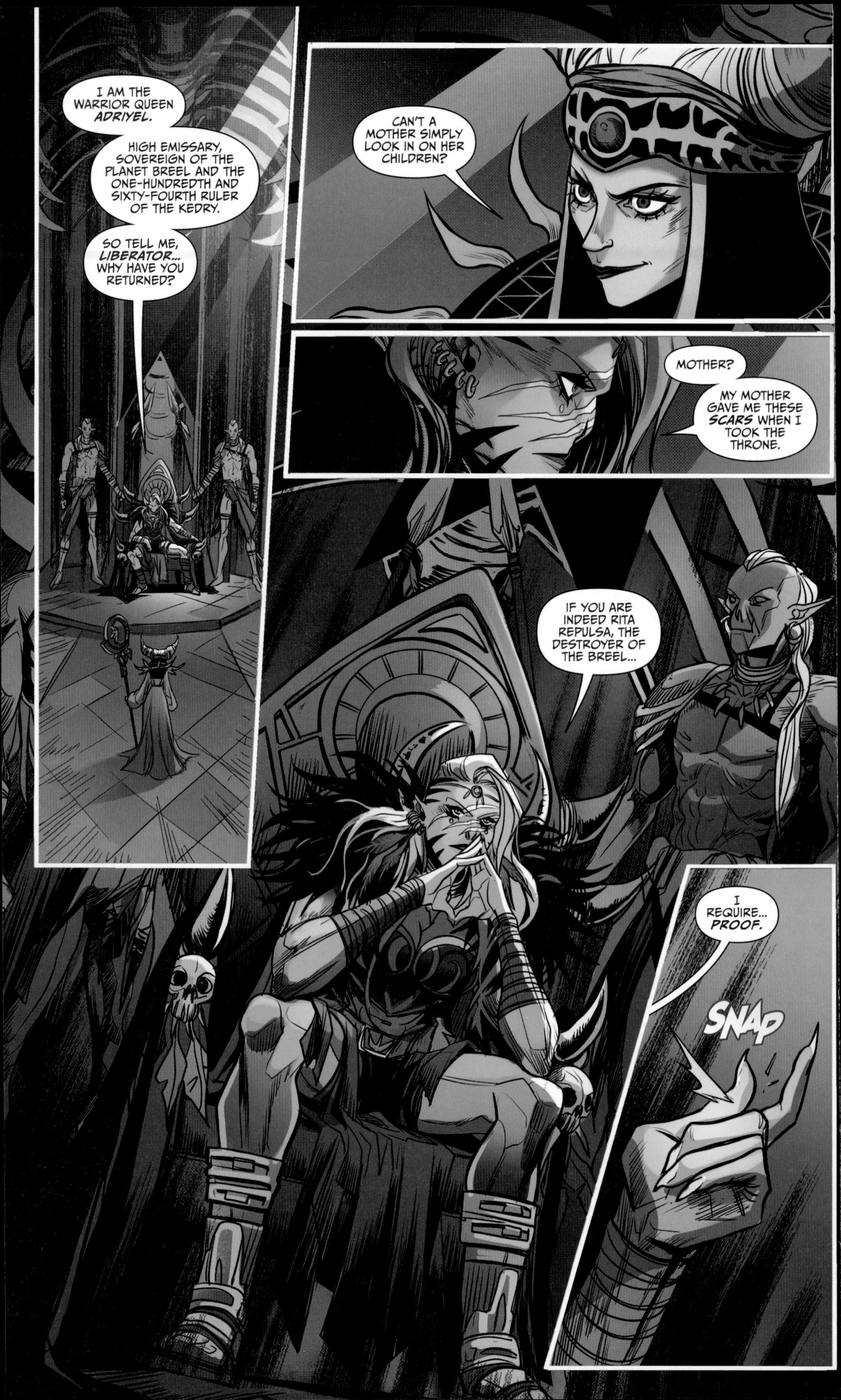
I AM THE WARRIOR QUEEN *ADRIYEL.*
HIGH EMISSARY, SOVEREIGN OF THE PLANET BREEL AND THE ONE-HUNDREDTH AND SIXTY-FOURTH RULER OF THE KEDRY.
SO TELL ME, *LIBERATOR...* WHY HAVE YOU RETURNED?
CAN'T A MOTHER SIMPLY LOOK IN ON HER CHILDREN?
MOTHER?
MY MOTHER GAVE ME THESE *SCARS* WHEN I TOOK THE THRONE.
IF YOU ARE INDEED RITA REPULSA, THE DESTROYER OF THE BREEL...
I REQUIRE... *PROOF.*
SNAP

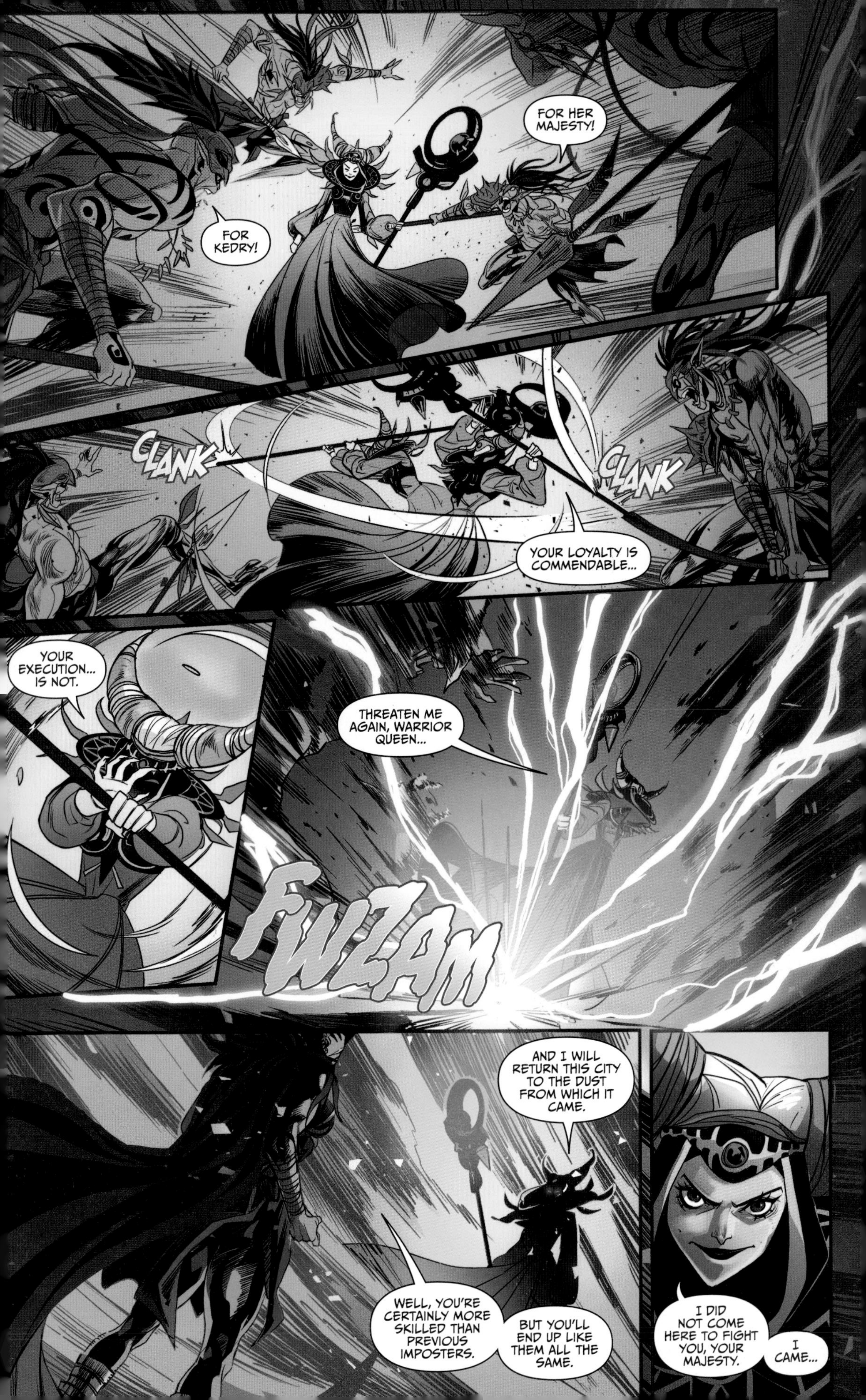
FOR HER MAJESTY!
FOR KEDRY!
CLANK
CLANK
YOUR LOYALTY IS COMMENDABLE...
YOUR EXECUTION... IS NOT.
THREATEN ME AGAIN, WARRIOR QUEEN...
FWZAM
AND I WILL RETURN THIS CITY TO THE DUST FROM WHICH IT CAME.
WELL, YOU'RE CERTAINLY MORE SKILLED THAN PREVIOUS IMPOSTERS.
BUT YOU'LL END UP LIKE THEM ALL THE SAME.
I DID NOT COME HERE TO FIGHT YOU, YOUR MAJESTY.
I CAME...

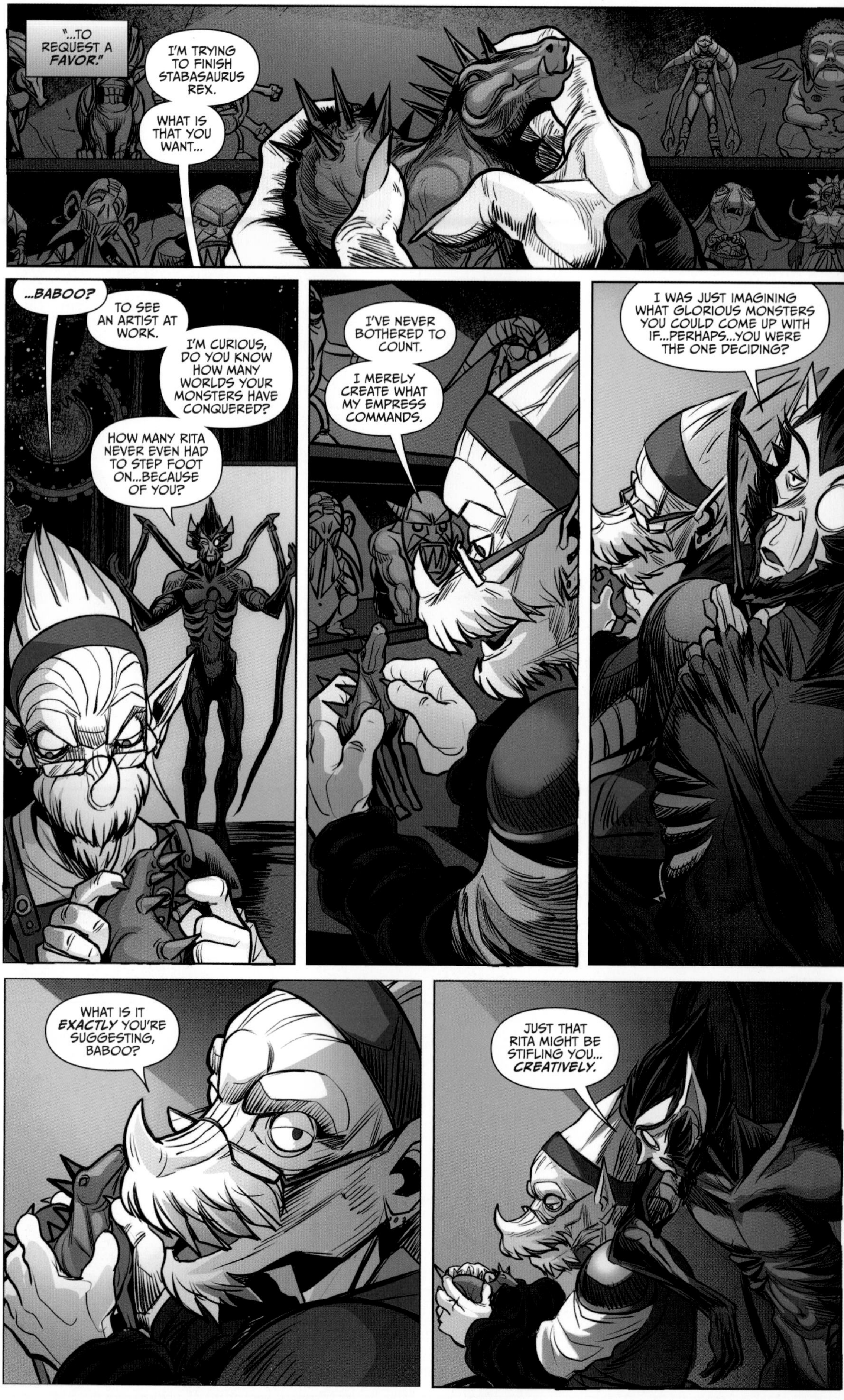
"...TO REQUEST A FAVOR."
I'M TRYING TO FINISH STABASAURUS REX.
WHAT IS THAT YOU WANT...
...BABOO?
TO SEE AN ARTIST AT WORK.
I'M CURIOUS, DO YOU KNOW HOW MANY WORLDS YOUR MONSTERS HAVE CONQUERED?
HOW MANY RITA NEVER EVEN HAD TO STEP FOOT ON...BECAUSE OF YOU?
I'VE NEVER BOTHERED TO COUNT.
I MERELY CREATE WHAT MY EMPRESS COMMANDS.
I WAS JUST IMAGINING WHAT GLORIOUS MONSTERS YOU COULD COME UP WITH IF...PERHAPS...YOU WERE THE ONE DECIDING?
WHAT IS IT EXACTLY YOU'RE SUGGESTING, BABOO?
JUST THAT RITA MIGHT BE STIFLING YOU... CREATIVELY.

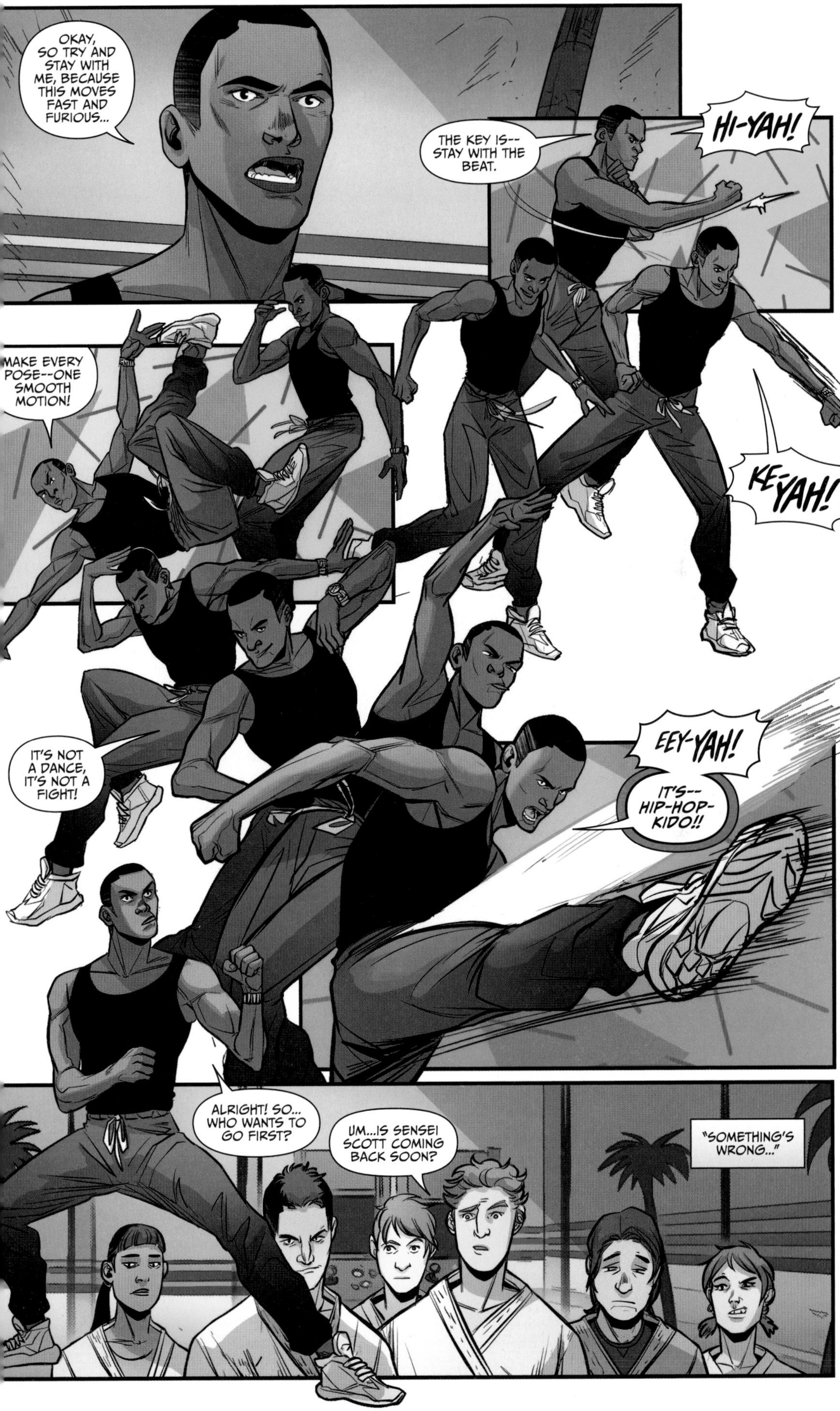
OKAY, SO TRY AND STAY WITH ME, BECAUSE THIS MOVES FAST AND FURIOUS...
THE KEY IS-- STAY WITH THE BEAT.
HI-YAH!
MAKE EVERY POSE--ONE SMOOTH MOTION!
KE-YAH!
IT'S NOT A DANCE, IT'S NOT A FIGHT!
EEY-YAH!
IT'S-- HIP-HOP-KIDO!!
ALRIGHT! SO... WHO WANTS TO GO FIRST?
UM...IS SENSEI SCOTT COMING BACK SOON?
"SOMETHING'S WRONG..."

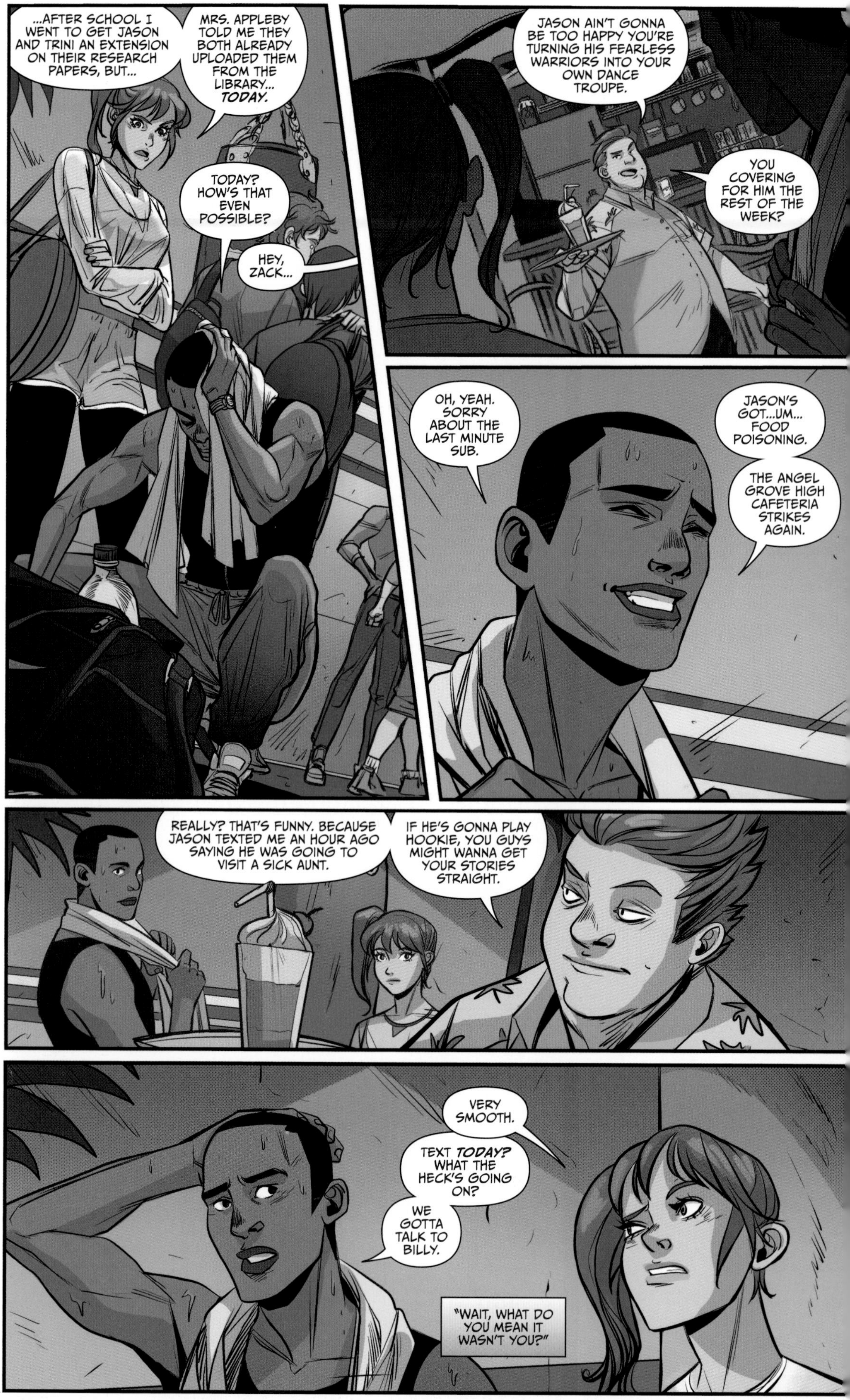
...AFTER SCHOOL I WENT TO GET JASON AND TRINI AN EXTENSION ON THEIR RESEARCH PAPERS, BUT...
MRS. APPLEBY TOLD ME THEY BOTH ALREADY UPLOADED THEM FROM THE LIBRARY... TODAY.
TODAY? HOW'S THAT EVEN POSSIBLE?
HEY, ZACK...
JASON AIN'T GONNA BE TOO HAPPY YOU'RE TURNING HIS FEARLESS WARRIORS INTO YOUR OWN DANCE TROUPE.
YOU COVERING FOR HIM THE REST OF THE WEEK?
OH, YEAH. SORRY ABOUT THE LAST MINUTE SUB.
JASON'S GOT...UM... FOOD POISONING.
THE ANGEL GROVE HIGH CAFETERIA STRIKES AGAIN.
REALLY? THAT'S FUNNY. BECAUSE JASON TEXTED ME AN HOUR AGO SAYING HE WAS GOING TO VISIT A SICK AUNT.
IF HE'S GONNA PLAY HOOKIE, YOU GUYS MIGHT WANNA GET YOUR STORIES STRAIGHT.
VERY SMOOTH.
TEXT TODAY? WHAT THE HECK'S GOING ON?
WE GOTTA TALK TO BILLY.
"WAIT, WHAT DO YOU MEAN IT WASN'T YOU?"

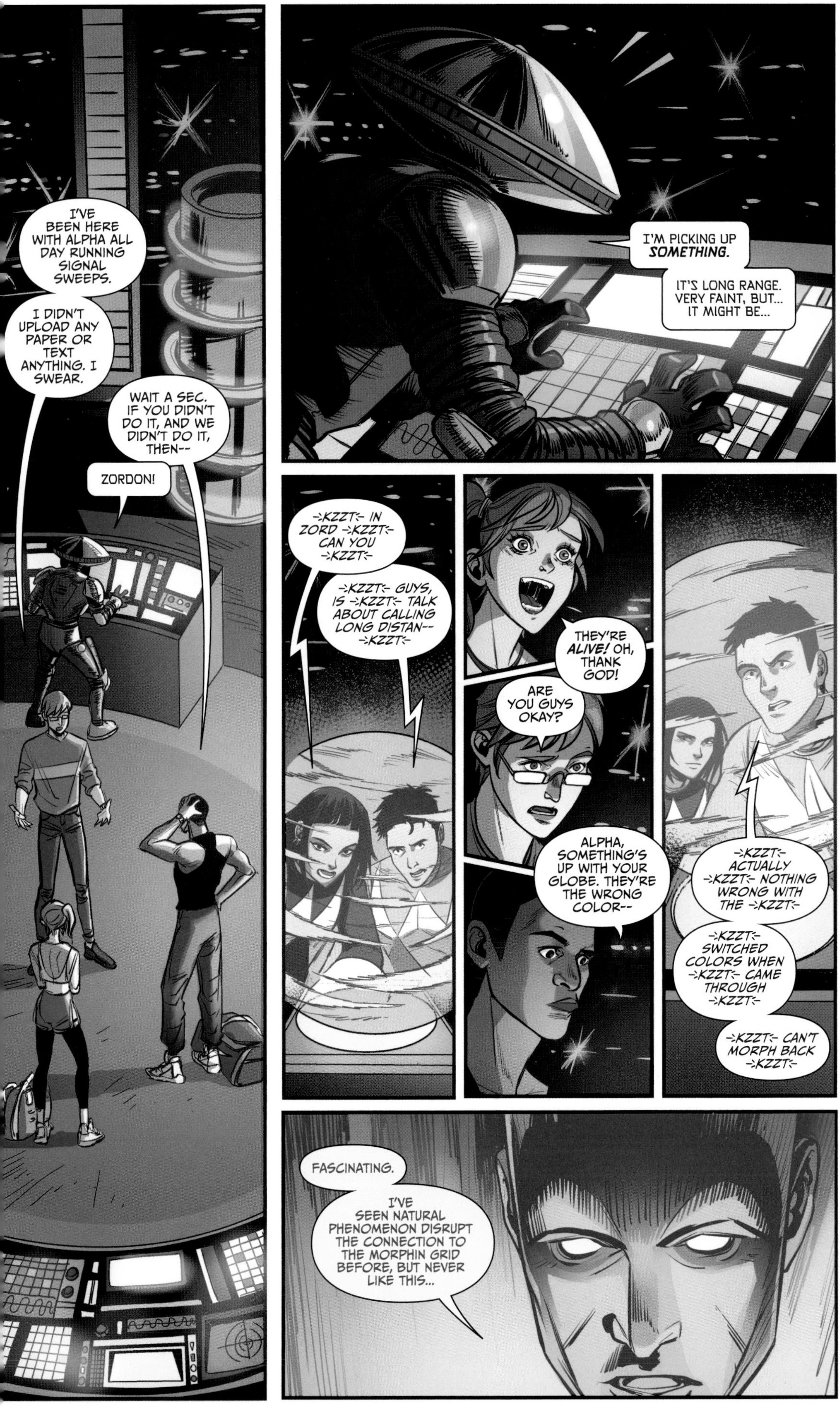
I'VE BEEN HERE WITH ALPHA ALL DAY RUNNING SIGNAL SWEEPS.
I DIDN'T UPLOAD ANY PAPER OR TEXT ANYTHING. I SWEAR.
WAIT A SEC. IF YOU DIDN'T DO IT, AND WE DIDN'T DO IT, THEN--
ZORDON!
I'M PICKING UP SOMETHING.
IT'S LONG RANGE. VERY FAINT, BUT... IT MIGHT BE...
-KZZT- IN ZORD -KZZT- CAN YOU -KZZT-
-KZZT- GUYS, IS -KZZT- TALK ABOUT CALLING LONG DISTAN-- -KZZT-
THEY'RE ALIVE! OH, THANK GOD!
ARE YOU GUYS OKAY?
ALPHA, SOMETHING'S UP WITH YOUR GLOBE. THEY'RE THE WRONG COLOR--
-KZZT- ACTUALLY -KZZT- NOTHING WRONG WITH THE -KZZT-
-KZZT- SWITCHED COLORS WHEN -KZZT- CAME THROUGH -KZZT-
-KZZT- CAN'T MORPH BACK -KZZT-
FASCINATING.
I'VE SEEN NATURAL PHENOMENON DISRUPT THE CONNECTION TO THE MORPHIN GRID BEFORE, BUT NEVER LIKE THIS...

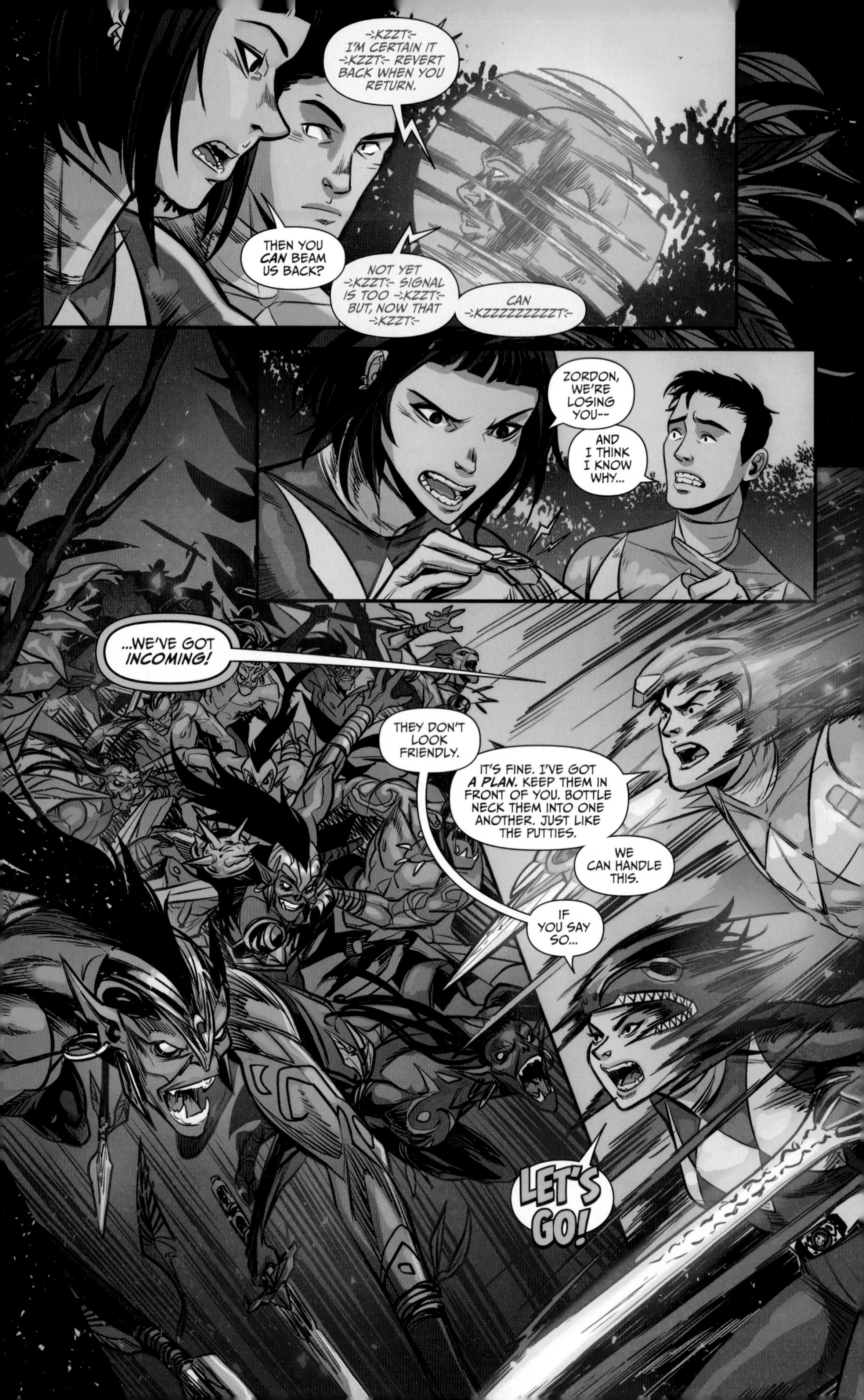

-KZZT- I'M CERTAIN IT -KZZT- REVERT BACK WHEN YOU RETURN.
THEN YOU CAN BEAM US BACK?
NOT YET -KZZT- SIGNAL IS TOO -KZZT- BUT, NOW THAT -KZZT-
CAN -KZZZZZZZZZT-
ZORDON, WE'RE LOSING YOU--
AND I THINK I KNOW WHY...
...WE'VE GOT INCOMING!
THEY DON'T LOOK FRIENDLY.
IT'S FINE. I'VE GOT A PLAN. KEEP THEM IN FRONT OF YOU. BOTTLE NECK THEM INTO ONE ANOTHER. JUST LIKE THE PUTTIES.
WE CAN HANDLE THIS.
IF YOU SAY SO...
LET'S GO!

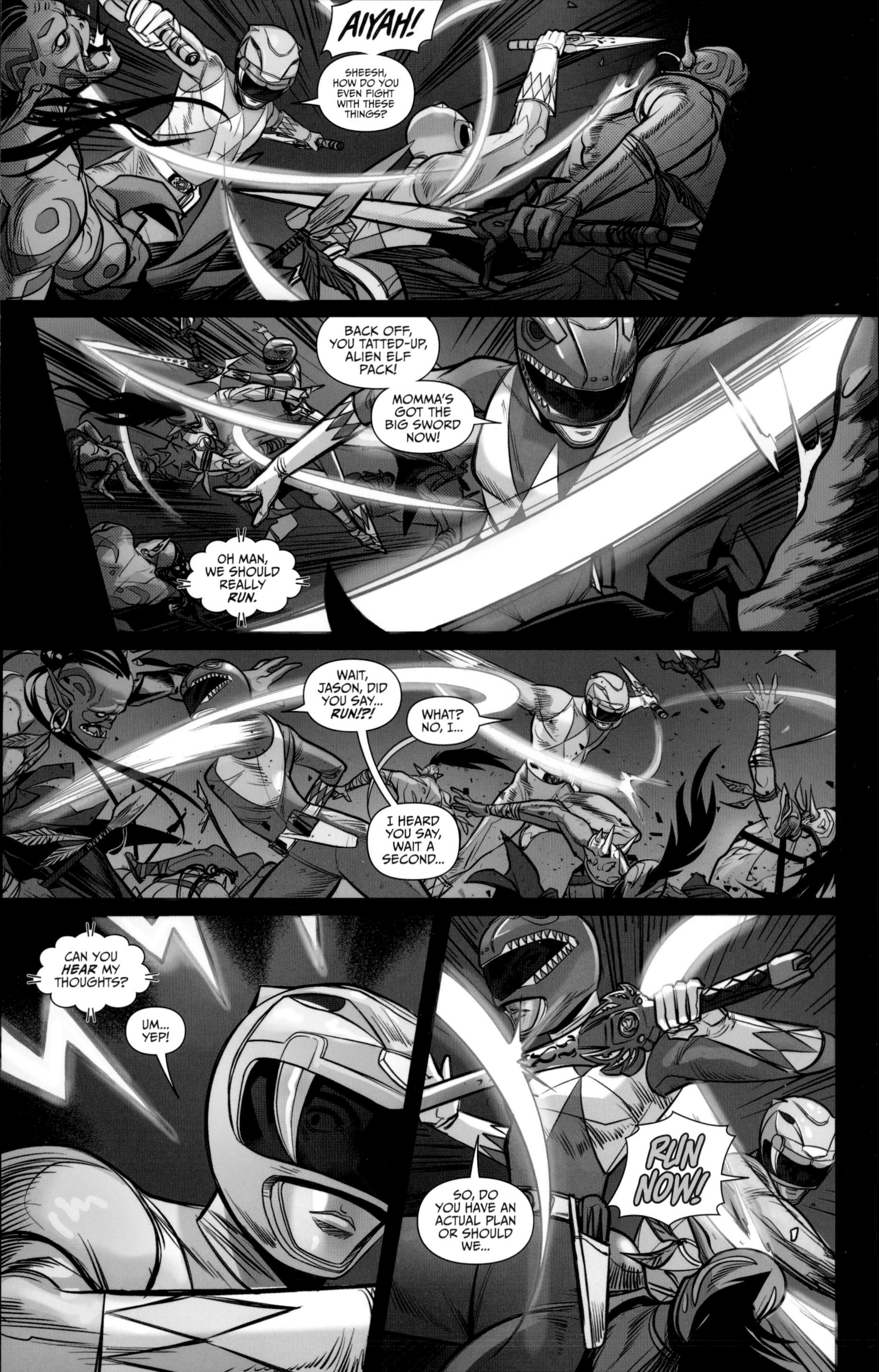
AIYAH!
SHEESH, HOW DO YOU EVEN FIGHT WITH THESE THINGS?
BACK OFF, YOU TATTED-UP, ALIEN ELF PACK!
MOMMA'S GOT THE BIG SWORD NOW!
OH MAN, WE SHOULD REALLY RUN.
WAIT, JASON, DID YOU SAY... RUN!?!
WHAT? NO, I...
I HEARD YOU SAY, WAIT A SECOND...
CAN YOU HEAR MY THOUGHTS?
UM... YEP!
SO, DO YOU HAVE AN ACTUAL PLAN OR SHOULD WE...
RUN NOW!

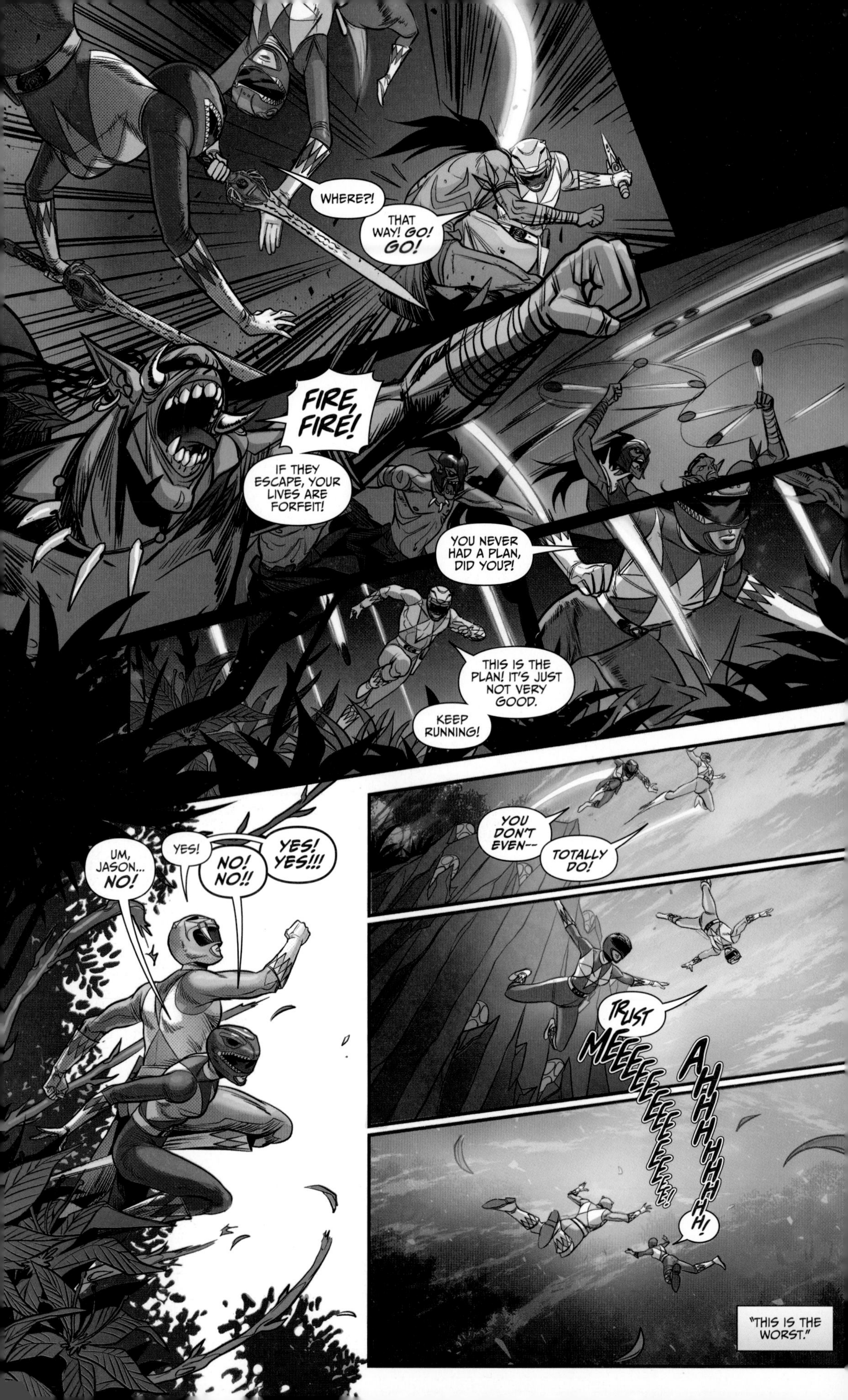
WHERE?!
THAT WAY! GO! GO!
FIRE, FIRE!
IF THEY ESCAPE, YOUR LIVES ARE FORFEIT!
YOU NEVER HAD A PLAN, DID YOU?!
THIS IS THE PLAN! IT'S JUST NOT VERY GOOD.
KEEP RUNNING!
UM, JASON... NO!
YES!
NO! NO!!
YES! YES!!!
YOU DON'T EVEN--
TOTALLY DO!
TRUST MEEEEEEEEEEEE!
AHHHHHHHHH!
"THIS IS THE WORST."

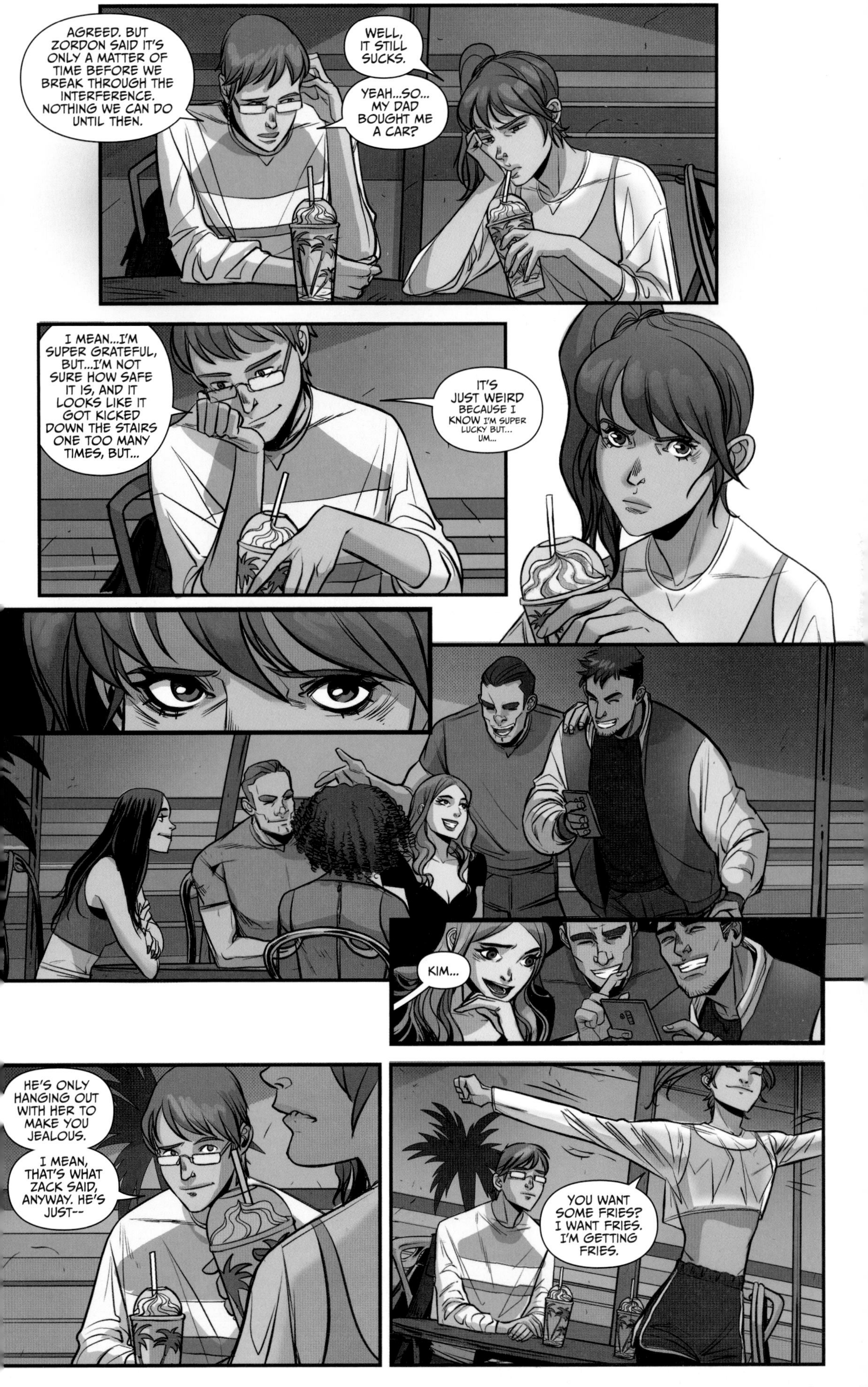
AGREED. BUT ZORDON SAID IT'S ONLY A MATTER OF TIME BEFORE WE BREAK THROUGH THE INTERFERENCE. NOTHING WE CAN DO UNTIL THEN.
WELL, IT STILL SUCKS.
YEAH...SO... MY DAD BOUGHT ME A CAR?
I MEAN...I'M SUPER GRATEFUL, BUT...I'M NOT SURE HOW SAFE IT IS, AND IT LOOKS LIKE IT GOT KICKED DOWN THE STAIRS ONE TOO MANY TIMES, BUT...
IT'S JUST WEIRD BECAUSE I KNOW I'M SUPER LUCKY BUT... UM...
KIM...
HE'S ONLY HANGING OUT WITH HER TO MAKE YOU JEALOUS.
I MEAN, THAT'S WHAT ZACK SAID, ANYWAY. HE'S JUST--
YOU WANT SOME FRIES? I WANT FRIES. I'M GETTING FRIES.

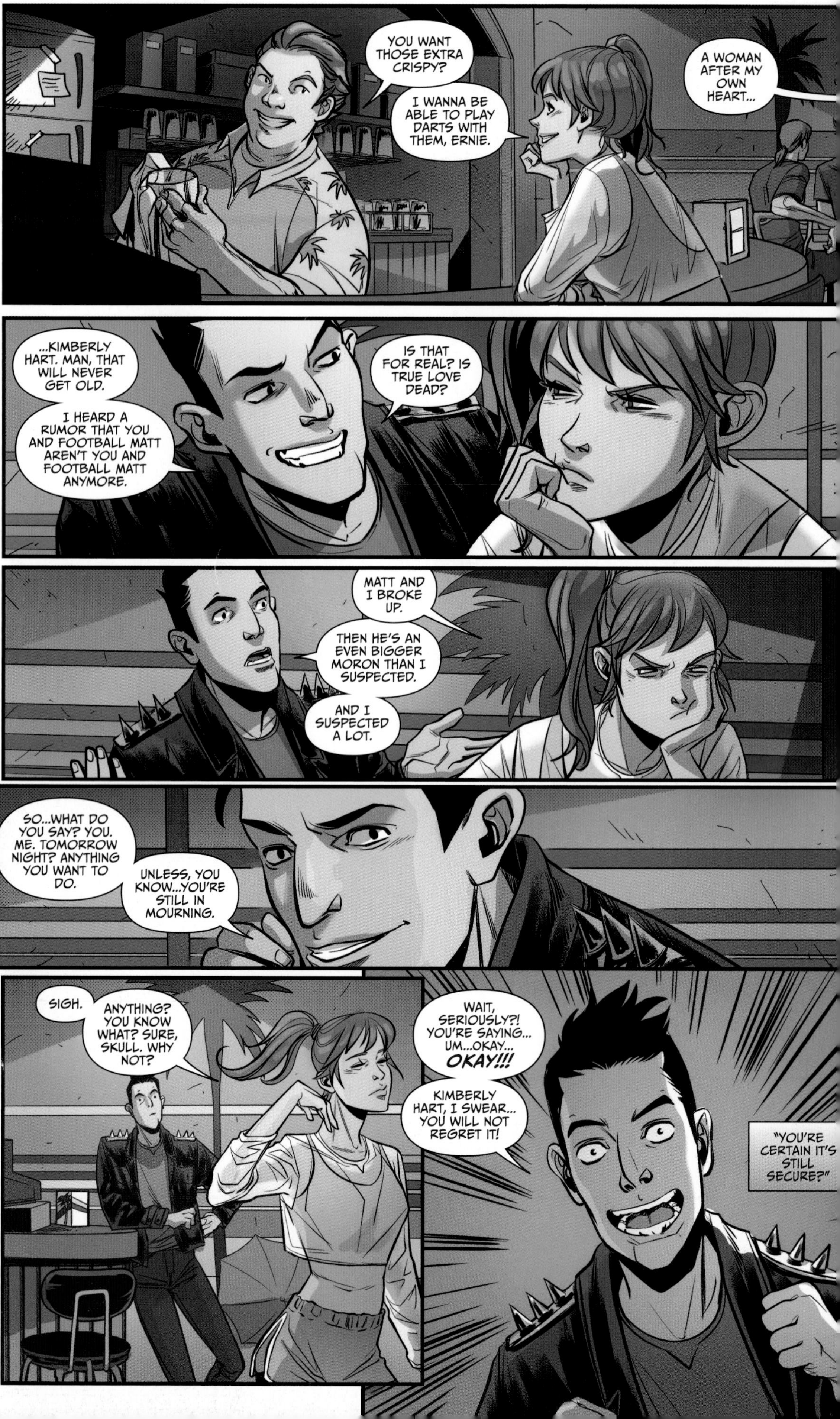

YOU WANT THOSE EXTRA CRISPY?
I WANNA BE ABLE TO PLAY DARTS WITH THEM, ERNIE.
A WOMAN AFTER MY OWN HEART...
...KIMBERLY HART. MAN, THAT WILL NEVER GET OLD.
I HEARD A RUMOR THAT YOU AND FOOTBALL MATT AREN'T YOU AND FOOTBALL MATT ANYMORE.
IS THAT FOR REAL? IS TRUE LOVE DEAD?
MATT AND I BROKE UP.
THEN HE'S AN EVEN BIGGER MORON THAN I SUSPECTED.
AND I SUSPECTED A LOT.
SO...WHAT DO YOU SAY? YOU. ME. TOMORROW NIGHT? ANYTHING YOU WANT TO DO.
UNLESS, YOU KNOW...YOU'RE STILL IN MOURNING.
SIGH.
ANYTHING? YOU KNOW WHAT? SURE, SKULL. WHY NOT?
WAIT, SERIOUSLY?! YOU'RE SAYING... UM...OKAY... OKAY!!!
KIMBERLY HART, I SWEAR... YOU WILL NOT REGRET IT!
"YOU'RE CERTAIN IT'S STILL SECURE?"

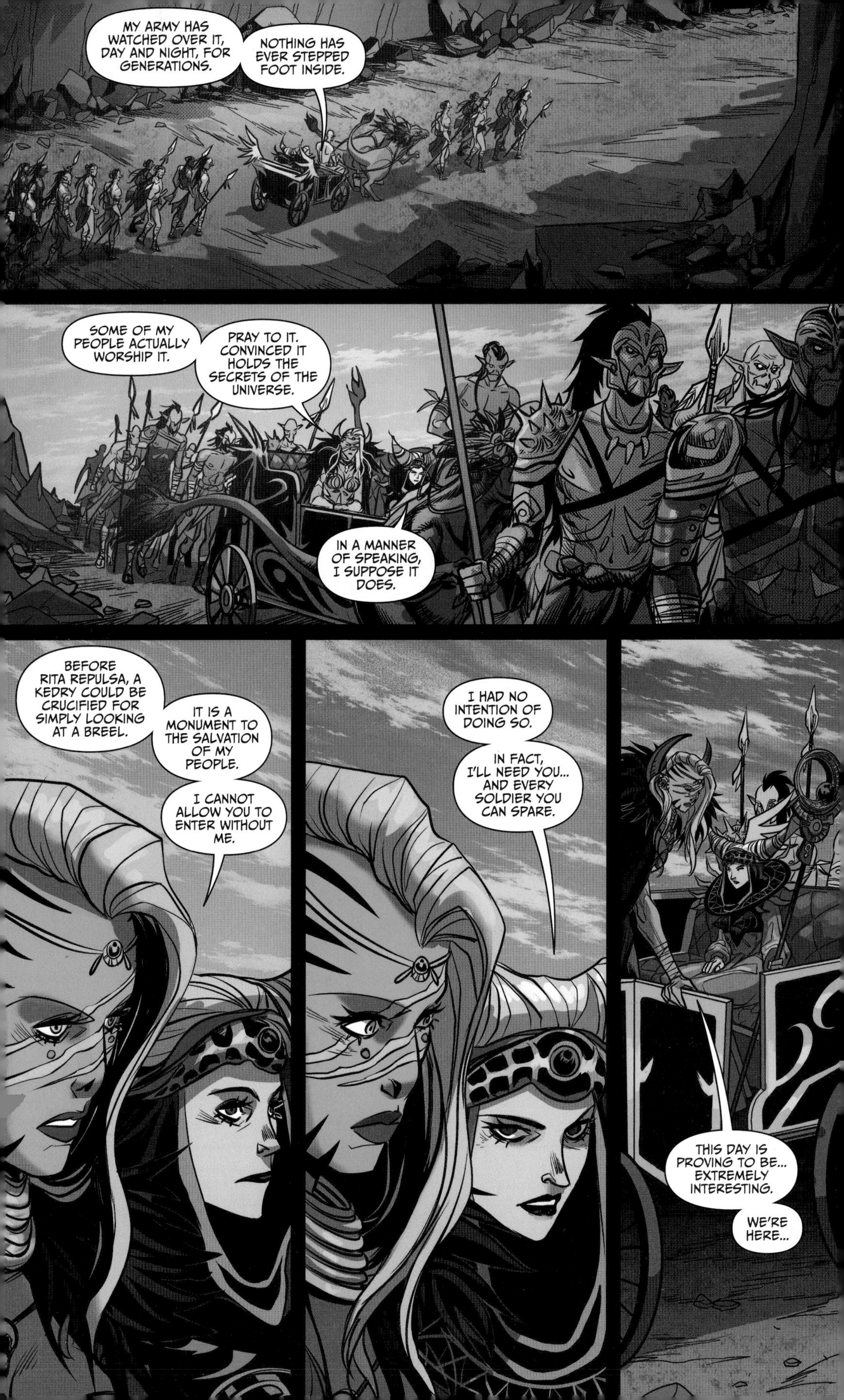

MY ARMY HAS WATCHED OVER IT, DAY AND NIGHT, FOR GENERATIONS.
NOTHING HAS EVER STEPPED FOOT INSIDE.
SOME OF MY PEOPLE ACTUALLY WORSHIP IT.
PRAY TO IT. CONVINCED IT HOLDS THE SECRETS OF THE UNIVERSE.
IN A MANNER OF SPEAKING, I SUPPOSE IT DOES.
BEFORE RITA REPULSA, A KEDRY COULD BE CRUCIFIED FOR SIMPLY LOOKING AT A BREEL.
IT IS A MONUMENT TO THE SALVATION OF MY PEOPLE.
I CANNOT ALLOW YOU TO ENTER WITHOUT ME.
I HAD NO INTENTION OF DOING SO.
IN FACT, I'LL NEED YOU... AND EVERY SOLDIER YOU CAN SPARE.
THIS DAY IS PROVING TO BE... EXTREMELY INTERESTING.
WE'RE HERE...

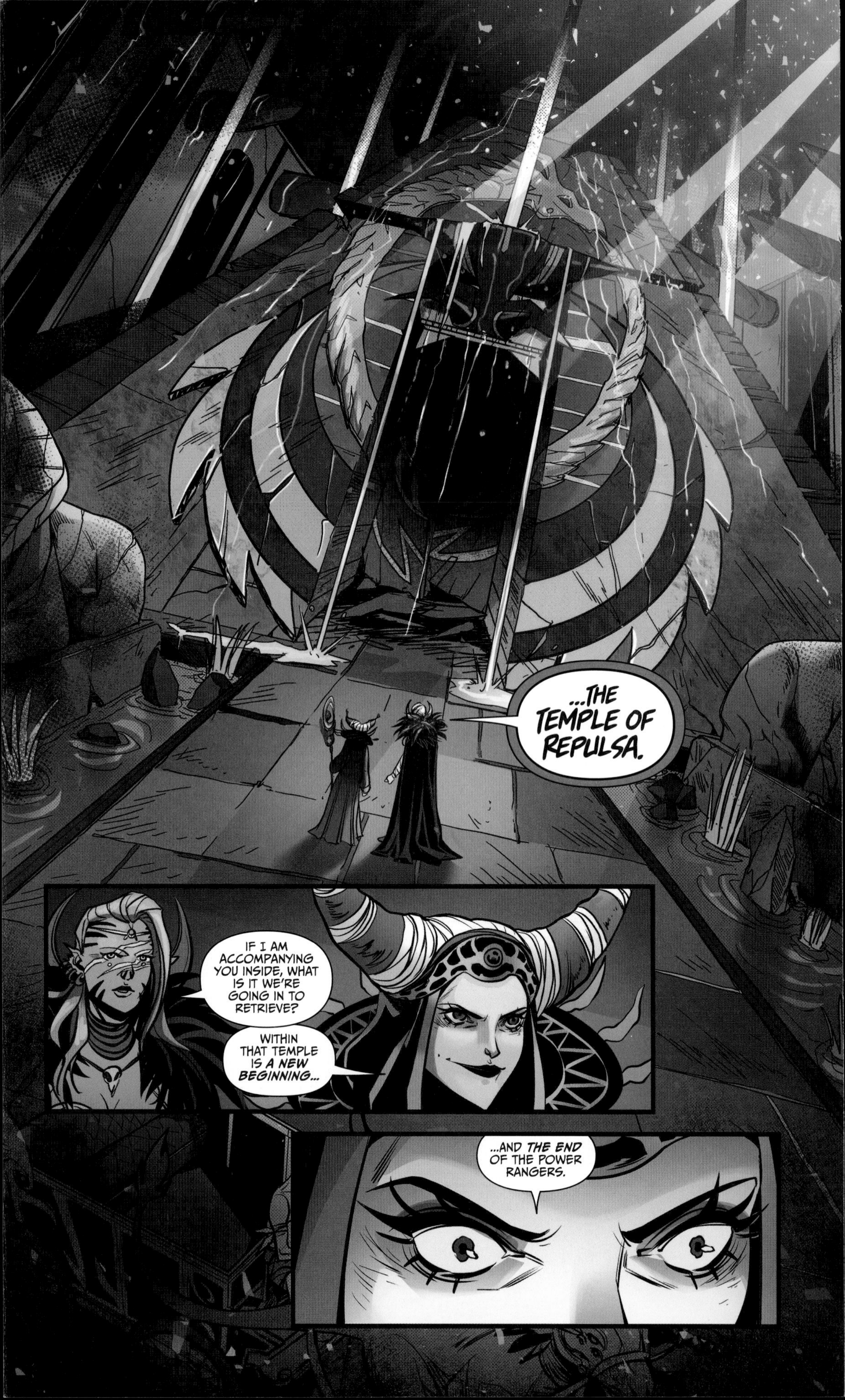
...THE TEMPLE OF REPULSA.
IF I AM ACCOMPANYING YOU INSIDE, WHAT IS IT WE'RE GOING IN TO RETRIEVE?
WITHIN THAT TEMPLE IS *A NEW BEGINNING...*
...AND *THE END* OF THE POWER RANGERS.

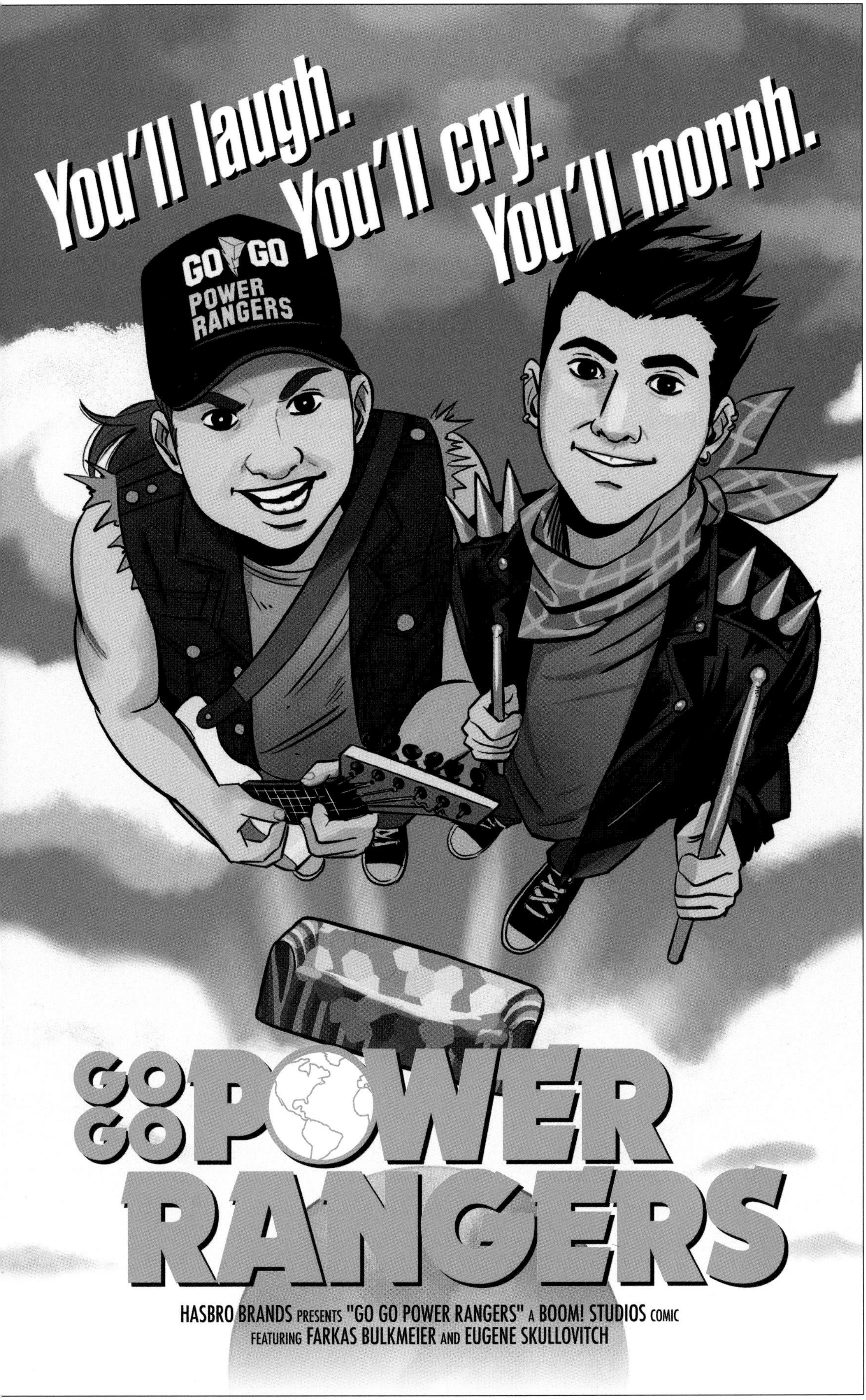
You'll laugh. You'll cry. You'll morph.
GO GO POWER RANGERS
GO GO POWER RANGERS
HASBRO BRANDS PRESENTS "GO GO POWER RANGERS" A BOOM! STUDIOS COMIC
FEATURING FARKAS BULKMEIER AND EUGENE SKULLOVITCH

NATACHA BUSTOS WITH DESIGN BY **DYLAN TODD** ISSUE FOURTEEN MOVIE HOMAGE VARIANT

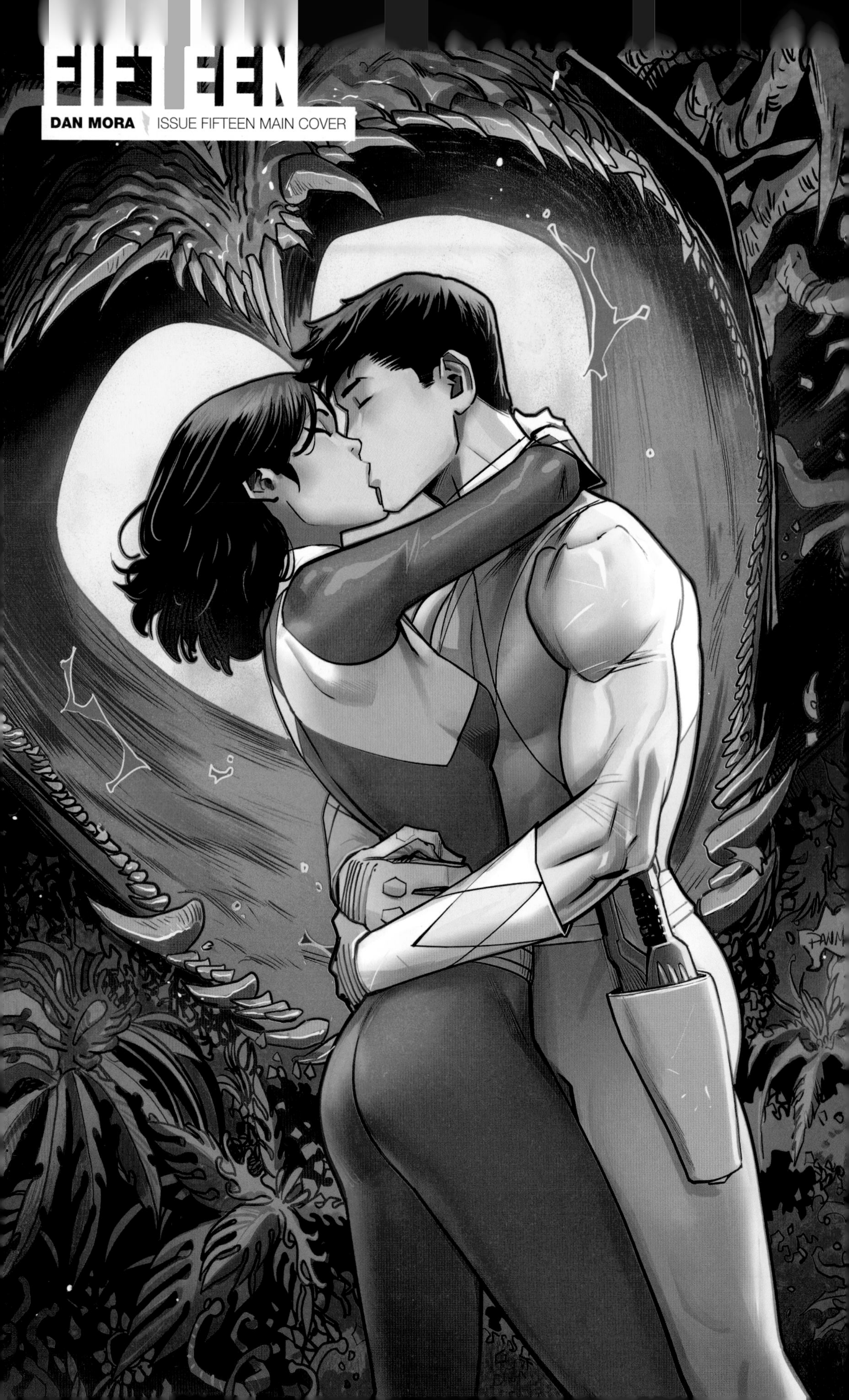
FIFTEEN
DAN MORA
ISSUE FIFTEEN MAIN COVER

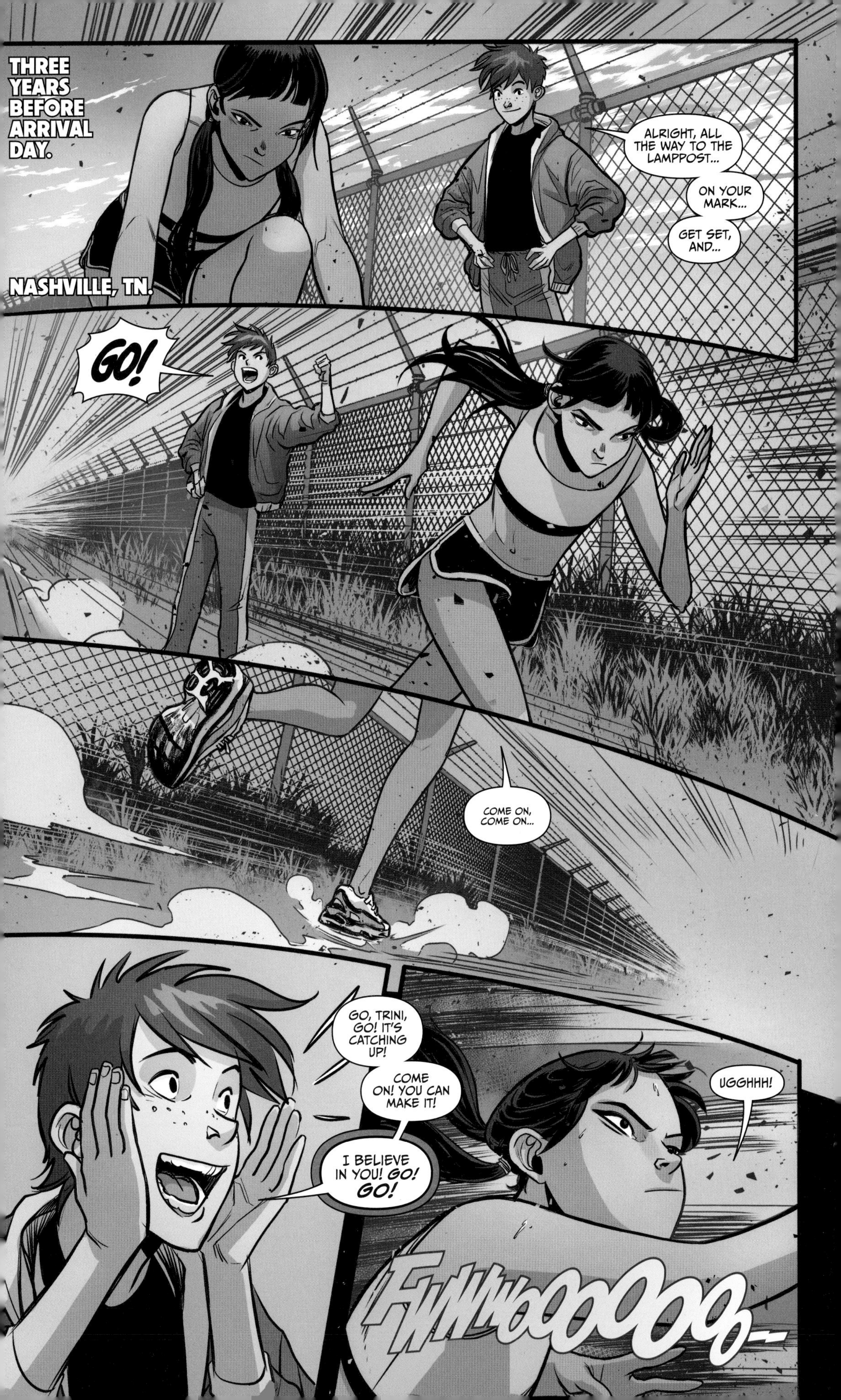
THREE YEARS BEFORE ARRIVAL DAY.
NASHVILLE, TN.
ALRIGHT, ALL THE WAY TO THE LAMPPOST...
ON YOUR MARK...
GET SET, AND...
GO!
COME ON, COME ON...
GO, TRINI, GO! IT'S CATCHING UP!
COME ON! YOU CAN MAKE IT!
I BELIEVE IN YOU! GO! GO!
UGGHHH!
FWWWOOOOOO-

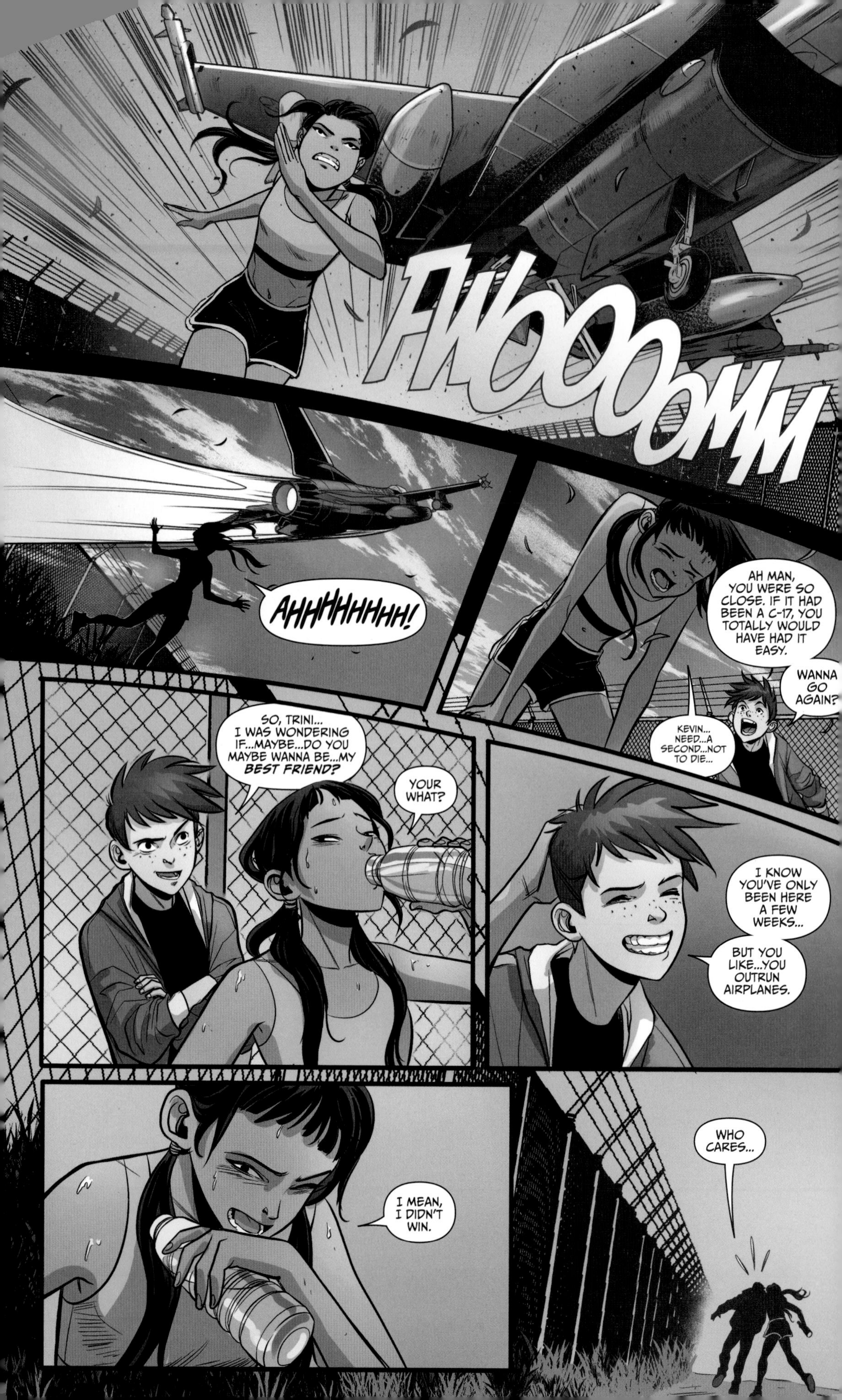

FWOOOOOMM
AHHHHHHHH!
AH MAN, YOU WERE SO CLOSE. IF IT HAD BEEN A C-17, YOU TOTALLY WOULD HAVE HAD IT EASY.
WANNA GO AGAIN?
KEVIN... NEED...A SECOND...NOT TO DIE...
SO, TRINI... I WAS WONDERING IF...MAYBE...DO YOU MAYBE WANNA BE...MY *BEST FRIEND?*
YOUR WHAT?
I KNOW YOU'VE ONLY BEEN HERE A FEW WEEKS...
BUT YOU LIKE...YOU OUTRUN AIRPLANES.
I MEAN, I DIDN'T WIN.
WHO CARES...

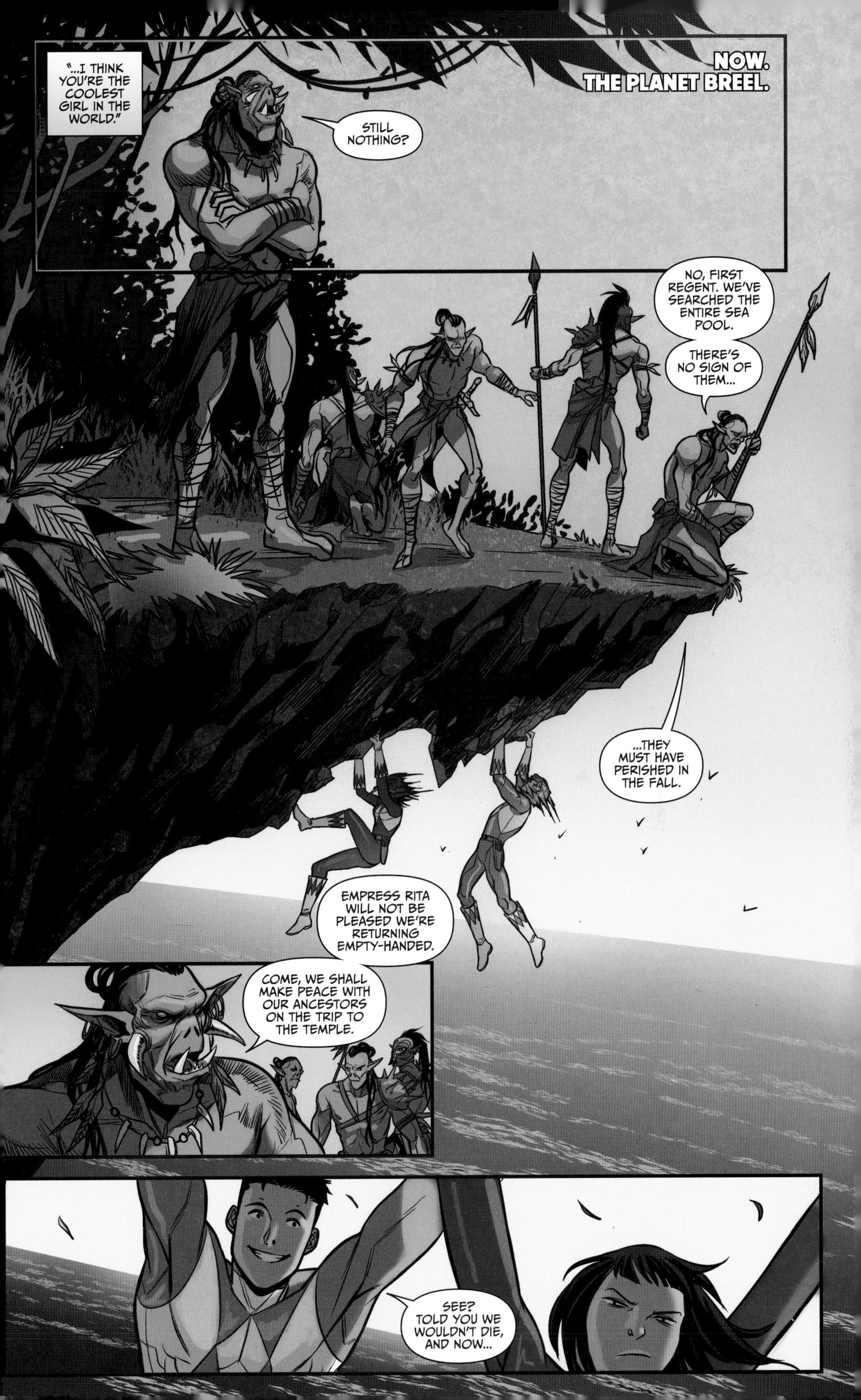
"...I THINK YOU'RE THE COOLEST GIRL IN THE WORLD."
NOW. THE PLANET BREEL.
STILL NOTHING?
NO, FIRST REGENT. WE'VE SEARCHED THE ENTIRE SEA POOL.
THERE'S NO SIGN OF THEM...
...THEY MUST HAVE PERISHED IN THE FALL.
EMPRESS RITA WILL NOT BE PLEASED WE'RE RETURNING EMPTY-HANDED.
COME, WE SHALL MAKE PEACE WITH OUR ANCESTORS ON THE TRIP TO THE TEMPLE.
SEE? TOLD YOU WE WOULDN'T DIE, AND NOW...

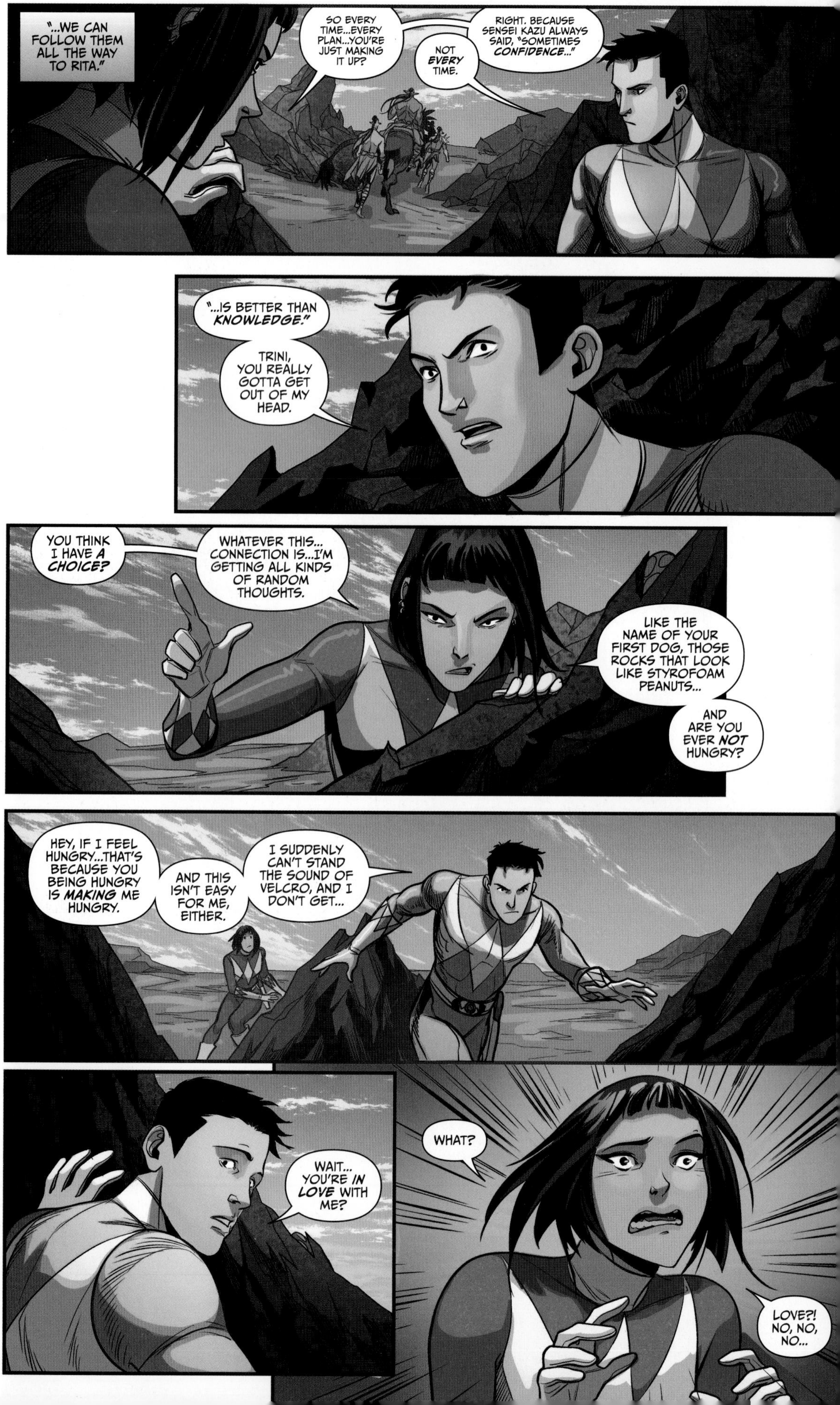
"...WE CAN FOLLOW THEM ALL THE WAY TO RITA."
SO EVERY TIME...EVERY PLAN...YOU'RE JUST MAKING IT UP?
NOT *EVERY* TIME.
RIGHT. BECAUSE SENSEI KAZU ALWAYS SAID, "SOMETIMES *CONFIDENCE...*"
"...IS BETTER THAN *KNOWLEDGE.*"
TRINI, YOU REALLY GOTTA GET OUT OF MY HEAD.
YOU THINK I HAVE *A CHOICE?*
WHATEVER THIS... CONNECTION IS...I'M GETTING ALL KINDS OF RANDOM THOUGHTS.
LIKE THE NAME OF YOUR FIRST DOG, THOSE ROCKS THAT LOOK LIKE STYROFOAM PEANUTS...
AND ARE YOU EVER *NOT* HUNGRY?
HEY, IF I FEEL HUNGRY...THAT'S BECAUSE YOU BEING HUNGRY IS *MAKING* ME HUNGRY.
AND THIS ISN'T EASY FOR ME, EITHER.
I SUDDENLY CAN'T STAND THE SOUND OF VELCRO, AND I DON'T GET...
WAIT... YOU'RE *IN LOVE* WITH ME?
WHAT?
LOVE?! NO, NO, NO...

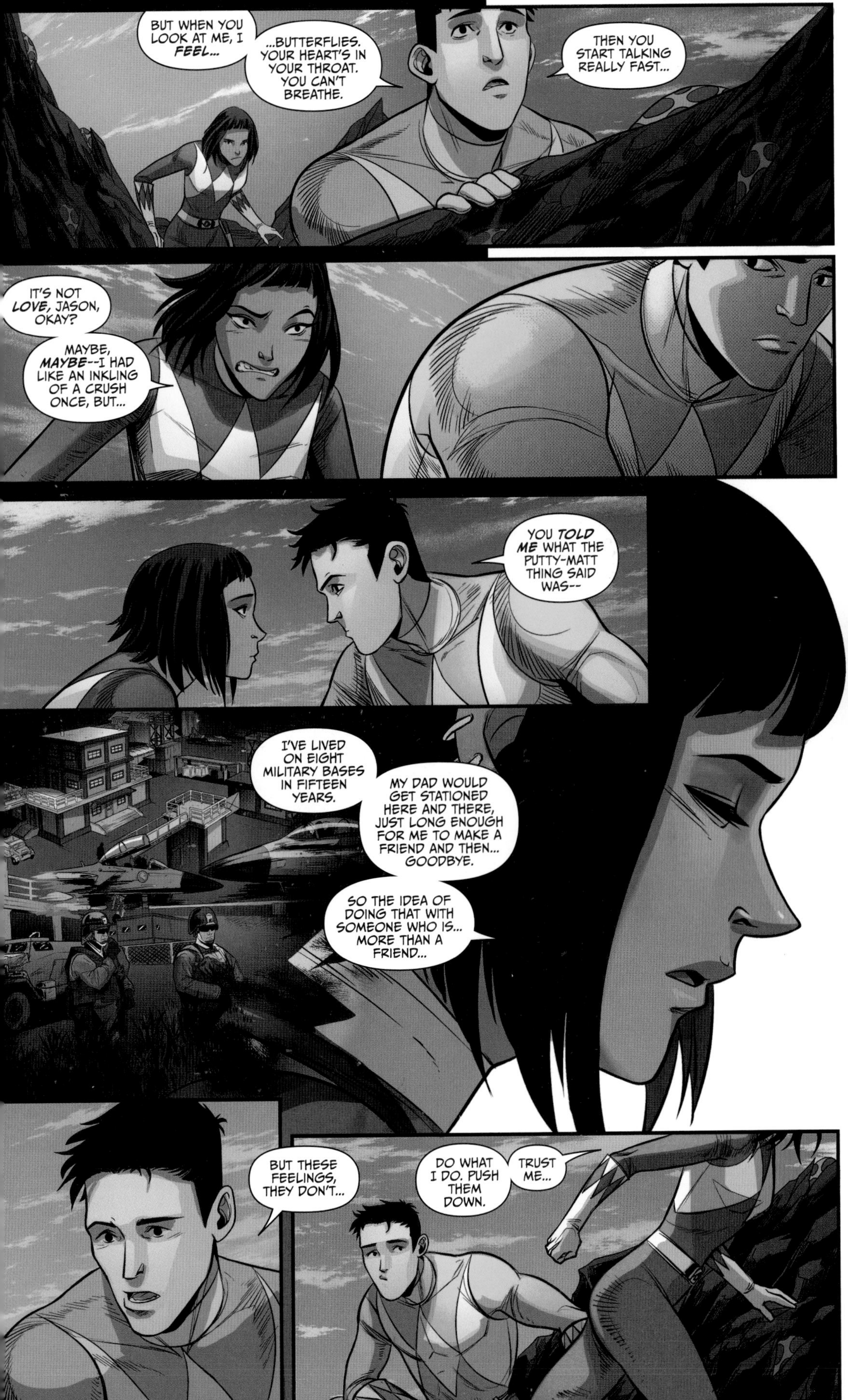

BUT WHEN YOU LOOK AT ME, I FEEL...
...BUTTERFLIES. YOUR HEART'S IN YOUR THROAT. YOU CAN'T BREATHE.
THEN YOU START TALKING REALLY FAST...
IT'S NOT LOVE, JASON, OKAY?
MAYBE, MAYBE--I HAD LIKE AN INKLING OF A CRUSH ONCE, BUT...
YOU TOLD ME WHAT THE PUTTY-MATT THING SAID WAS--
I'VE LIVED ON EIGHT MILITARY BASES IN FIFTEEN YEARS.
MY DAD WOULD GET STATIONED HERE AND THERE, JUST LONG ENOUGH FOR ME TO MAKE A FRIEND AND THEN... GOODBYE.
SO THE IDEA OF DOING THAT WITH SOMEONE WHO IS... MORE THAN A FRIEND...
BUT THESE FEELINGS, THEY DON'T...
DO WHAT I DO. PUSH THEM DOWN.
TRUST ME...

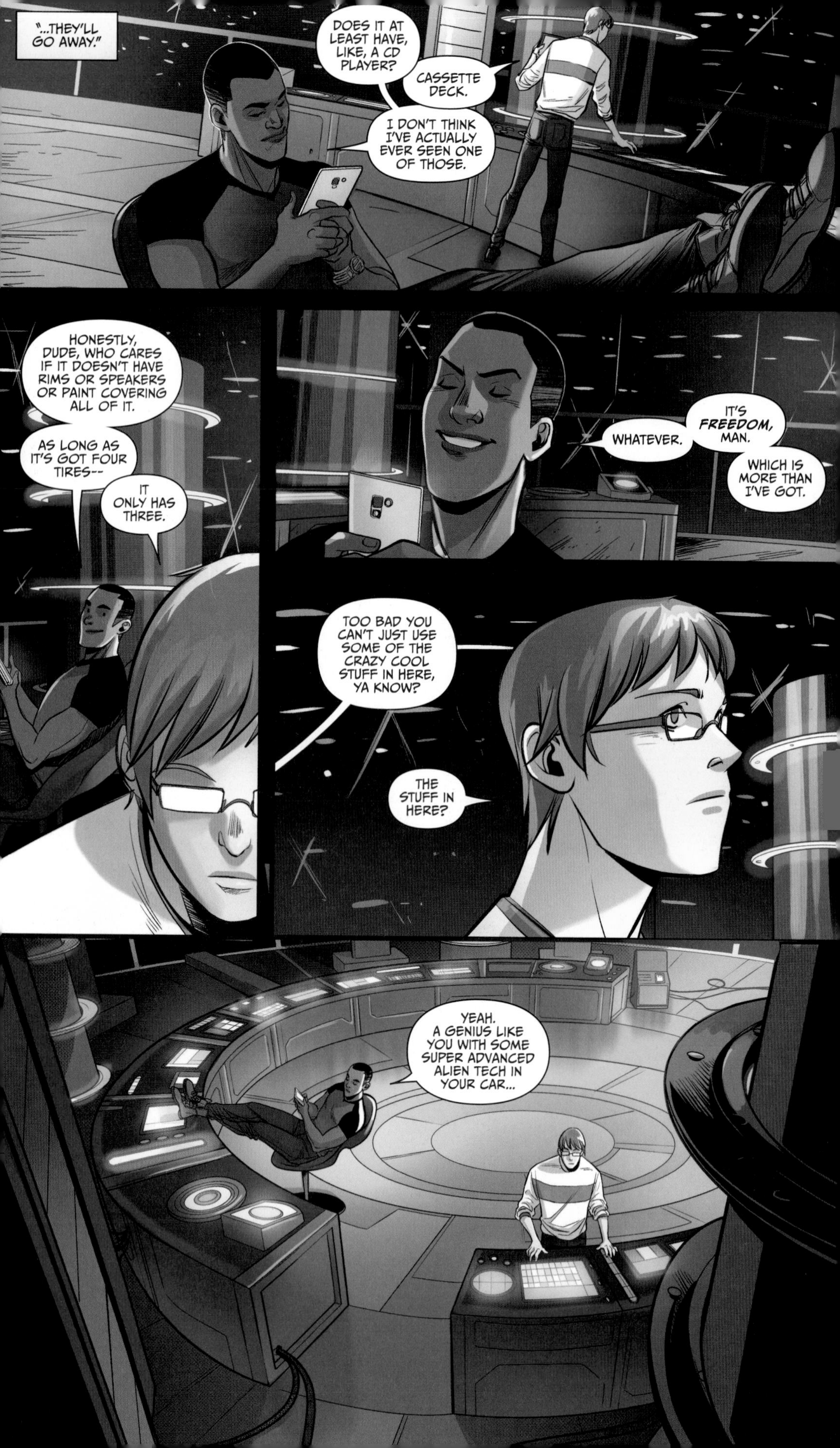
"...THEY'LL GO AWAY."
DOES IT AT LEAST HAVE, LIKE, A CD PLAYER?
CASSETTE DECK.
I DON'T THINK I'VE ACTUALLY EVER SEEN ONE OF THOSE.
HONESTLY, DUDE, WHO CARES IF IT DOESN'T HAVE RIMS OR SPEAKERS OR PAINT COVERING ALL OF IT.
AS LONG AS IT'S GOT FOUR TIRES--
IT ONLY HAS THREE.
WHATEVER.
IT'S *FREEDOM*, MAN.
WHICH IS MORE THAN I'VE GOT.
TOO BAD YOU CAN'T JUST USE SOME OF THE CRAZY COOL STUFF IN HERE, YA KNOW?
THE STUFF IN HERE?
YEAH. A GENIUS LIKE YOU WITH SOME SUPER ADVANCED ALIEN TECH IN YOUR CAR...

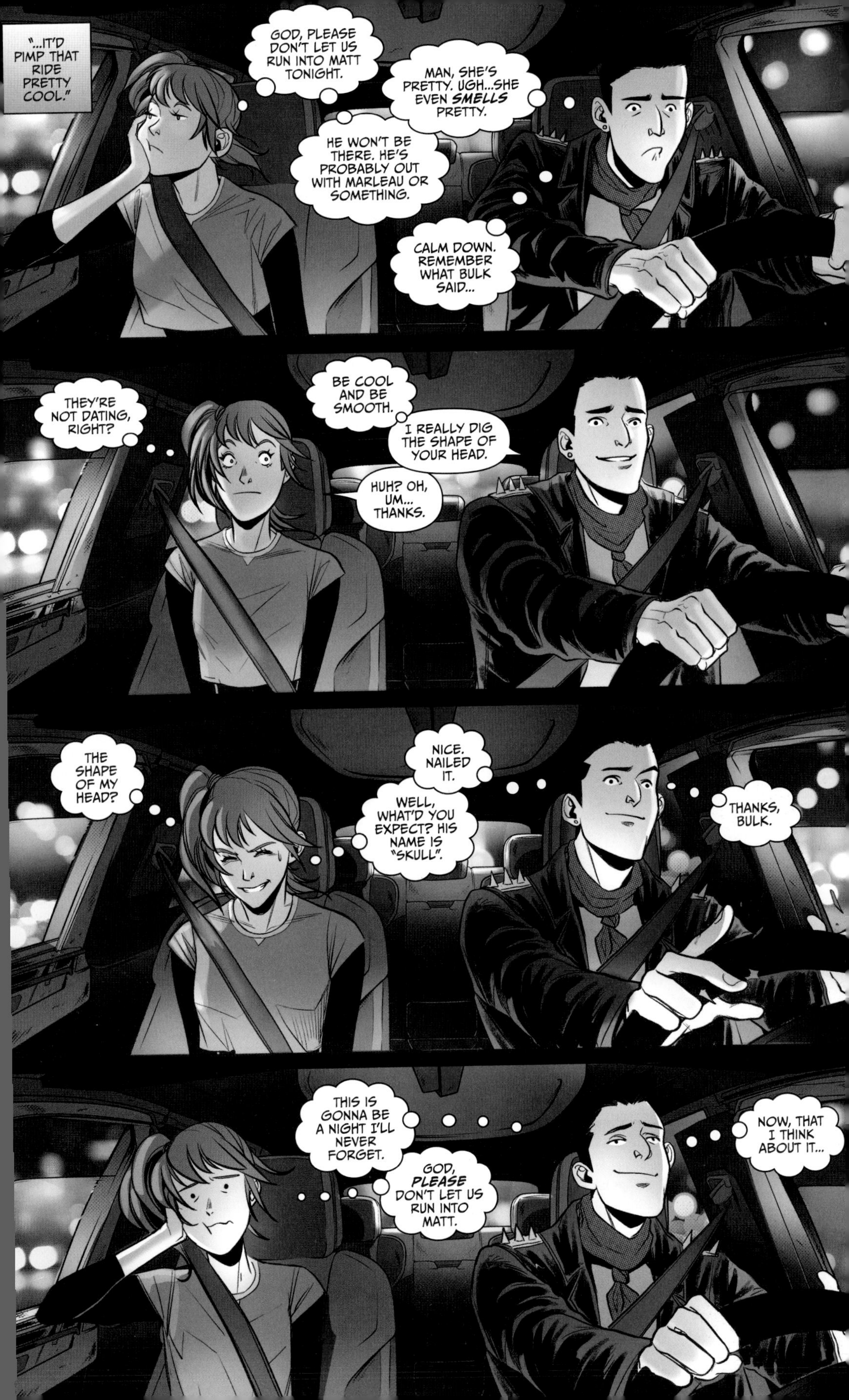
"...IT'D PIMP THAT RIDE PRETTY COOL."
GOD, PLEASE DON'T LET US RUN INTO MATT TONIGHT.
MAN, SHE'S PRETTY. UGH...SHE EVEN SMELLS PRETTY.
HE WON'T BE THERE. HE'S PROBABLY OUT WITH MARLEAU OR SOMETHING.
CALM DOWN. REMEMBER WHAT BULK SAID...
THEY'RE NOT DATING, RIGHT?
BE COOL AND BE SMOOTH.
I REALLY DIG THE SHAPE OF YOUR HEAD.
HUH? OH, UM... THANKS.
THE SHAPE OF MY HEAD?
NICE. NAILED IT.
WELL, WHAT'D YOU EXPECT? HIS NAME IS "SKULL".
THANKS, BULK.
THIS IS GONNA BE A NIGHT I'LL NEVER FORGET.
GOD, PLEASE DON'T LET US RUN INTO MATT.
NOW, THAT I THINK ABOUT IT...

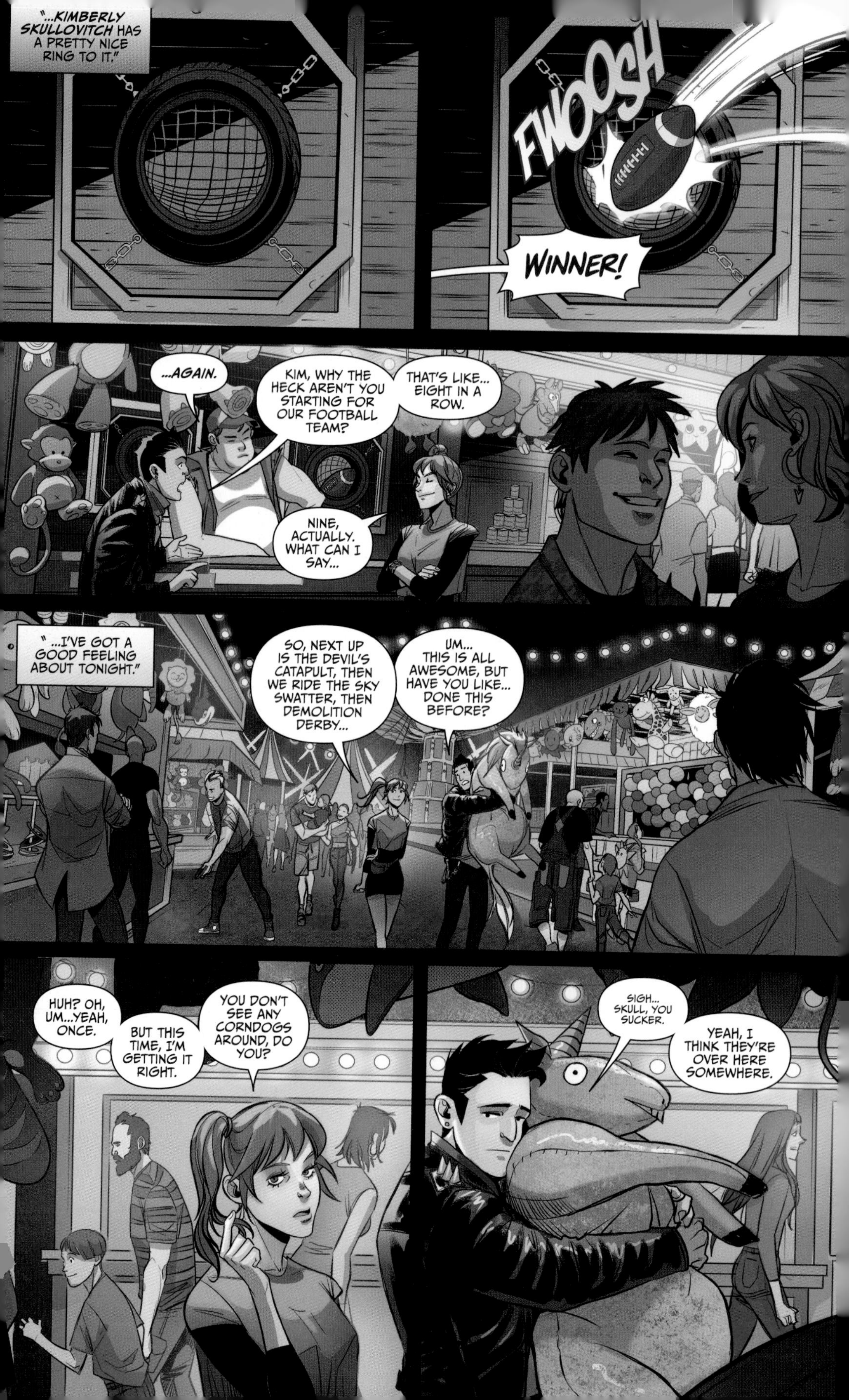
"...KIMBERLY SKULLOVITCH HAS A PRETTY NICE RING TO IT."
FWOOSH
WINNER!
...AGAIN.
KIM, WHY THE HECK AREN'T YOU STARTING FOR OUR FOOTBALL TEAM?
THAT'S LIKE... EIGHT IN A ROW.
NINE, ACTUALLY. WHAT CAN I SAY...
"...I'VE GOT A GOOD FEELING ABOUT TONIGHT."
SO, NEXT UP IS THE DEVIL'S CATAPULT, THEN WE RIDE THE SKY SWATTER, THEN DEMOLITION DERBY...
UM... THIS IS ALL AWESOME, BUT HAVE YOU LIKE... DONE THIS BEFORE?
HUH? OH, UM...YEAH, ONCE.
BUT THIS TIME, I'M GETTING IT RIGHT.
YOU DON'T SEE ANY CORNDOGS AROUND, DO YOU?
SIGH... SKULL, YOU SUCKER.
YEAH, I THINK THEY'RE OVER HERE SOMEWHERE.

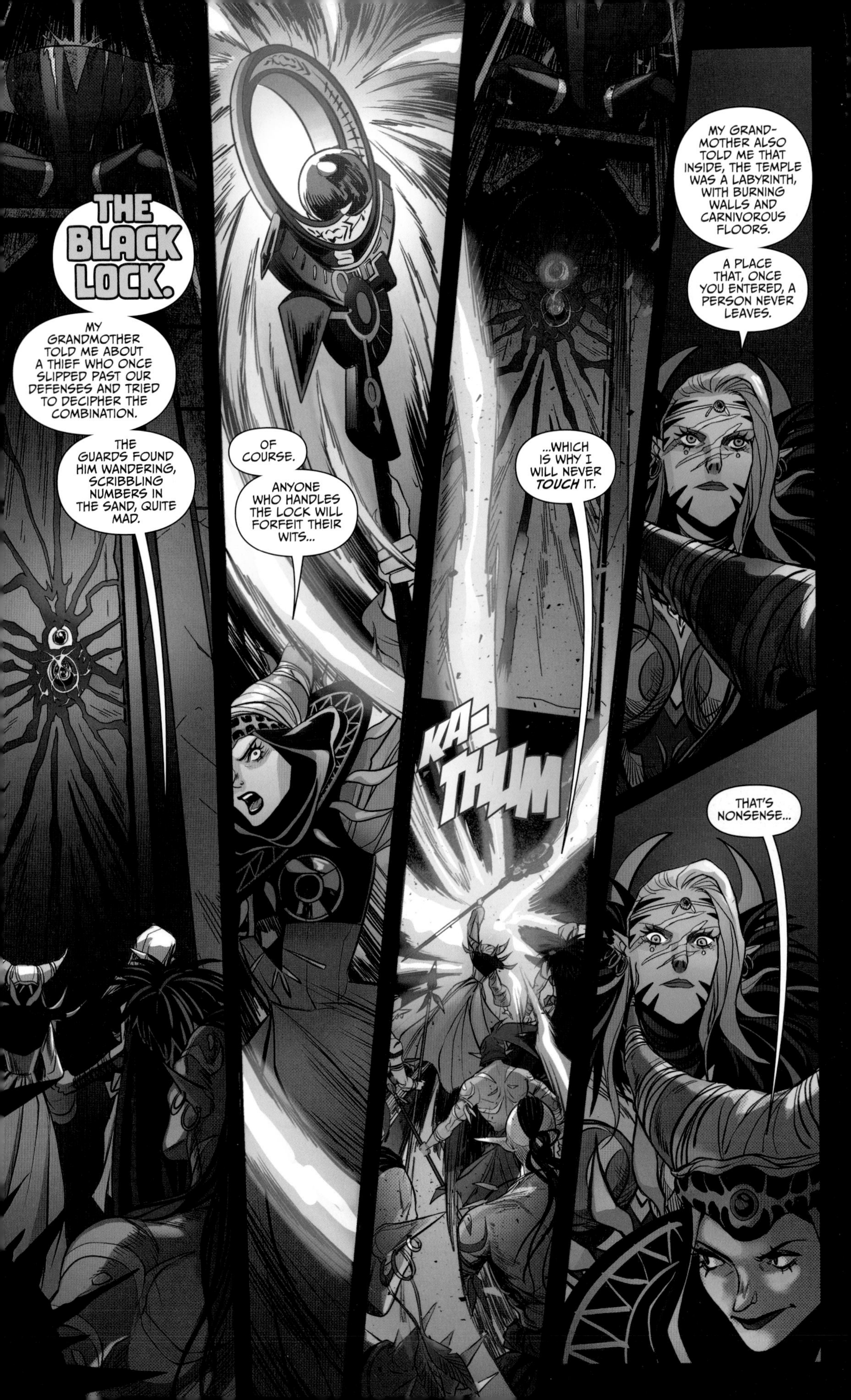
THE BLACK LOCK.
MY GRANDMOTHER TOLD ME ABOUT A THIEF WHO ONCE SLIPPED PAST OUR DEFENSES AND TRIED TO DECIPHER THE COMBINATION.
THE GUARDS FOUND HIM WANDERING, SCRIBBLING NUMBERS IN THE SAND, QUITE MAD.
OF COURSE.
ANYONE WHO HANDLES THE LOCK WILL FORFEIT THEIR WITS...
...WHICH IS WHY I WILL NEVER *TOUCH* IT.
KA-THUM
MY GRAND-MOTHER ALSO TOLD ME THAT INSIDE, THE TEMPLE WAS A LABYRINTH, WITH BURNING WALLS AND CARNIVOROUS FLOORS.
A PLACE THAT, ONCE YOU ENTERED, A PERSON NEVER LEAVES.
THAT'S NONSENSE...

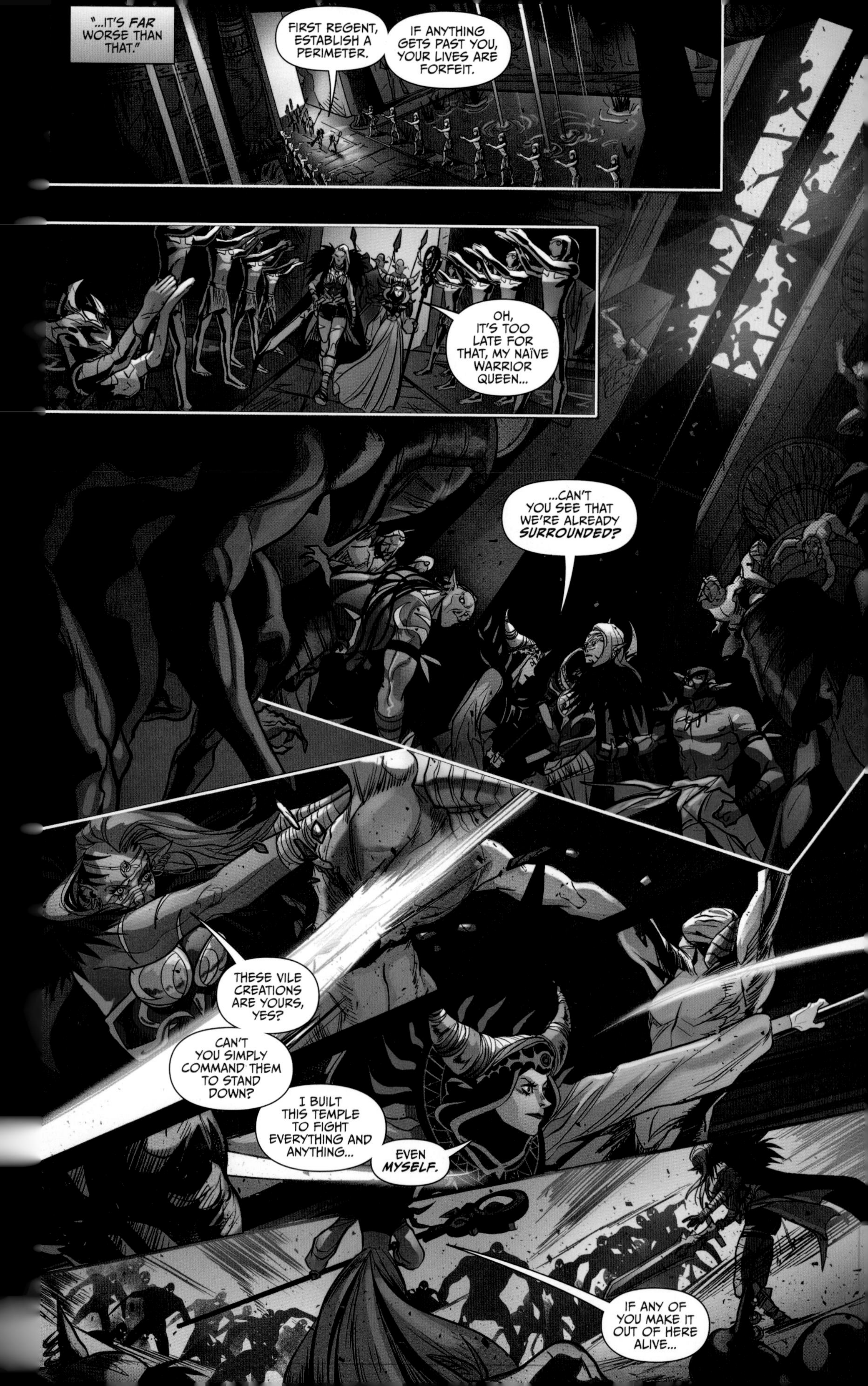
"...IT'S FAR WORSE THAN THAT."
FIRST REGENT, ESTABLISH A PERIMETER.
IF ANYTHING GETS PAST YOU, YOUR LIVES ARE FORFEIT.
OH, IT'S TOO LATE FOR THAT, MY NAÏVE WARRIOR QUEEN...
...CAN'T YOU SEE THAT WE'RE ALREADY SURROUNDED?
THESE VILE CREATIONS ARE YOURS, YES?
CAN'T YOU SIMPLY COMMAND THEM TO STAND DOWN?
I BUILT THIS TEMPLE TO FIGHT EVERYTHING AND ANYTHING...
EVEN MYSELF.
IF ANY OF YOU MAKE IT OUT OF HERE ALIVE...

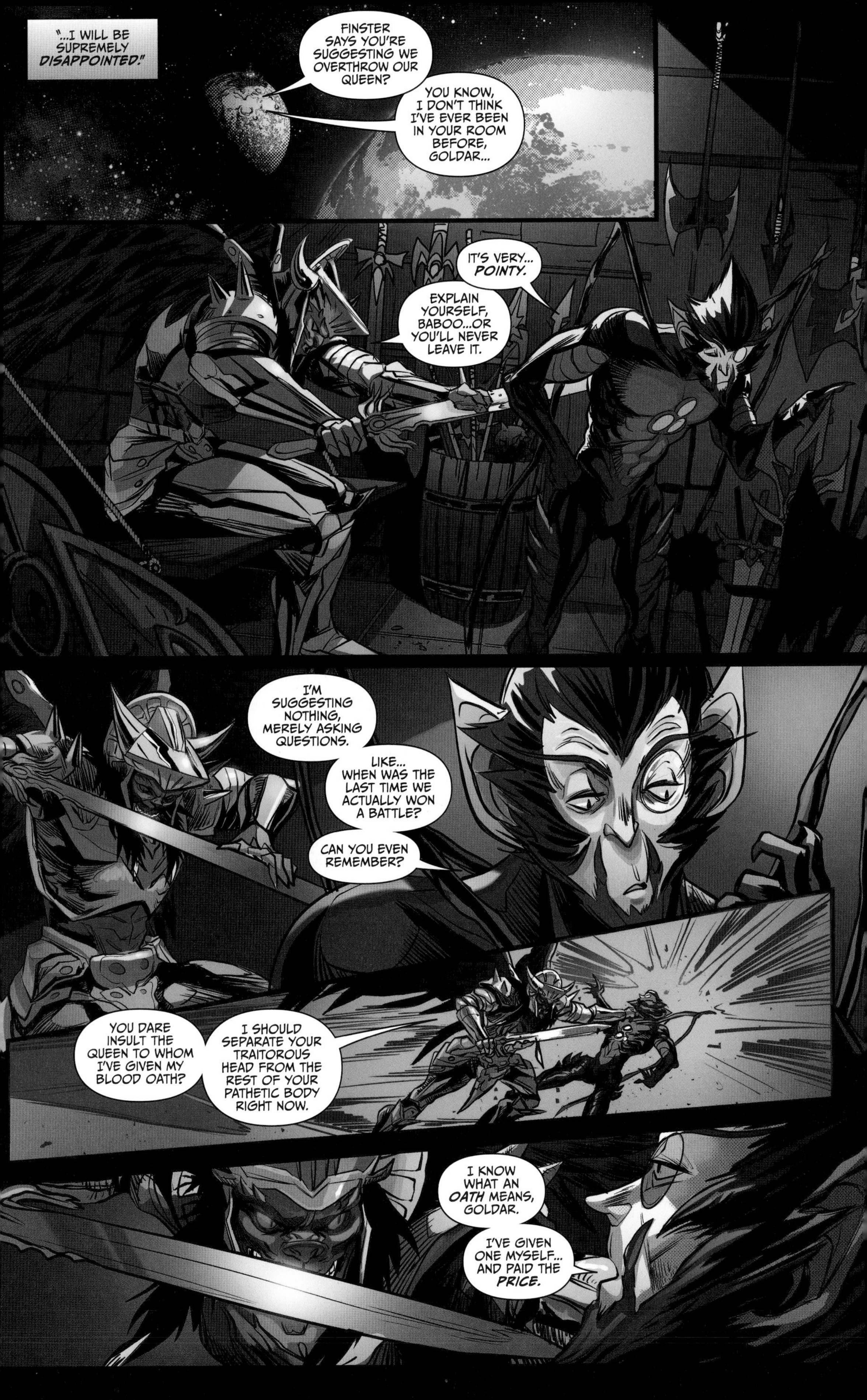
"...I WILL BE SUPREMELY *DISAPPOINTED.*"
FINSTER SAYS YOU'RE SUGGESTING WE OVERTHROW OUR QUEEN?
YOU KNOW, I DON'T THINK I'VE EVER BEEN IN YOUR ROOM BEFORE, GOLDAR...
IT'S VERY... *POINTY.*
EXPLAIN YOURSELF, BABOO...OR YOU'LL NEVER LEAVE IT.
I'M SUGGESTING NOTHING, MERELY ASKING QUESTIONS.
LIKE... WHEN WAS THE LAST TIME WE ACTUALLY WON A BATTLE?
CAN YOU EVEN REMEMBER?
YOU DARE INSULT THE QUEEN TO WHOM I'VE GIVEN MY BLOOD OATH?
I SHOULD SEPARATE YOUR TRAITOROUS HEAD FROM THE REST OF YOUR PATHETIC BODY RIGHT NOW.
I KNOW WHAT AN *OATH* MEANS, GOLDAR.
I'VE GIVEN ONE MYSELF... AND PAID THE *PRICE.*

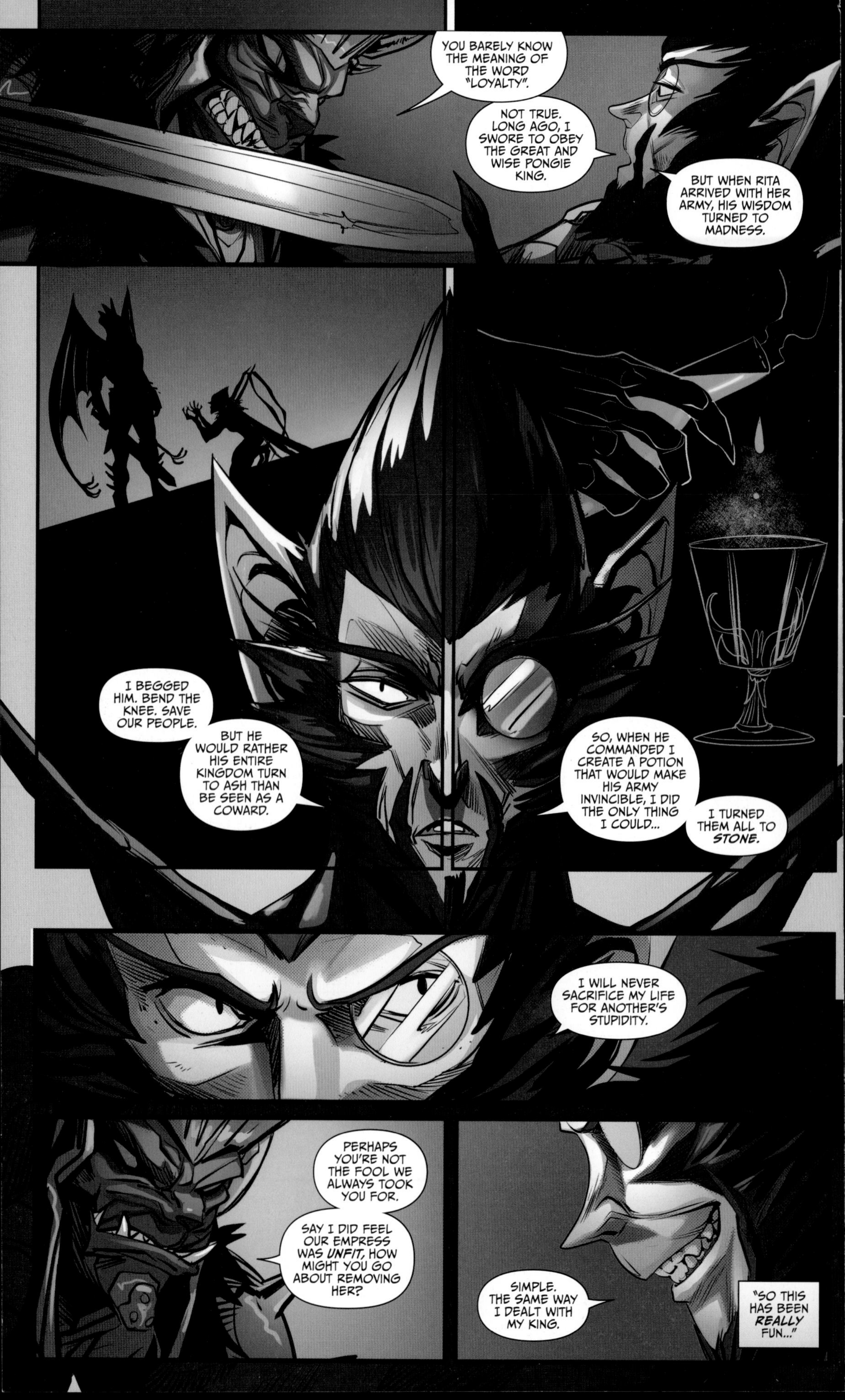
YOU BARELY KNOW THE MEANING OF THE WORD "LOYALTY".
NOT TRUE. LONG AGO, I SWORE TO OBEY THE GREAT AND WISE PONGIE KING.
BUT WHEN RITA ARRIVED WITH HER ARMY, HIS WISDOM TURNED TO MADNESS.
I BEGGED HIM. BEND THE KNEE. SAVE OUR PEOPLE.
BUT HE WOULD RATHER HIS ENTIRE KINGDOM TURN TO ASH THAN BE SEEN AS A COWARD.
SO, WHEN HE COMMANDED I CREATE A POTION THAT WOULD MAKE HIS ARMY INVINCIBLE, I DID THE ONLY THING I COULD...
I TURNED THEM ALL TO STONE.
I WILL NEVER SACRIFICE MY LIFE FOR ANOTHER'S STUPIDITY.
PERHAPS YOU'RE NOT THE FOOL WE ALWAYS TOOK YOU FOR.
SAY I DID FEEL OUR EMPRESS WAS UNFIT, HOW MIGHT YOU GO ABOUT REMOVING HER?
SIMPLE. THE SAME WAY I DEALT WITH MY KING.
"SO THIS HAS BEEN REALLY FUN..."

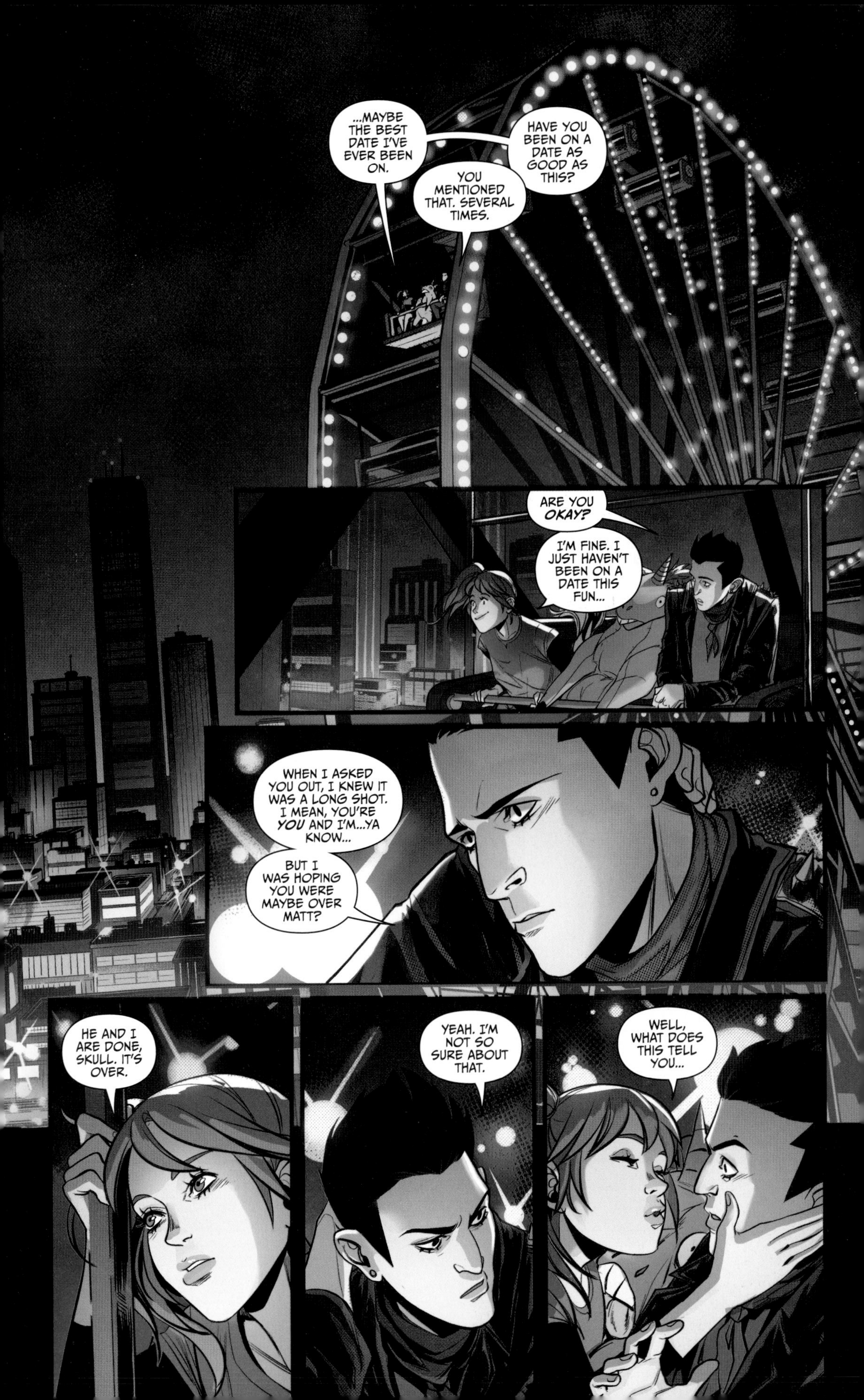
...MAYBE THE BEST DATE I'VE EVER BEEN ON.
HAVE YOU BEEN ON A DATE AS GOOD AS THIS?
YOU MENTIONED THAT. SEVERAL TIMES.
ARE YOU *OKAY?*
I'M FINE. I JUST HAVEN'T BEEN ON A DATE THIS FUN...
WHEN I ASKED YOU OUT, I KNEW IT WAS A LONG SHOT. I MEAN, YOU'RE *YOU* AND I'M...YA KNOW...
BUT I WAS HOPING YOU WERE MAYBE OVER MATT?
HE AND I ARE DONE, SKULL. IT'S OVER.
YEAH. I'M NOT SO SURE ABOUT THAT.
WELL, WHAT DOES THIS TELL YOU...

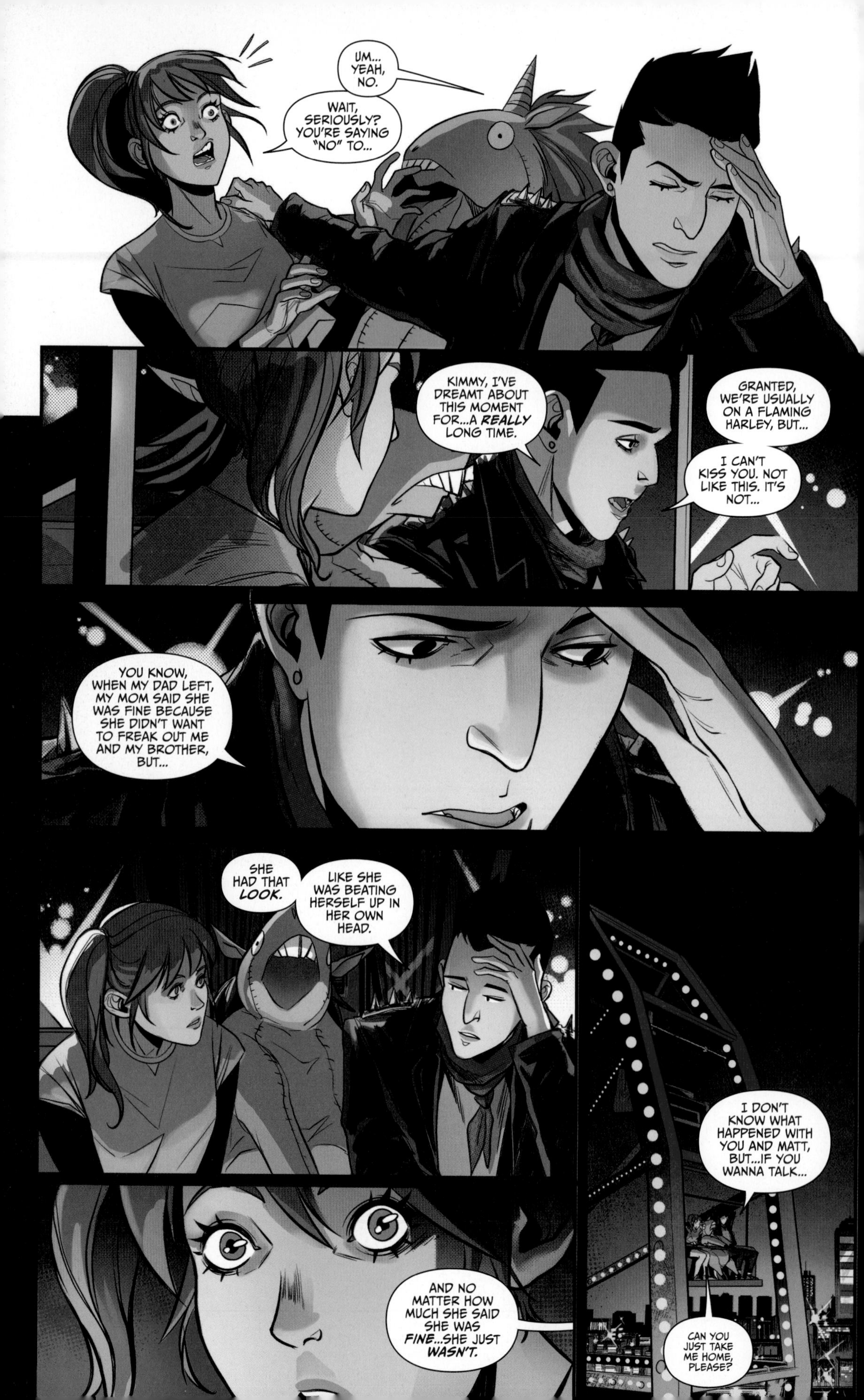
UM... YEAH, NO.
WAIT, SERIOUSLY? YOU'RE SAYING "NO" TO...
KIMMY, I'VE DREAMT ABOUT THIS MOMENT FOR...A *REALLY* LONG TIME.
GRANTED, WE'RE USUALLY ON A FLAMING HARLEY, BUT...
I CAN'T KISS YOU. NOT LIKE THIS. IT'S NOT...
YOU KNOW, WHEN MY DAD LEFT, MY MOM SAID SHE WAS FINE BECAUSE SHE DIDN'T WANT TO FREAK OUT ME AND MY BROTHER, BUT...
SHE HAD THAT *LOOK.*
LIKE SHE WAS BEATING HERSELF UP IN HER OWN HEAD.
AND NO MATTER HOW MUCH SHE SAID SHE WAS *FINE*...SHE JUST *WASN'T.*
I DON'T KNOW WHAT HAPPENED WITH YOU AND MATT, BUT...IF YOU WANNA TALK...
CAN YOU JUST TAKE ME HOME, PLEASE?

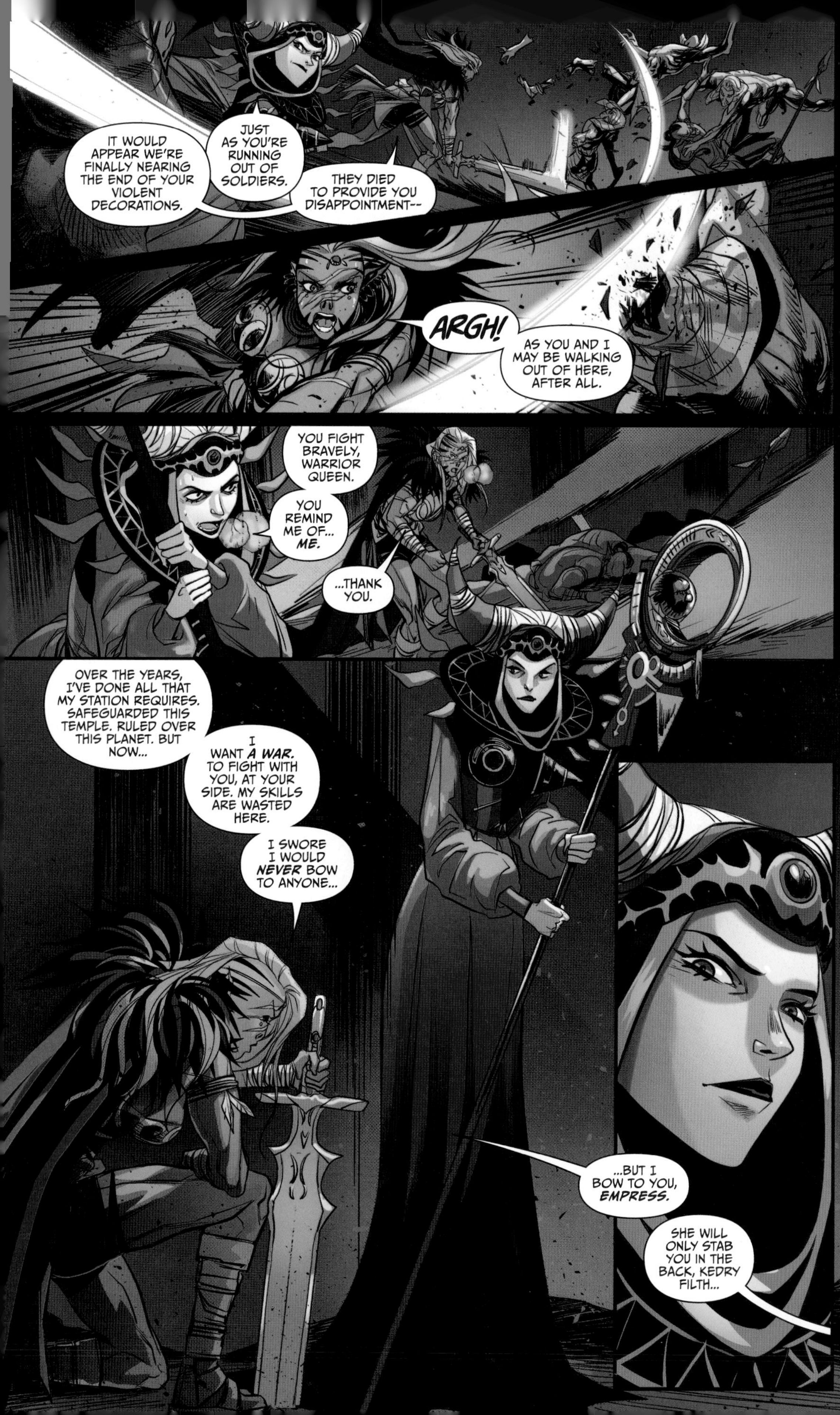
IT WOULD APPEAR WE'RE FINALLY NEARING THE END OF YOUR VIOLENT DECORATIONS.
JUST AS YOU'RE RUNNING OUT OF SOLDIERS.
THEY DIED TO PROVIDE YOU DISAPPOINTMENT--
ARGH!
AS YOU AND I MAY BE WALKING OUT OF HERE, AFTER ALL.
YOU FIGHT BRAVELY, WARRIOR QUEEN.
YOU REMIND ME OF... ME.
...THANK YOU.
OVER THE YEARS, I'VE DONE ALL THAT MY STATION REQUIRES. SAFEGUARDED THIS TEMPLE. RULED OVER THIS PLANET. BUT NOW...
I WANT A WAR. TO FIGHT WITH YOU, AT YOUR SIDE. MY SKILLS ARE WASTED HERE.
I SWORE I WOULD NEVER BOW TO ANYONE...
...BUT I BOW TO YOU, EMPRESS.
SHE WILL ONLY STAB YOU IN THE BACK, KEDRY FILTH...

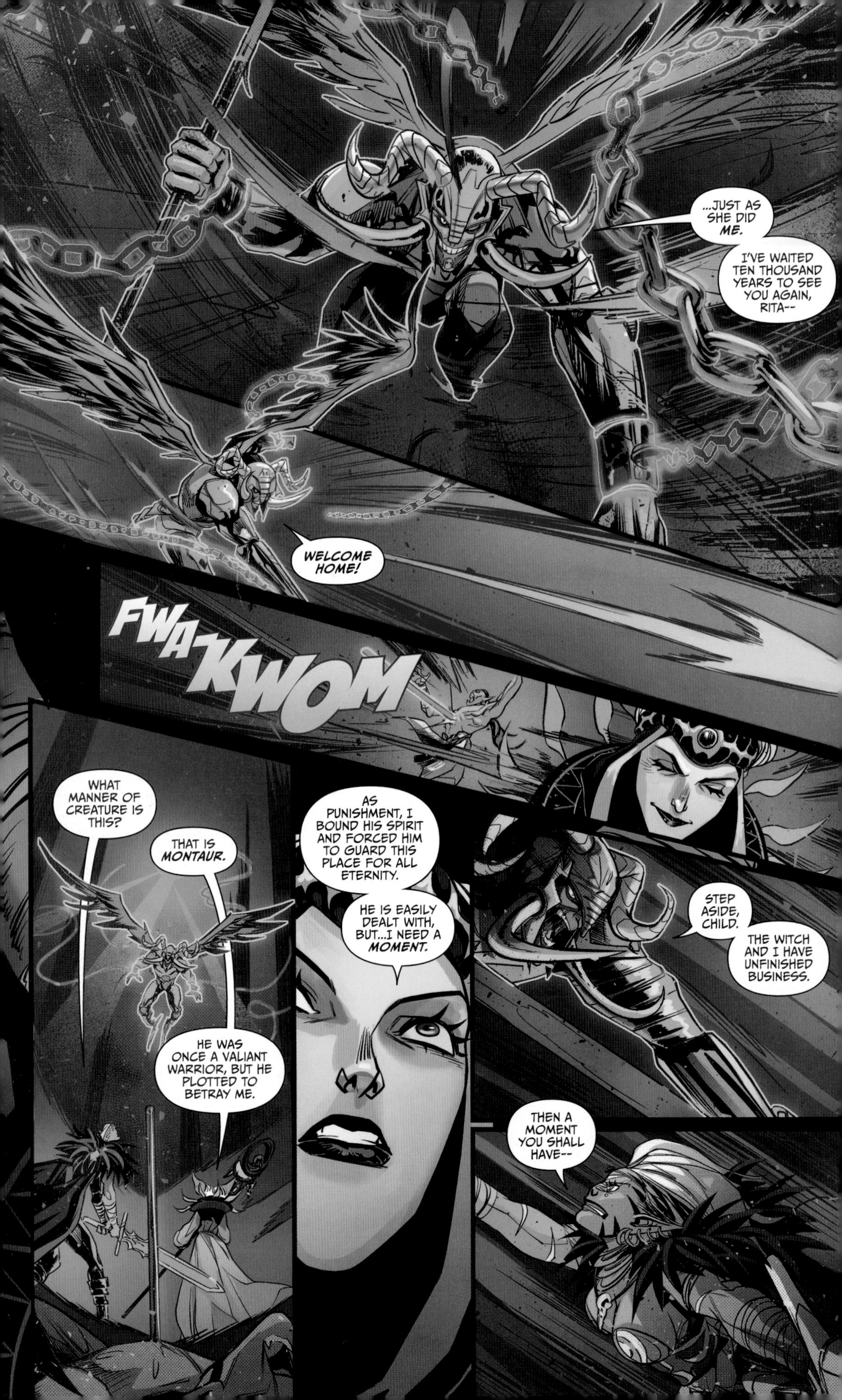
...JUST AS SHE DID ME.
I'VE WAITED TEN THOUSAND YEARS TO SEE YOU AGAIN, RITA--
WELCOME HOME!
FWA-KWOM
WHAT MANNER OF CREATURE IS THIS?
THAT IS MONTAUR.
HE WAS ONCE A VALIANT WARRIOR, BUT HE PLOTTED TO BETRAY ME.
AS PUNISHMENT, I BOUND HIS SPIRIT AND FORCED HIM TO GUARD THIS PLACE FOR ALL ETERNITY.
HE IS EASILY DEALT WITH, BUT...I NEED A MOMENT.
STEP ASIDE, CHILD.
THE WITCH AND I HAVE UNFINISHED BUSINESS.
THEN A MOMENT YOU SHALL HAVE--

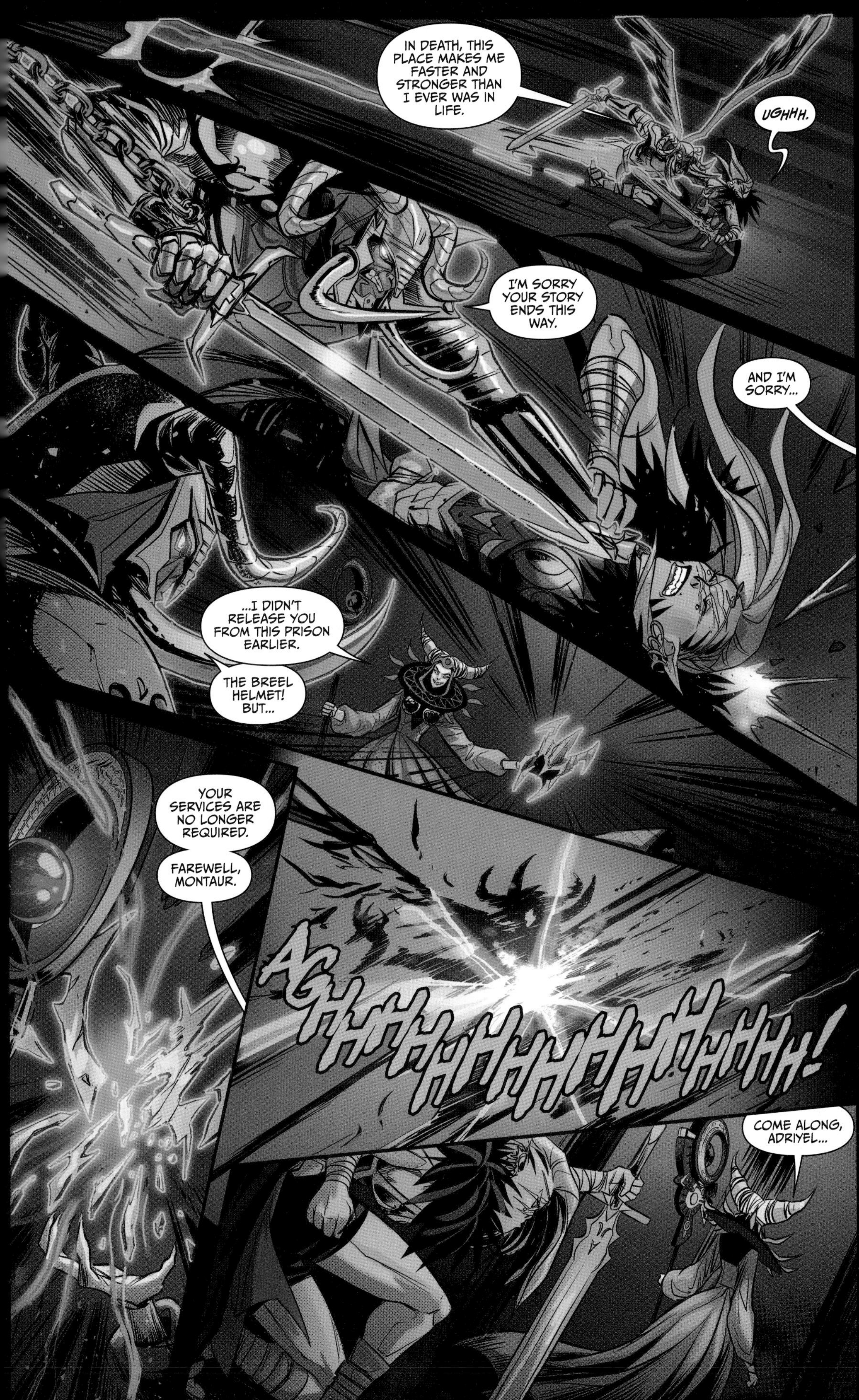
IN DEATH, THIS PLACE MAKES ME FASTER AND STRONGER THAN I EVER WAS IN LIFE.
UGHHH.
I'M SORRY YOUR STORY ENDS THIS WAY.
AND I'M SORRY...
...I DIDN'T RELEASE YOU FROM THIS PRISON EARLIER.
THE BREEL HELMET! BUT...
YOUR SERVICES ARE NO LONGER REQUIRED.
FAREWELL, MONTAUR.
AGHHHHHHHHHHHHHHHH!
COME ALONG, ADRIYEL...

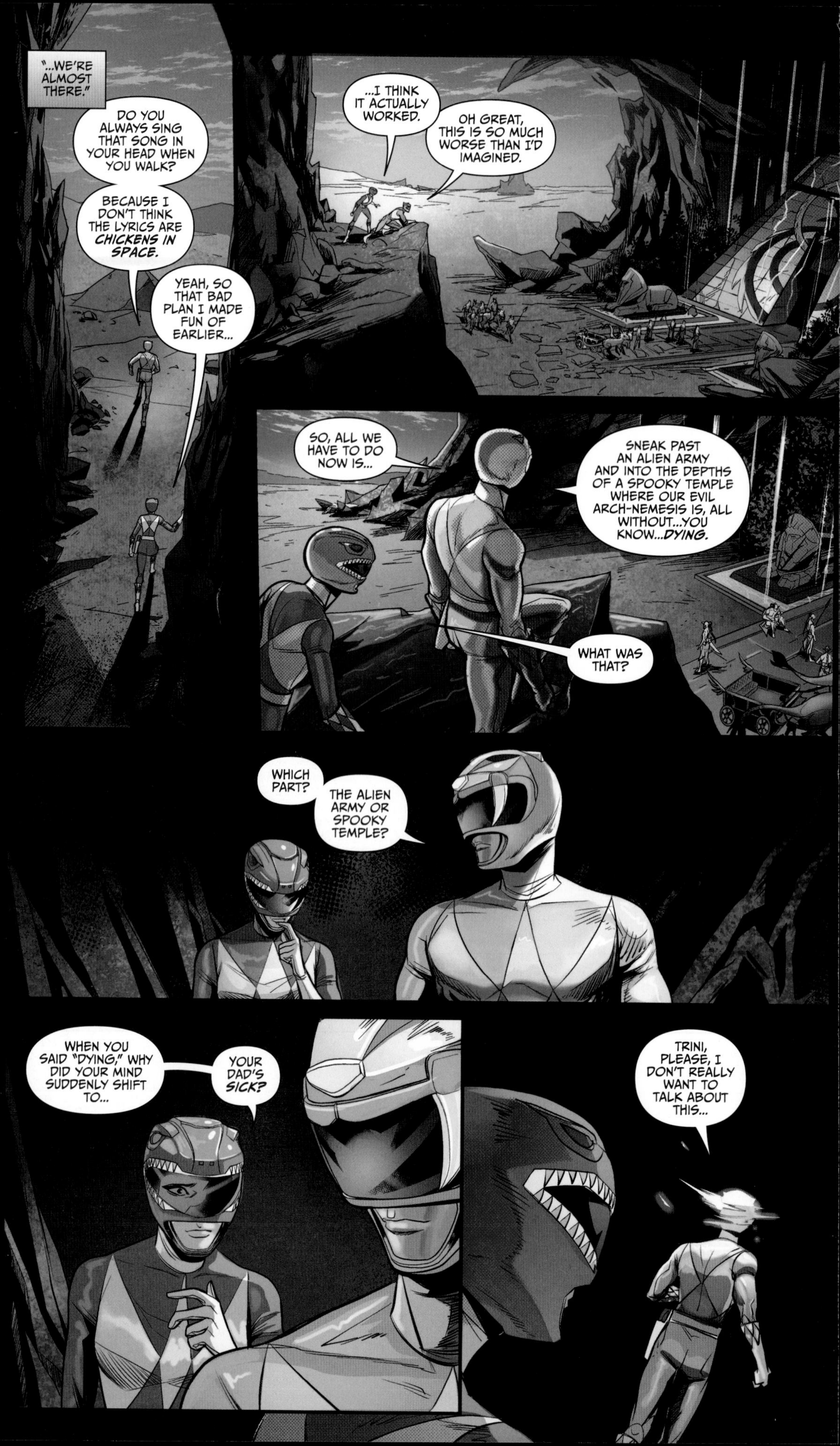
"...WE'RE ALMOST THERE."
DO YOU ALWAYS SING THAT SONG IN YOUR HEAD WHEN YOU WALK?
BECAUSE I DON'T THINK THE LYRICS ARE *CHICKENS IN SPACE.*
YEAH, SO THAT BAD PLAN I MADE FUN OF EARLIER...
...I THINK IT ACTUALLY WORKED.
OH GREAT, THIS IS SO MUCH WORSE THAN I'D IMAGINED.
SO, ALL WE HAVE TO DO NOW IS...
SNEAK PAST AN ALIEN ARMY AND INTO THE DEPTHS OF A SPOOKY TEMPLE WHERE OUR EVIL ARCH-NEMESIS IS, ALL WITHOUT...YOU KNOW...*DYING.*
WHAT WAS THAT?
WHICH PART?
THE ALIEN ARMY OR SPOOKY TEMPLE?
WHEN YOU SAID "DYING," WHY DID YOUR MIND SUDDENLY SHIFT TO...
YOUR DAD'S *SICK?*
TRINI, PLEASE, I DON'T REALLY WANT TO TALK ABOUT THIS...

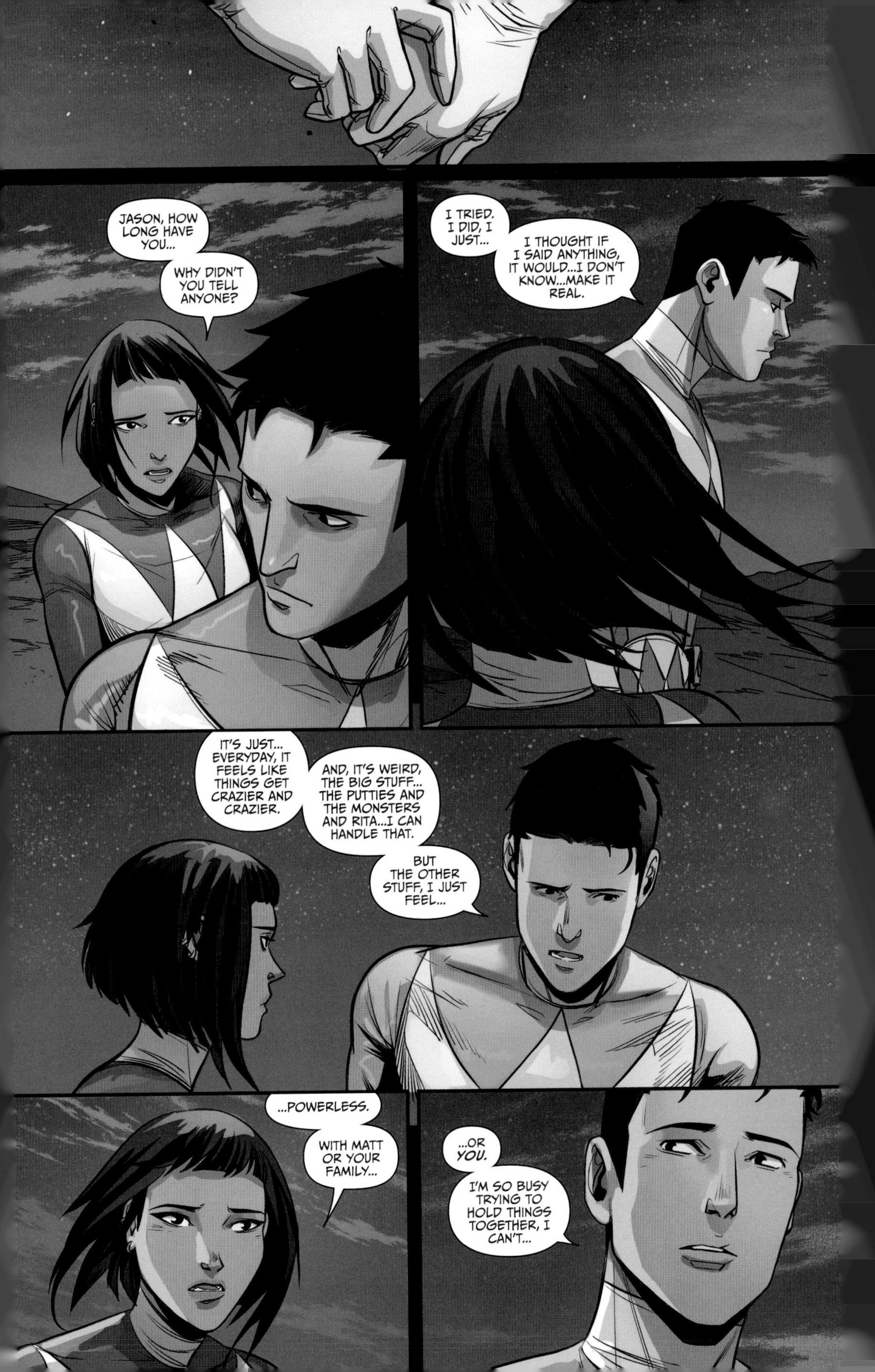
JASON, HOW LONG HAVE YOU...
WHY DIDN'T YOU TELL ANYONE?
I TRIED. I DID, I JUST...
I THOUGHT IF I SAID ANYTHING, IT WOULD...I DON'T KNOW...MAKE IT REAL.
IT'S JUST... EVERYDAY, IT FEELS LIKE THINGS GET CRAZIER AND CRAZIER.
AND, IT'S WEIRD, THE BIG STUFF... THE PUTTIES AND THE MONSTERS AND RITA...I CAN HANDLE THAT.
BUT THE OTHER STUFF, I JUST FEEL...
...POWERLESS.
WITH MATT OR YOUR FAMILY...
...OR YOU.
I'M SO BUSY TRYING TO HOLD THINGS TOGETHER, I CAN'T...

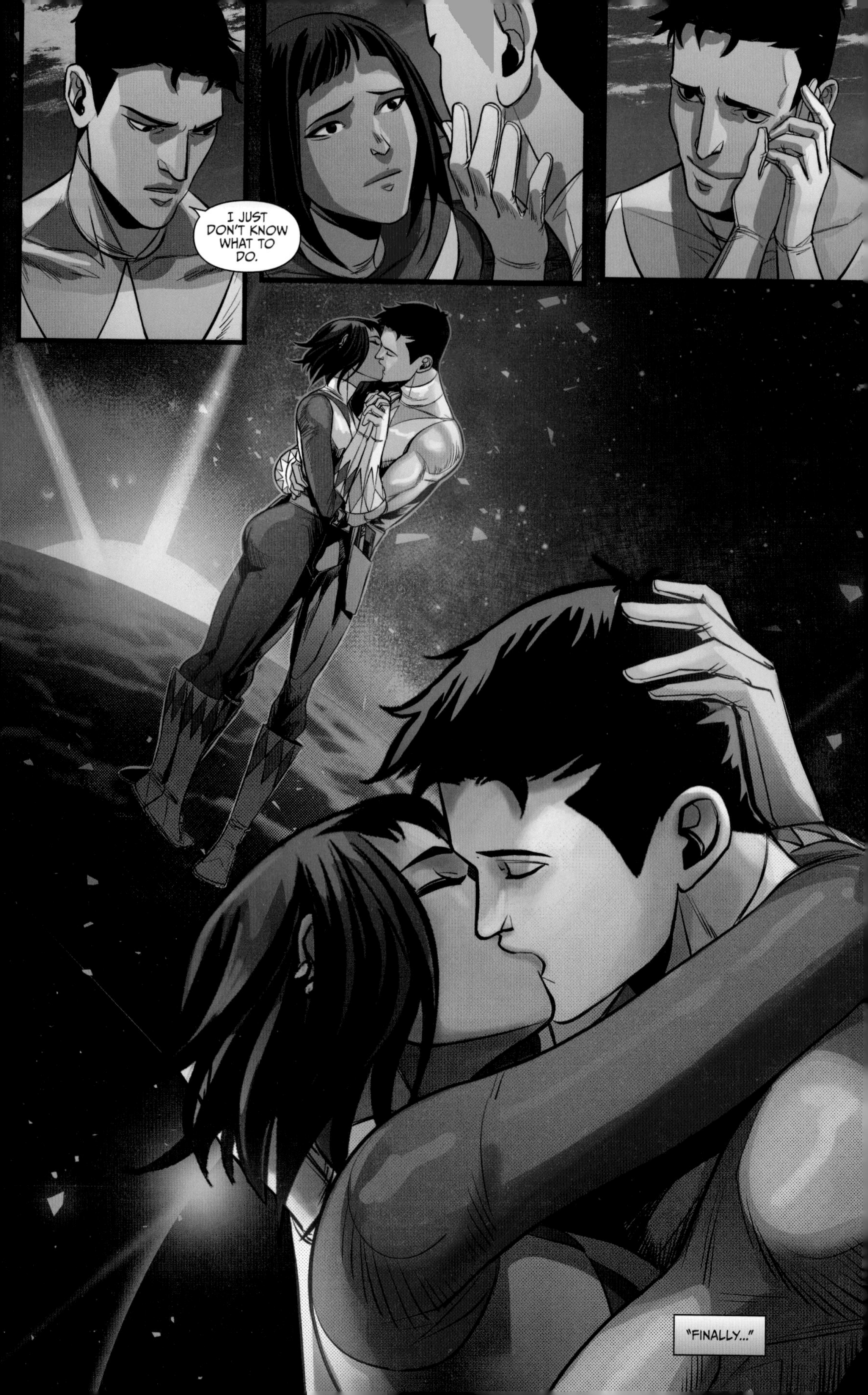
I JUST DON'T KNOW WHAT TO DO.
"FINALLY..."

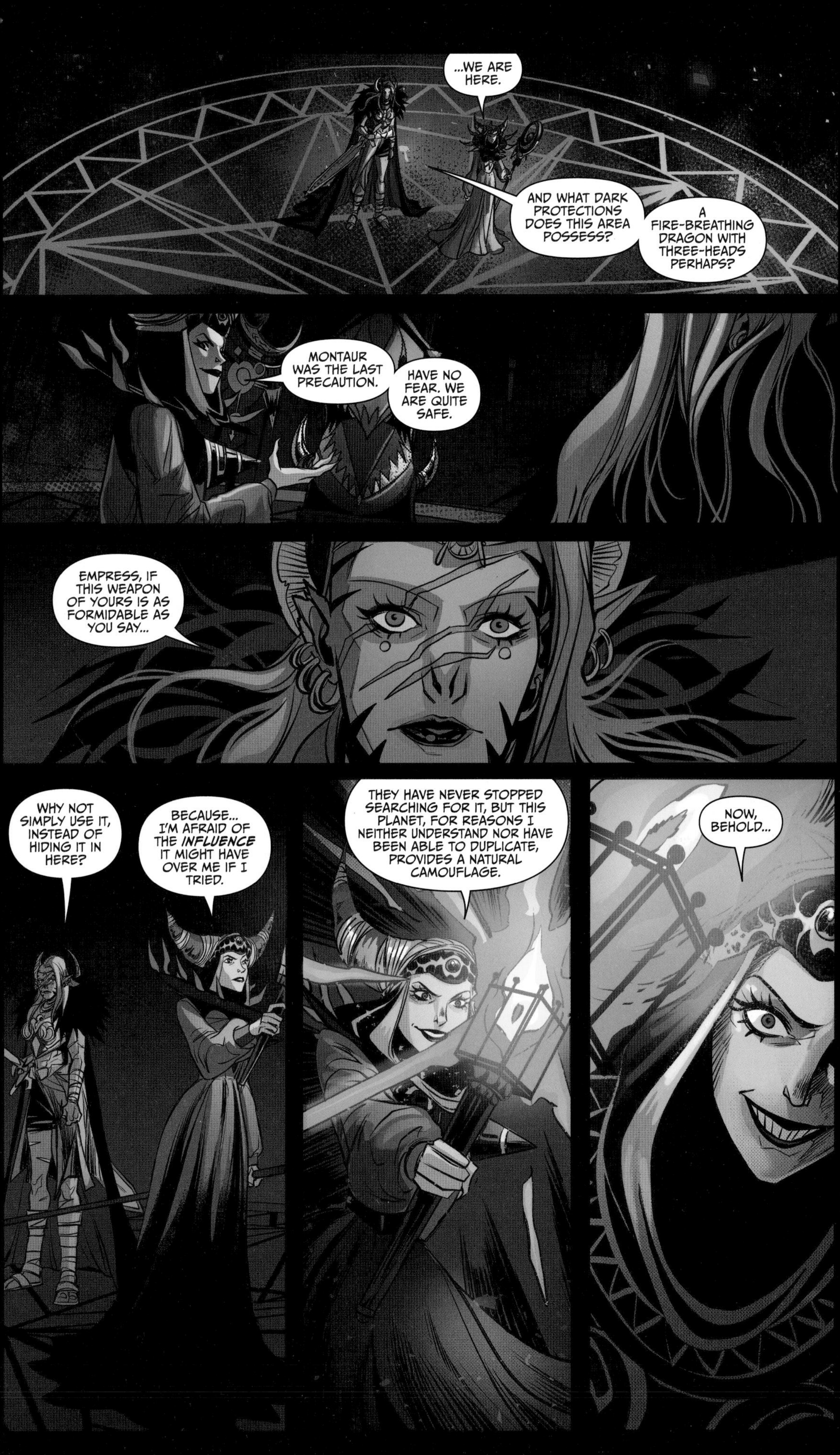
...WE ARE HERE.
AND WHAT DARK PROTECTIONS DOES THIS AREA POSSESS?
A FIRE-BREATHING DRAGON WITH THREE-HEADS PERHAPS?
MONTAUR WAS THE LAST PRECAUTION.
HAVE NO FEAR. WE ARE QUITE SAFE.
EMPRESS, IF THIS WEAPON OF YOURS IS AS FORMIDABLE AS YOU SAY...
WHY NOT SIMPLY USE IT, INSTEAD OF HIDING IT IN HERE?
BECAUSE... I'M AFRAID OF THE INFLUENCE IT MIGHT HAVE OVER ME IF I TRIED.
THEY HAVE NEVER STOPPED SEARCHING FOR IT, BUT THIS PLANET, FOR REASONS I NEITHER UNDERSTAND NOR HAVE BEEN ABLE TO DUPLICATE, PROVIDES A NATURAL CAMOUFLAGE.
NOW, BEHOLD...

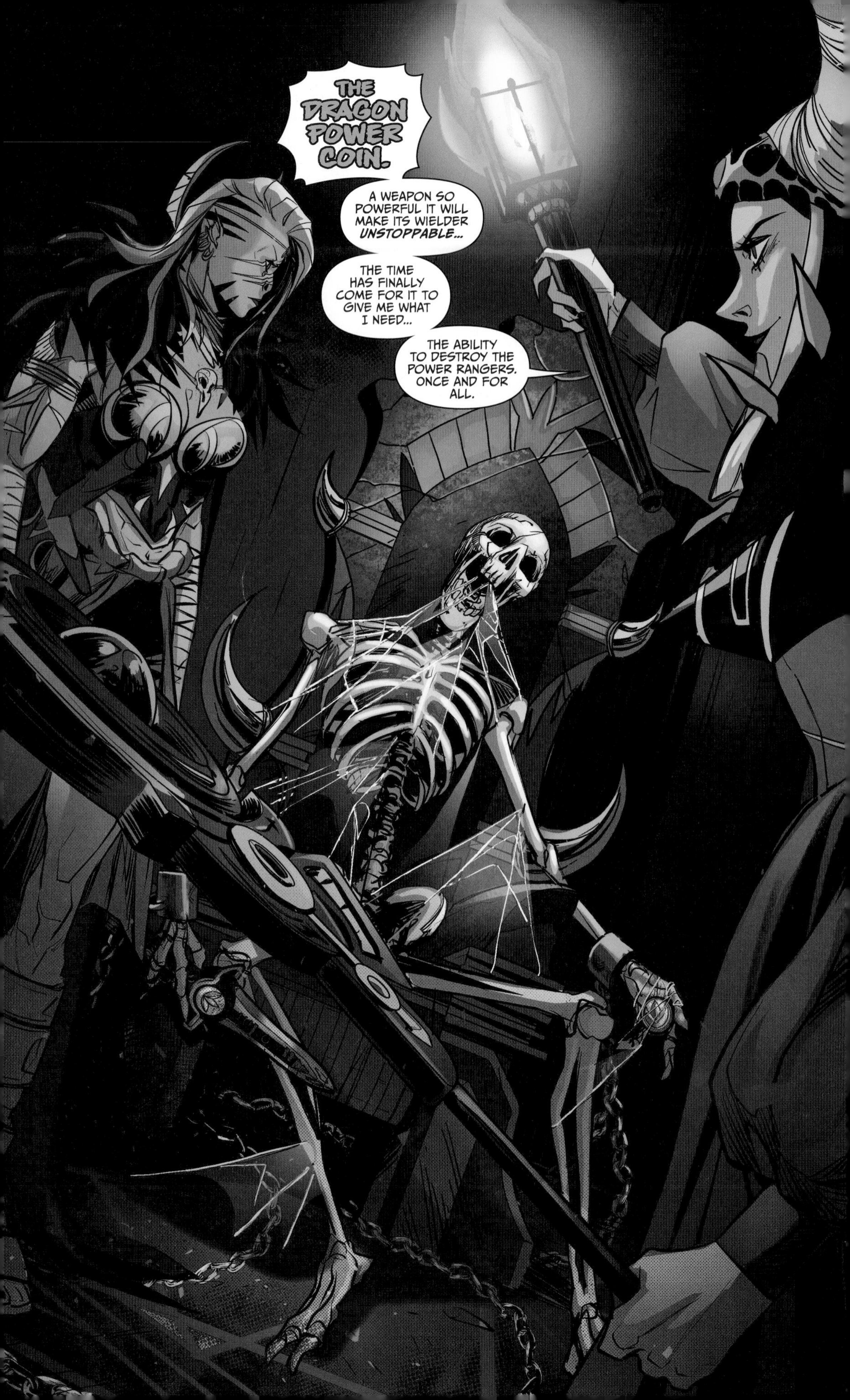
THE DRAGON POWER COIN.
A WEAPON SO POWERFUL IT WILL MAKE ITS WIELDER UNSTOPPABLE...
THE TIME HAS FINALLY COME FOR IT TO GIVE ME WHAT I NEED...
THE ABILITY TO DESTROY THE POWER RANGERS. ONCE AND FOR ALL.

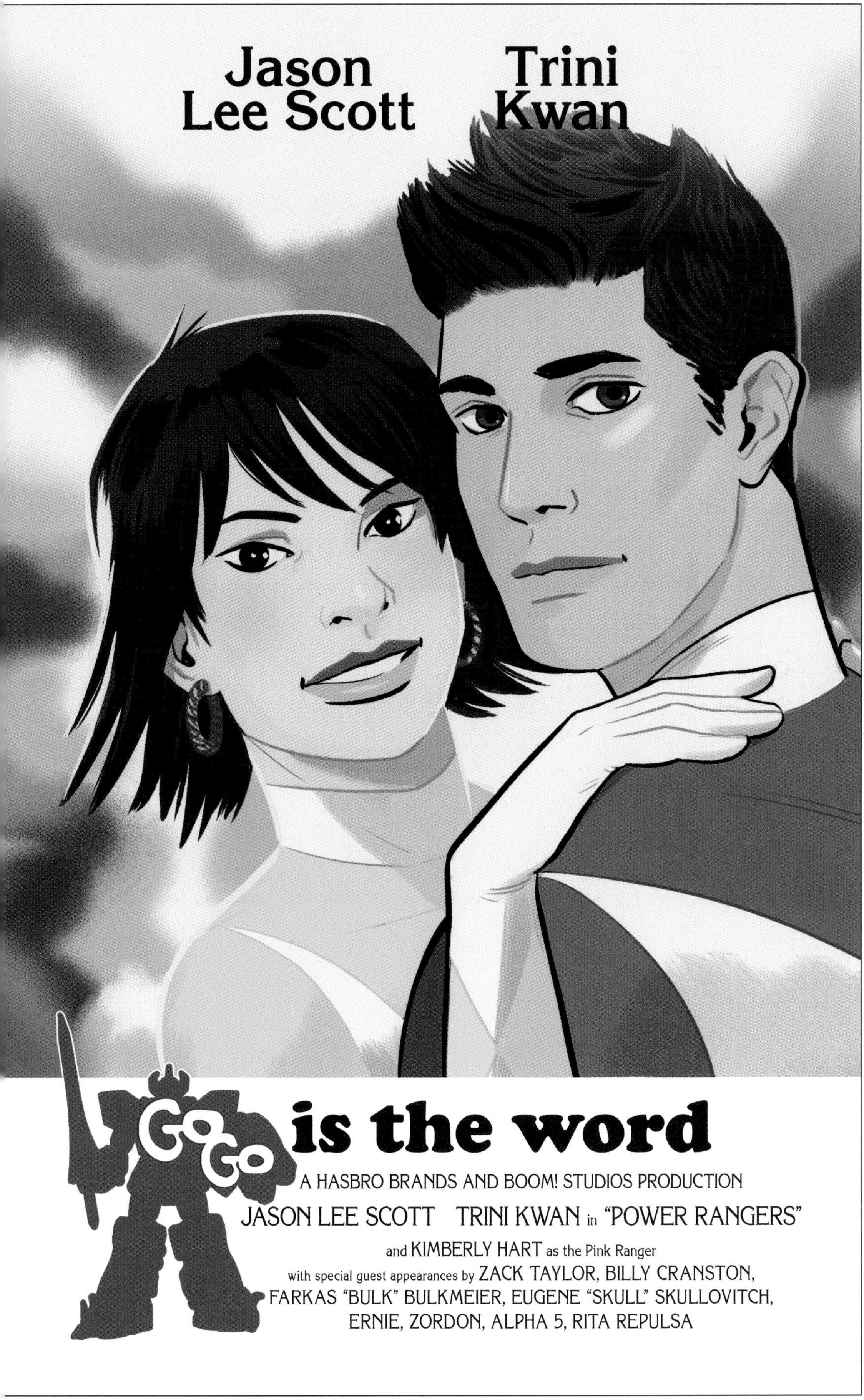
Jason
Lee Scott
Trini
Kwan
GO GO
is the word
A HASBRO BRANDS AND BOOM! STUDIOS PRODUCTION
JASON LEE SCOTT TRINI KWAN in "POWER RANGERS"
and KIMBERLY HART as the Pink Ranger
with special guest appearances by ZACK TAYLOR, BILLY CRANSTON,
FARKAS "BULK" BULKMEIER, EUGENE "SKULL" SKULLOVITCH,
ERNIE, ZORDON, ALPHA 5, RITA REPULSA

NATACHA BUSTOS WITH DESIGN BY **DYLAN TODD** ISSUE FIFTEEN MOVIE HOMAGE VARIANT

SIXTEEN

DAN MORA | ISSUE SIXTEEN MAIN COVER

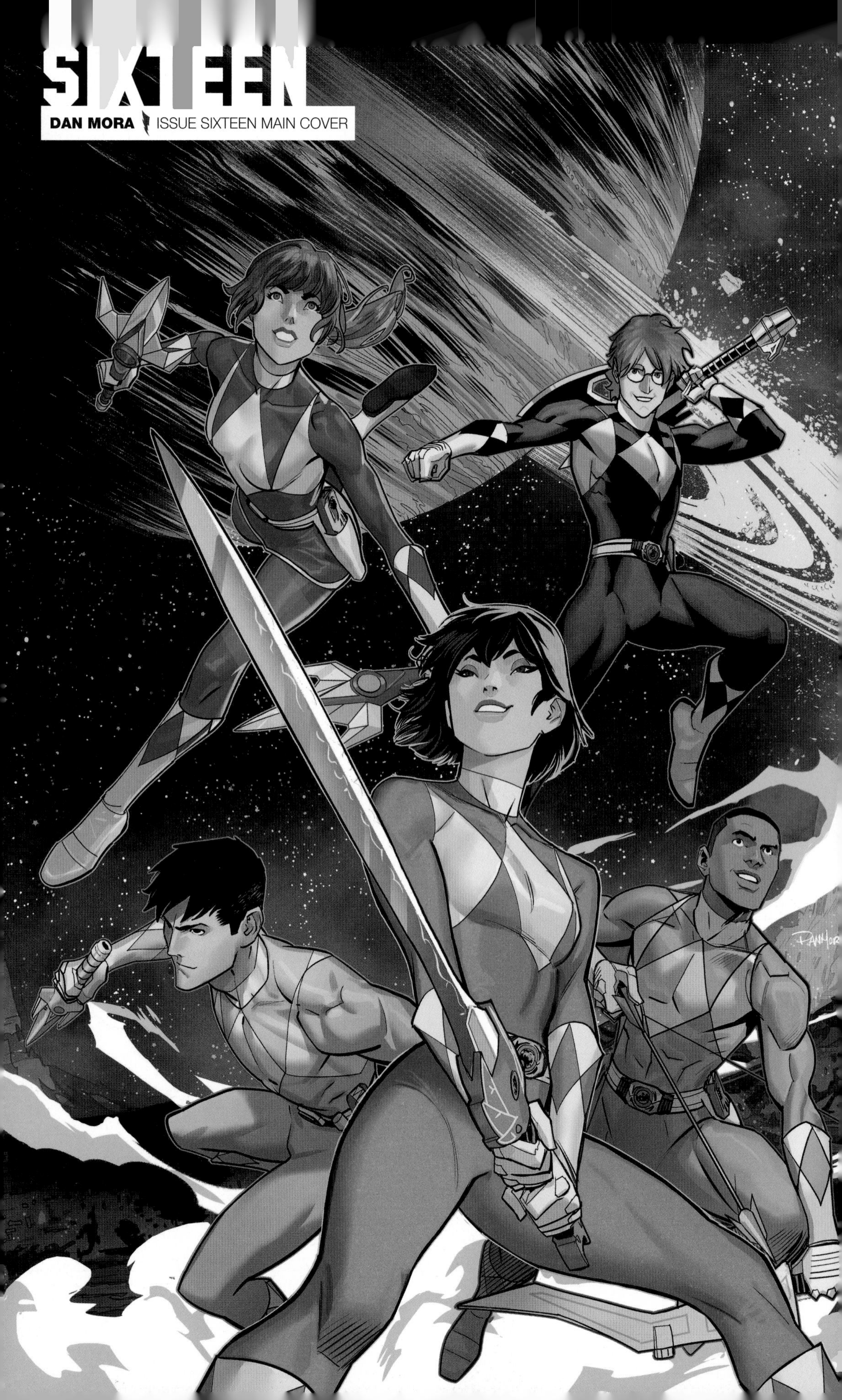

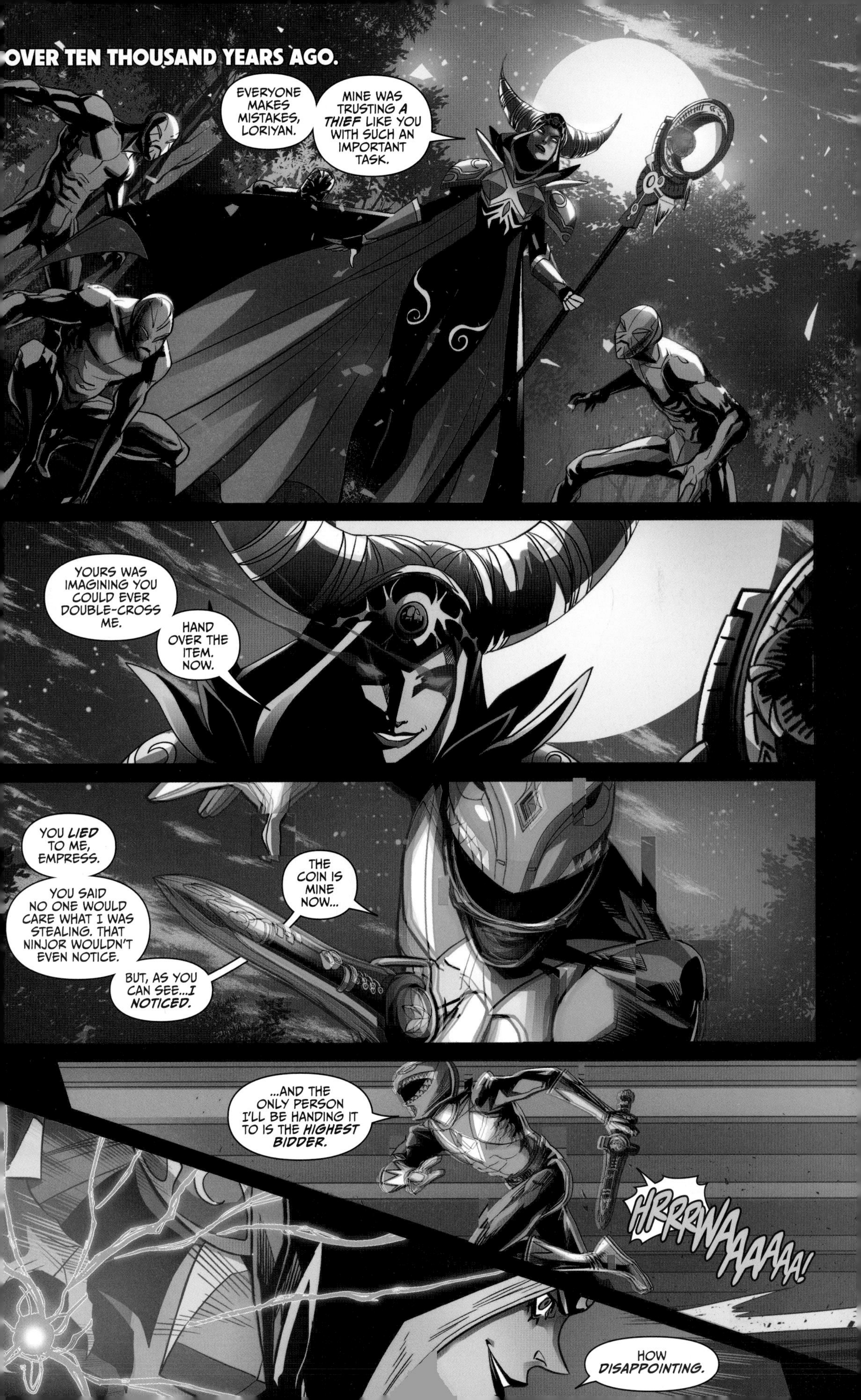
OVER TEN THOUSAND YEARS AGO.
EVERYONE MAKES MISTAKES, LORIYAN.
MINE WAS TRUSTING A THIEF LIKE YOU WITH SUCH AN IMPORTANT TASK.
YOURS WAS IMAGINING YOU COULD EVER DOUBLE-CROSS ME.
HAND OVER THE ITEM. NOW.
YOU LIED TO ME, EMPRESS.
YOU SAID NO ONE WOULD CARE WHAT I WAS STEALING. THAT NINJOR WOULDN'T EVEN NOTICE.
BUT, AS YOU CAN SEE...I NOTICED.
THE COIN IS MINE NOW...
...AND THE ONLY PERSON I'LL BE HANDING IT TO IS THE HIGHEST BIDDER.
HRRRWAAAAAA!
HOW DISAPPOINTING.

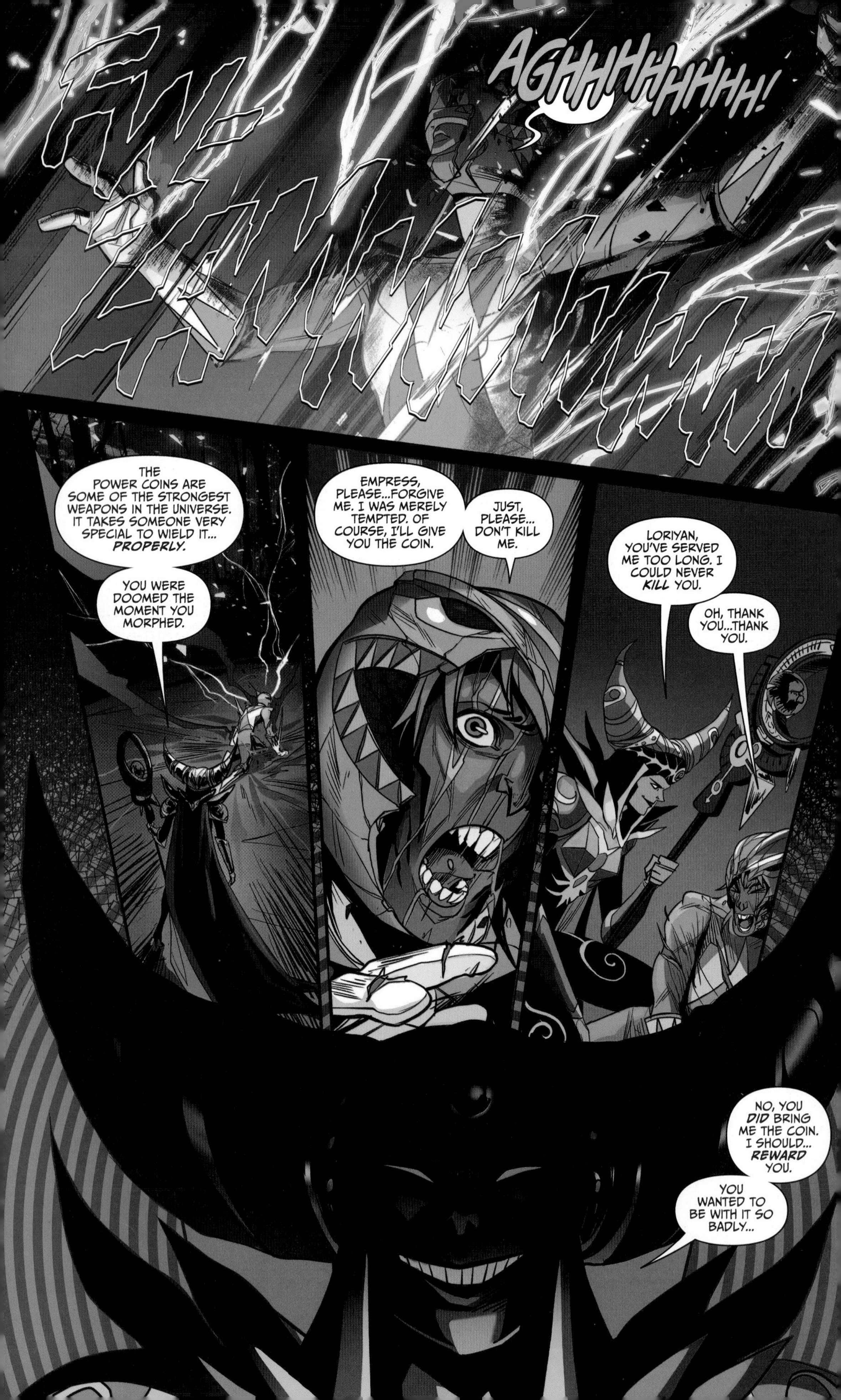
AGHHHHHHHH!
THE POWER COINS ARE SOME OF THE STRONGEST WEAPONS IN THE UNIVERSE. IT TAKES SOMEONE VERY SPECIAL TO WIELD IT... PROPERLY.
YOU WERE DOOMED THE MOMENT YOU MORPHED.
EMPRESS, PLEASE...FORGIVE ME. I WAS MERELY TEMPTED. OF COURSE, I'LL GIVE YOU THE COIN.
JUST, PLEASE... DON'T KILL ME.
LORIYAN, YOU'VE SERVED ME TOO LONG. I COULD NEVER KILL YOU.
OH, THANK YOU...THANK YOU.
NO, YOU DID BRING ME THE COIN. I SHOULD... REWARD YOU.
YOU WANTED TO BE WITH IT SO BADLY...

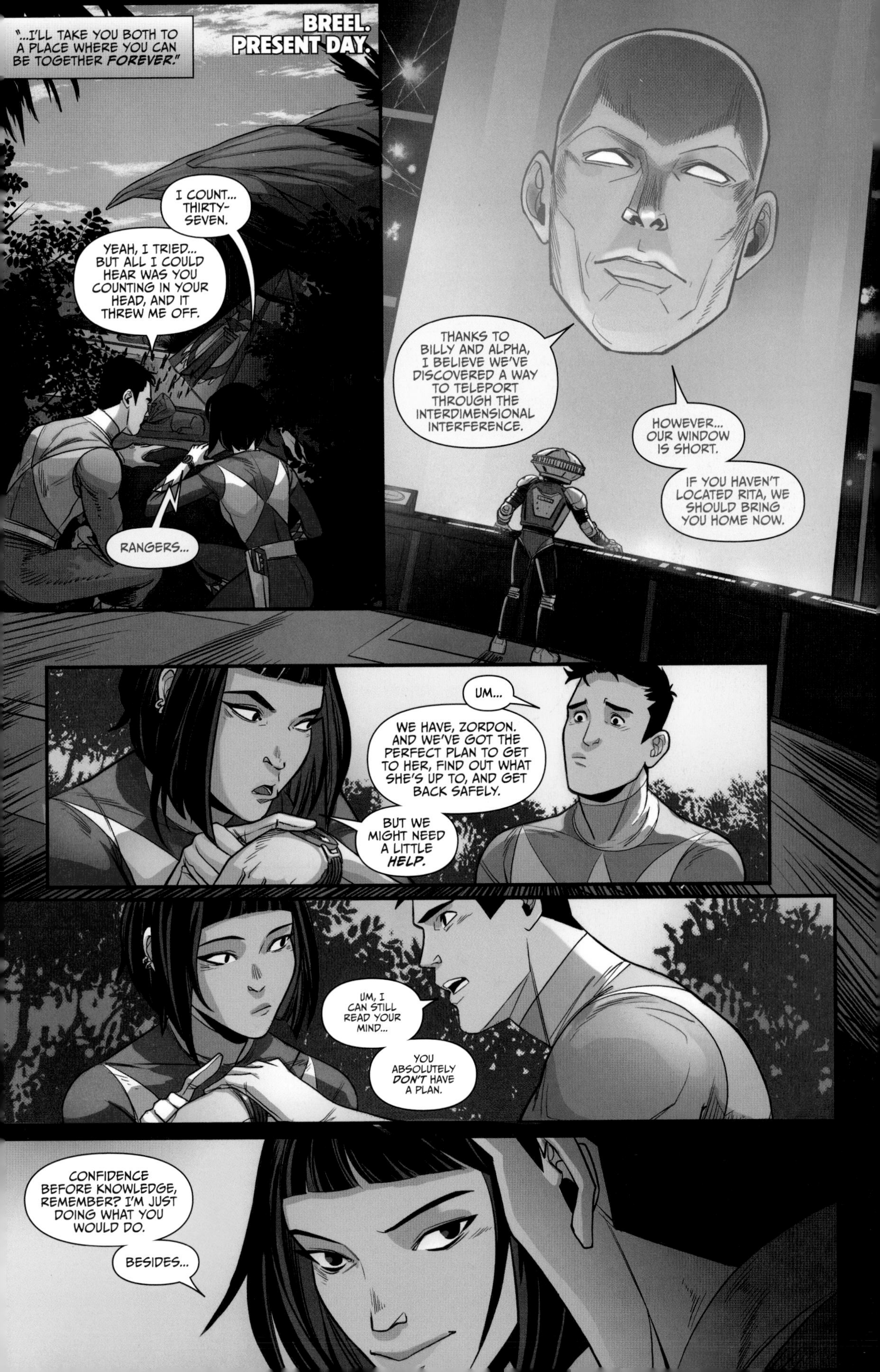
"...I'LL TAKE YOU BOTH TO A PLACE WHERE YOU CAN BE TOGETHER *FOREVER*."
BREEL. PRESENT DAY.
I COUNT... THIRTY-SEVEN.
YEAH, I TRIED... BUT ALL I COULD HEAR WAS YOU COUNTING IN YOUR HEAD, AND IT THREW ME OFF.
RANGERS...
THANKS TO BILLY AND ALPHA, I BELIEVE WE'VE DISCOVERED A WAY TO TELEPORT THROUGH THE INTERDIMENSIONAL INTERFERENCE.
HOWEVER... OUR WINDOW IS SHORT.
IF YOU HAVEN'T LOCATED RITA, WE SHOULD BRING YOU HOME NOW.
UM...
WE HAVE, ZORDON. AND WE'VE GOT THE PERFECT PLAN TO GET TO HER, FIND OUT WHAT SHE'S UP TO, AND GET BACK SAFELY.
BUT WE MIGHT NEED A LITTLE ***HELP.***
UM, I CAN STILL READ YOUR MIND...
YOU ABSOLUTELY *DON'T* HAVE A PLAN.
CONFIDENCE BEFORE KNOWLEDGE, REMEMBER? I'M JUST DOING WHAT YOU WOULD DO.
BESIDES...

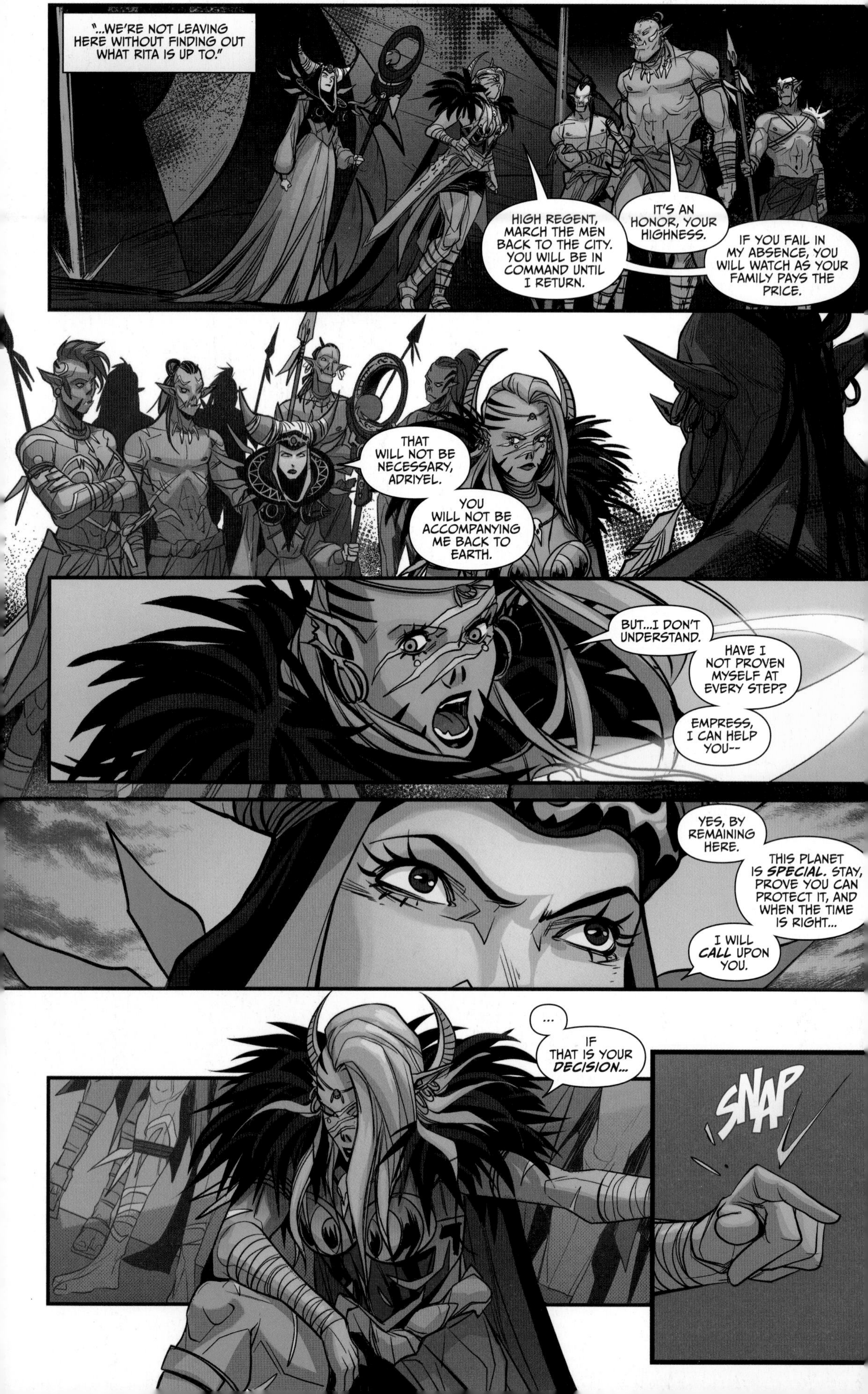
"...WE'RE NOT LEAVING HERE WITHOUT FINDING OUT WHAT RITA IS UP TO."
HIGH REGENT, MARCH THE MEN BACK TO THE CITY. YOU WILL BE IN COMMAND UNTIL I RETURN.
IT'S AN HONOR, YOUR HIGHNESS.
IF YOU FAIL IN MY ABSENCE, YOU WILL WATCH AS YOUR FAMILY PAYS THE PRICE.
THAT WILL NOT BE NECESSARY, ADRIYEL.
YOU WILL NOT BE ACCOMPANYING ME BACK TO EARTH.
BUT...I DON'T UNDERSTAND.
HAVE I NOT PROVEN MYSELF AT EVERY STEP?
EMPRESS, I CAN HELP YOU--
YES, BY REMAINING HERE.
THIS PLANET IS *SPECIAL.* STAY, PROVE YOU CAN PROTECT IT, AND WHEN THE TIME IS RIGHT...
I WILL *CALL* UPON YOU.
...
IF THAT IS YOUR *DECISION...*
SNAP

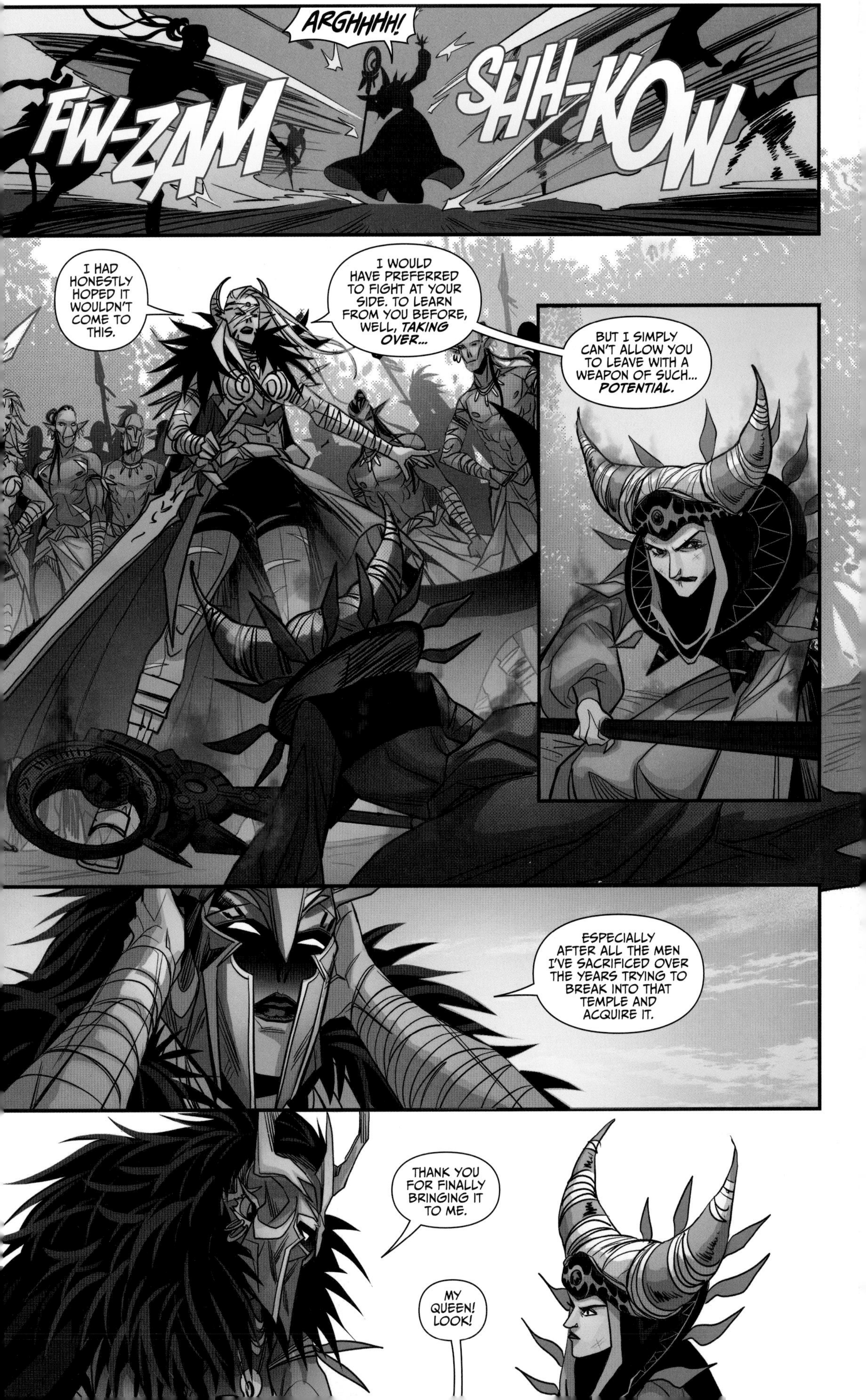
ARGHHHH!
FW-ZAM
SHH-KOW
I HAD HONESTLY HOPED IT WOULDN'T COME TO THIS.
I WOULD HAVE PREFERRED TO FIGHT AT YOUR SIDE. TO LEARN FROM YOU BEFORE, WELL, *TAKING OVER...*
BUT I SIMPLY CAN'T ALLOW YOU TO LEAVE WITH A WEAPON OF SUCH... *POTENTIAL.*
ESPECIALLY AFTER ALL THE MEN I'VE SACRIFICED OVER THE YEARS TRYING TO BREAK INTO THAT TEMPLE AND ACQUIRE IT.
THANK YOU FOR FINALLY BRINGING IT TO ME.
MY QUEEN! LOOK!

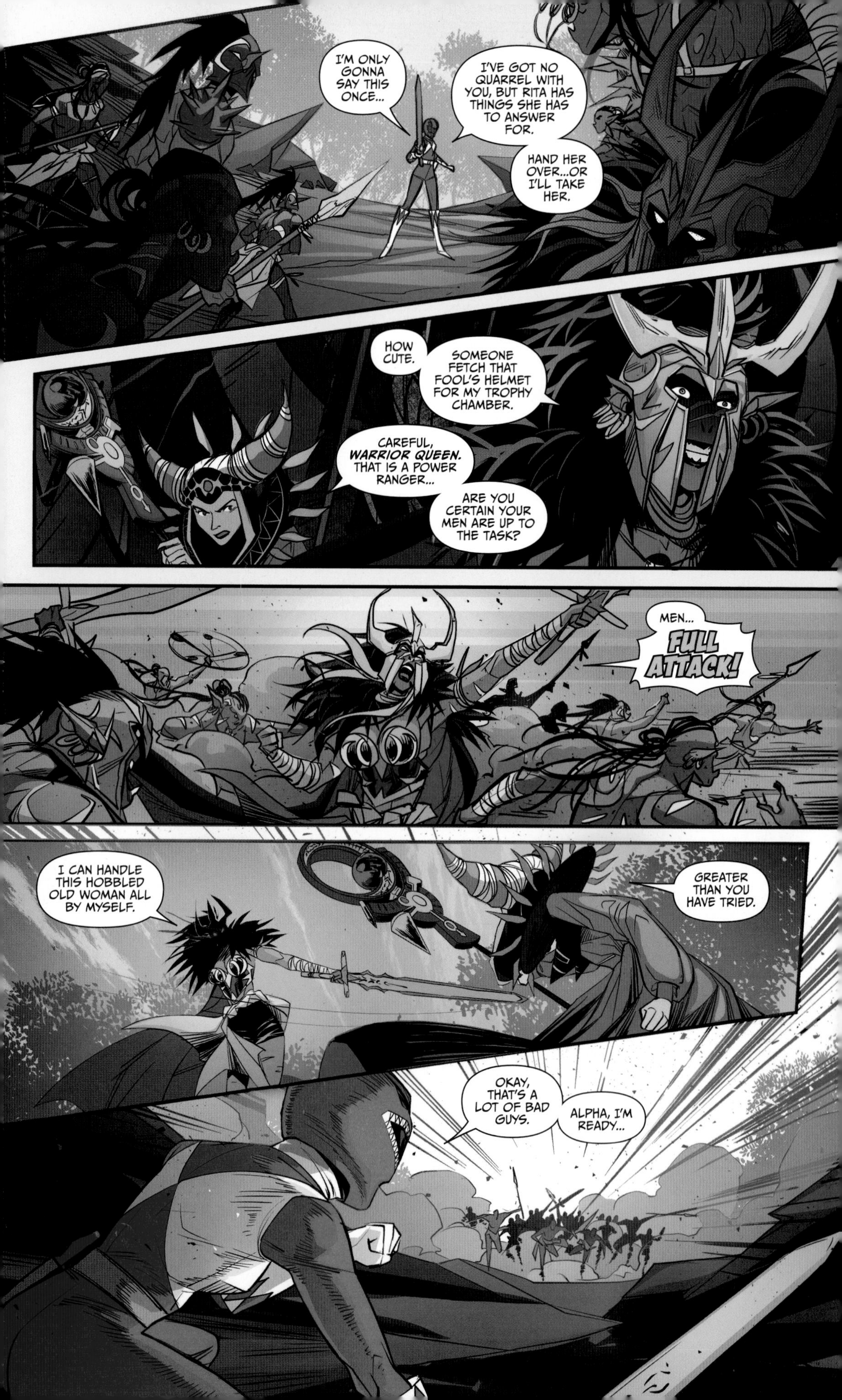

I'M ONLY GONNA SAY THIS ONCE...
I'VE GOT NO QUARREL WITH YOU, BUT RITA HAS THINGS SHE HAS TO ANSWER FOR.
HAND HER OVER...OR I'LL TAKE HER.
HOW CUTE.
SOMEONE FETCH THAT FOOL'S HELMET FOR MY TROPHY CHAMBER.
CAREFUL, *WARRIOR QUEEN.* THAT IS A POWER RANGER...
ARE YOU CERTAIN YOUR MEN ARE UP TO THE TASK?
MEN...
FULL ATTACK!
I CAN HANDLE THIS HOBBLED OLD WOMAN ALL BY MYSELF.
GREATER THAN YOU HAVE TRIED.
OKAY, THAT'S A LOT OF BAD GUYS.
ALPHA, I'M READY...

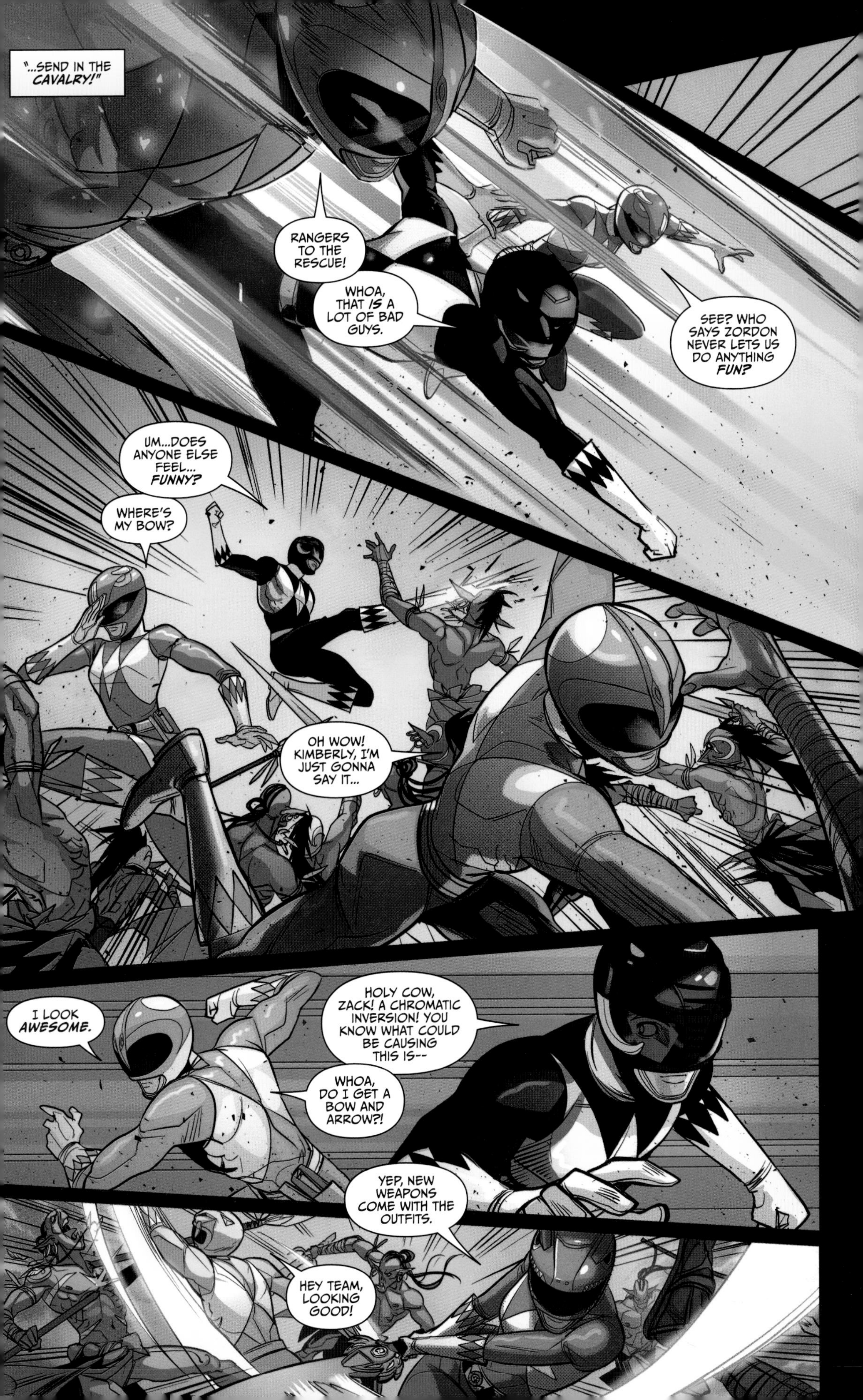
"...SEND IN THE CAVALRY!"
RANGERS TO THE RESCUE!
WHOA, THAT *IS* A LOT OF BAD GUYS.
SEE? WHO SAYS ZORDON NEVER LETS US DO ANYTHING *FUN?*
UM...DOES ANYONE ELSE FEEL... *FUNNY?*
WHERE'S MY BOW?
OH WOW! KIMBERLY, I'M JUST GONNA SAY IT...
I LOOK *AWESOME.*
HOLY COW, ZACK! A CHROMATIC INVERSION! YOU KNOW WHAT COULD BE CAUSING THIS IS--
WHOA, DO I GET A BOW AND ARROW?!
YEP, NEW WEAPONS COME WITH THE OUTFITS.
HEY TEAM, LOOKING GOOD!

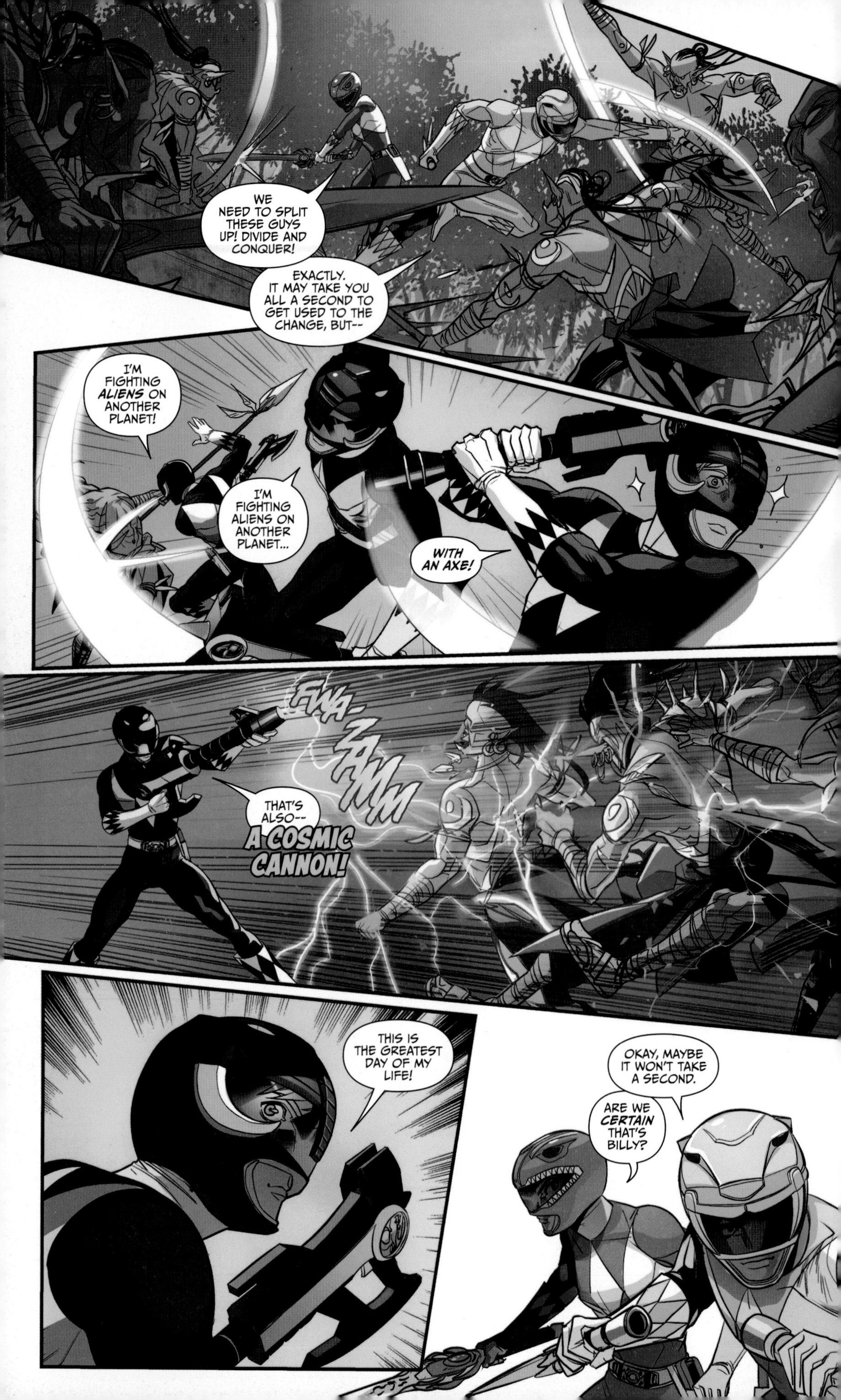

WE NEED TO SPLIT THESE GUYS UP! DIVIDE AND CONQUER!
EXACTLY. IT MAY TAKE YOU ALL A SECOND TO GET USED TO THE CHANGE, BUT--
I'M FIGHTING ALIENS ON ANOTHER PLANET!
I'M FIGHTING ALIENS ON ANOTHER PLANET...
WITH AN AXE!
THAT'S ALSO-- A COSMIC CANNON!
FWA-ZAMM
THIS IS THE GREATEST DAY OF MY LIFE!
OKAY, MAYBE IT WON'T TAKE A SECOND.
ARE WE CERTAIN THAT'S BILLY?

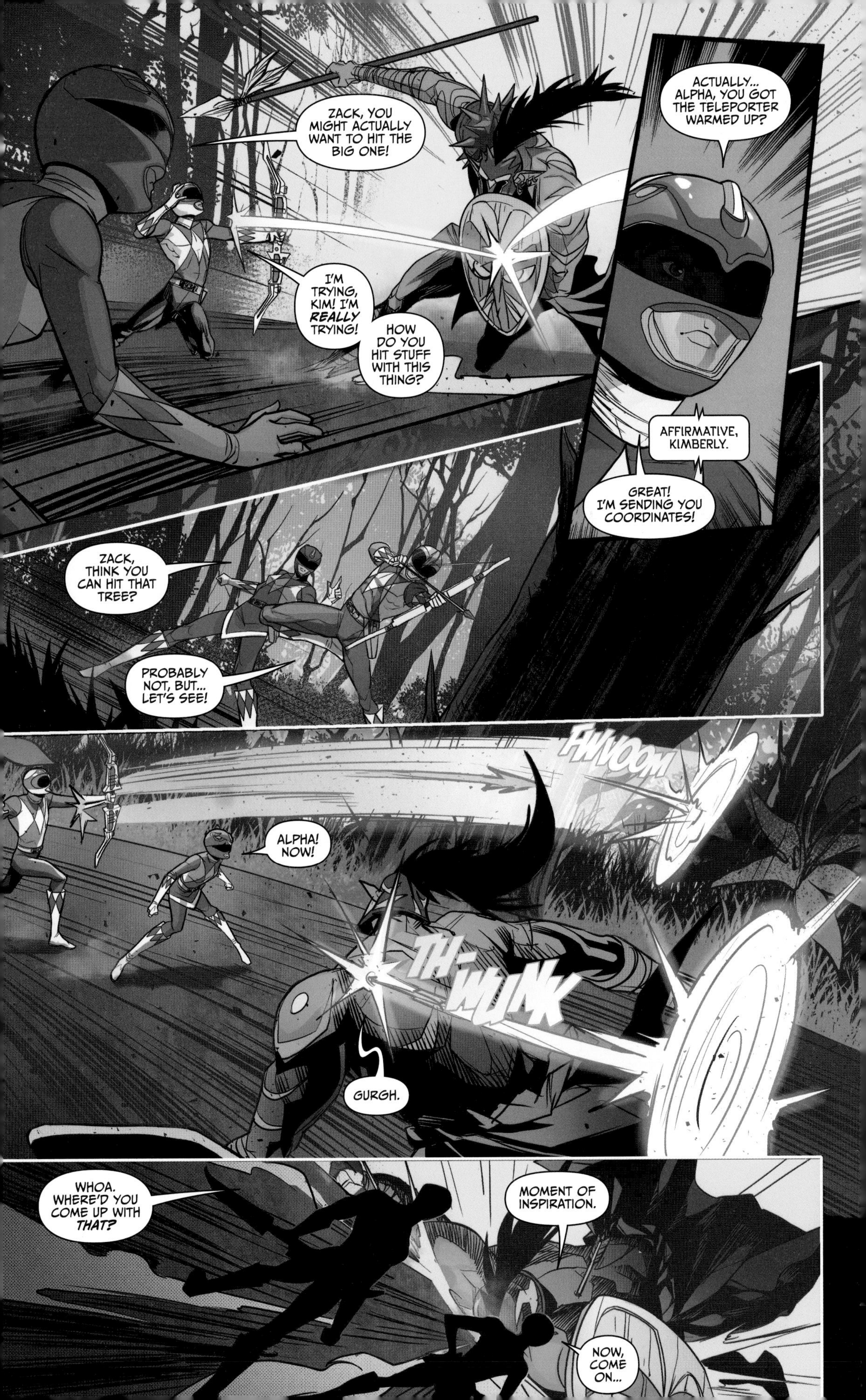
ZACK, YOU MIGHT ACTUALLY WANT TO HIT THE BIG ONE!
I'M TRYING, KIM! I'M REALLY TRYING!
HOW DO YOU HIT STUFF WITH THIS THING?
ACTUALLY... ALPHA, YOU GOT THE TELEPORTER WARMED UP?
AFFIRMATIVE, KIMBERLY.
GREAT! I'M SENDING YOU COORDINATES!
ZACK, THINK YOU CAN HIT THAT TREE?
PROBABLY NOT, BUT... LET'S SEE!
FWOOM
ALPHA! NOW!
TH-WUNK
GURGH.
WHOA. WHERE'D YOU COME UP WITH THAT?
MOMENT OF INSPIRATION.
NOW, COME ON...

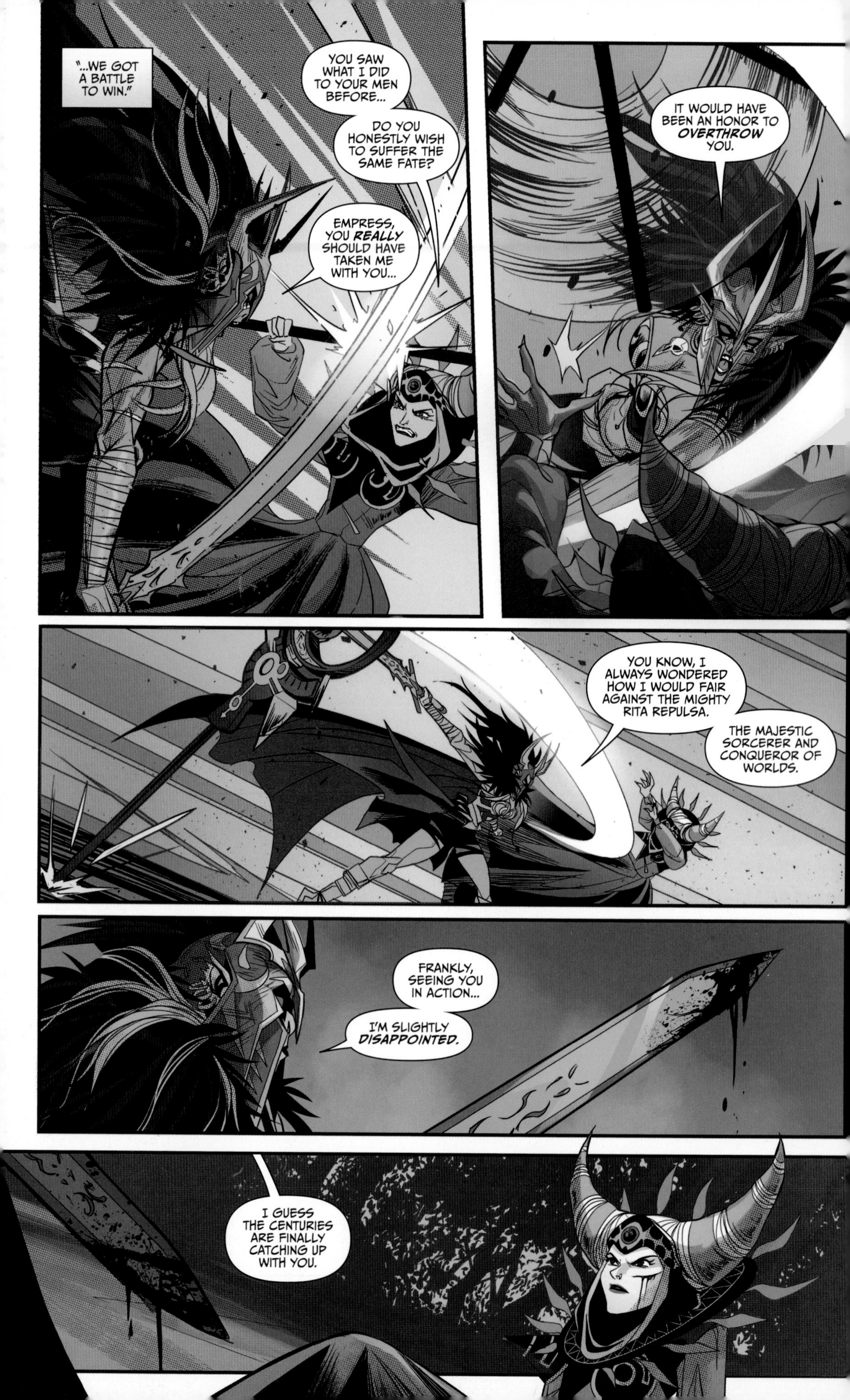
"...WE GOT A BATTLE TO WIN."
YOU SAW WHAT I DID TO YOUR MEN BEFORE...
DO YOU HONESTLY WISH TO SUFFER THE SAME FATE?
EMPRESS, YOU REALLY SHOULD HAVE TAKEN ME WITH YOU...
IT WOULD HAVE BEEN AN HONOR TO OVERTHROW YOU.
YOU KNOW, I ALWAYS WONDERED HOW I WOULD FAIR AGAINST THE MIGHTY RITA REPULSA.
THE MAJESTIC SORCERER AND CONQUEROR OF WORLDS.
FRANKLY, SEEING YOU IN ACTION...
I'M SLIGHTLY DISAPPOINTED.
I GUESS THE CENTURIES ARE FINALLY CATCHING UP WITH YOU.

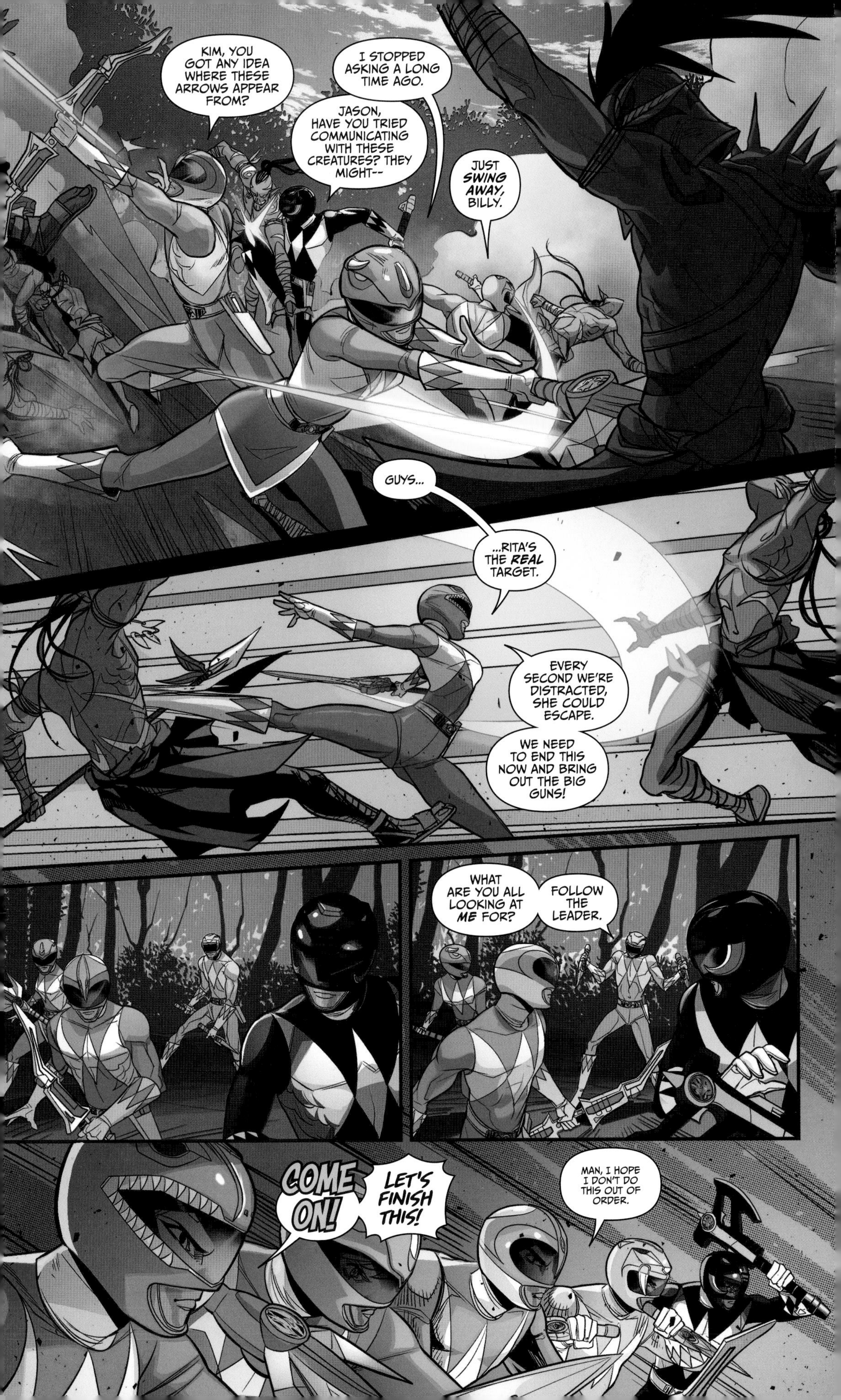
KIM, YOU GOT ANY IDEA WHERE THESE ARROWS APPEAR FROM?
I STOPPED ASKING A LONG TIME AGO.
JASON, HAVE YOU TRIED COMMUNICATING WITH THESE CREATURES? THEY MIGHT--
JUST SWING AWAY, BILLY.
GUYS...
...RITA'S THE REAL TARGET.
EVERY SECOND WE'RE DISTRACTED, SHE COULD ESCAPE.
WE NEED TO END THIS NOW AND BRING OUT THE BIG GUNS!
WHAT ARE YOU ALL LOOKING AT ME FOR?
FOLLOW THE LEADER.
COME ON!
LET'S FINISH THIS!
MAN, I HOPE I DON'T DO THIS OUT OF ORDER.

POWER AXE!
POWER BOW!
POWER DAGGERS!
POWER LANCE!
POWER SWORD
POWER BLASTER!

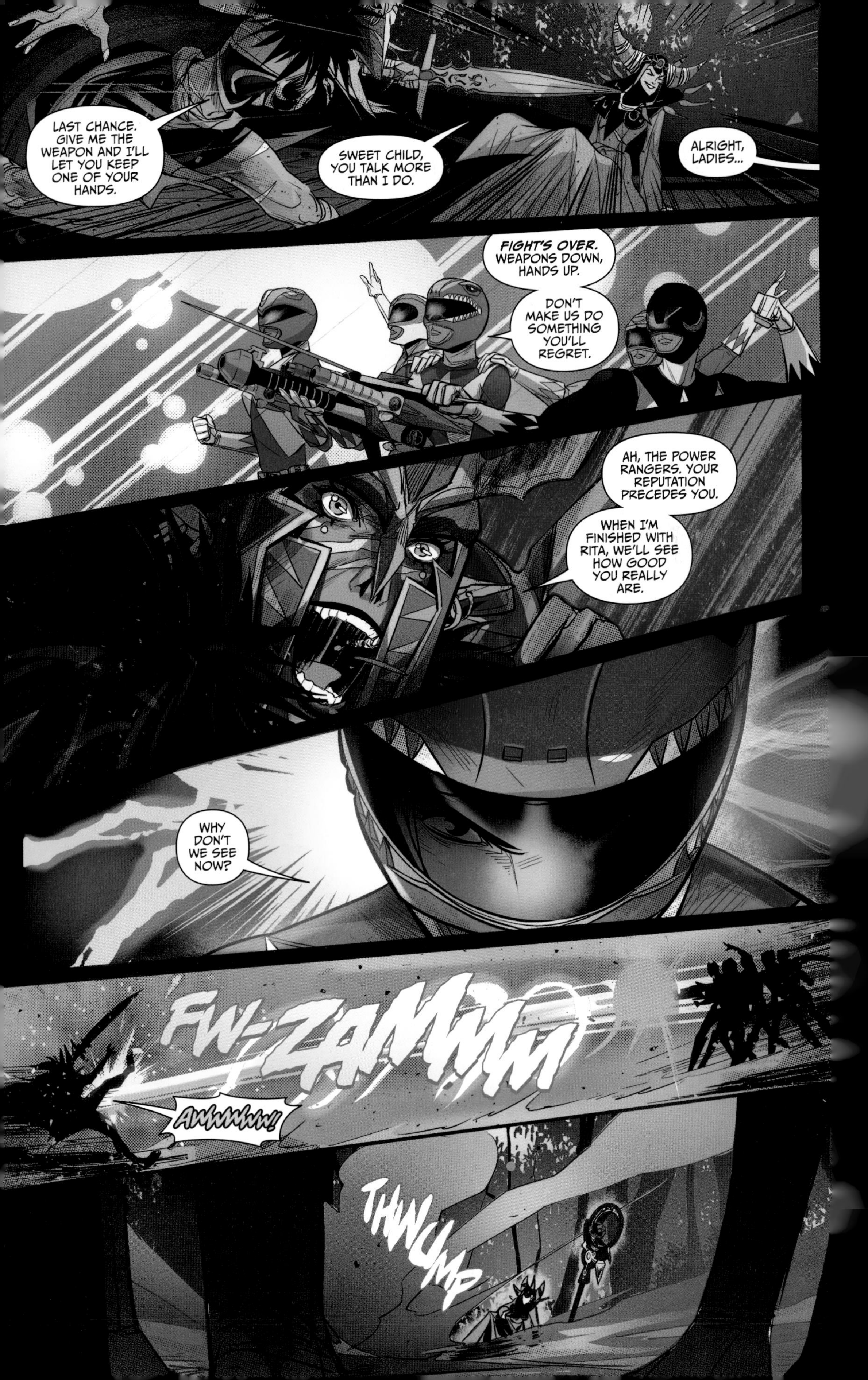
LAST CHANCE. GIVE ME THE WEAPON AND I'LL LET YOU KEEP ONE OF YOUR HANDS.
SWEET CHILD, YOU TALK MORE THAN I DO.
ALRIGHT, LADIES...
FIGHT'S OVER. WEAPONS DOWN, HANDS UP.
DON'T MAKE US DO SOMETHING YOU'LL REGRET.
AH, THE POWER RANGERS. YOUR REPUTATION PRECEDES YOU.
WHEN I'M FINISHED WITH RITA, WE'LL SEE HOW GOOD YOU REALLY ARE.
WHY DON'T WE SEE NOW?
FW-ZAMMMM
AWHWHW!
THWUMP

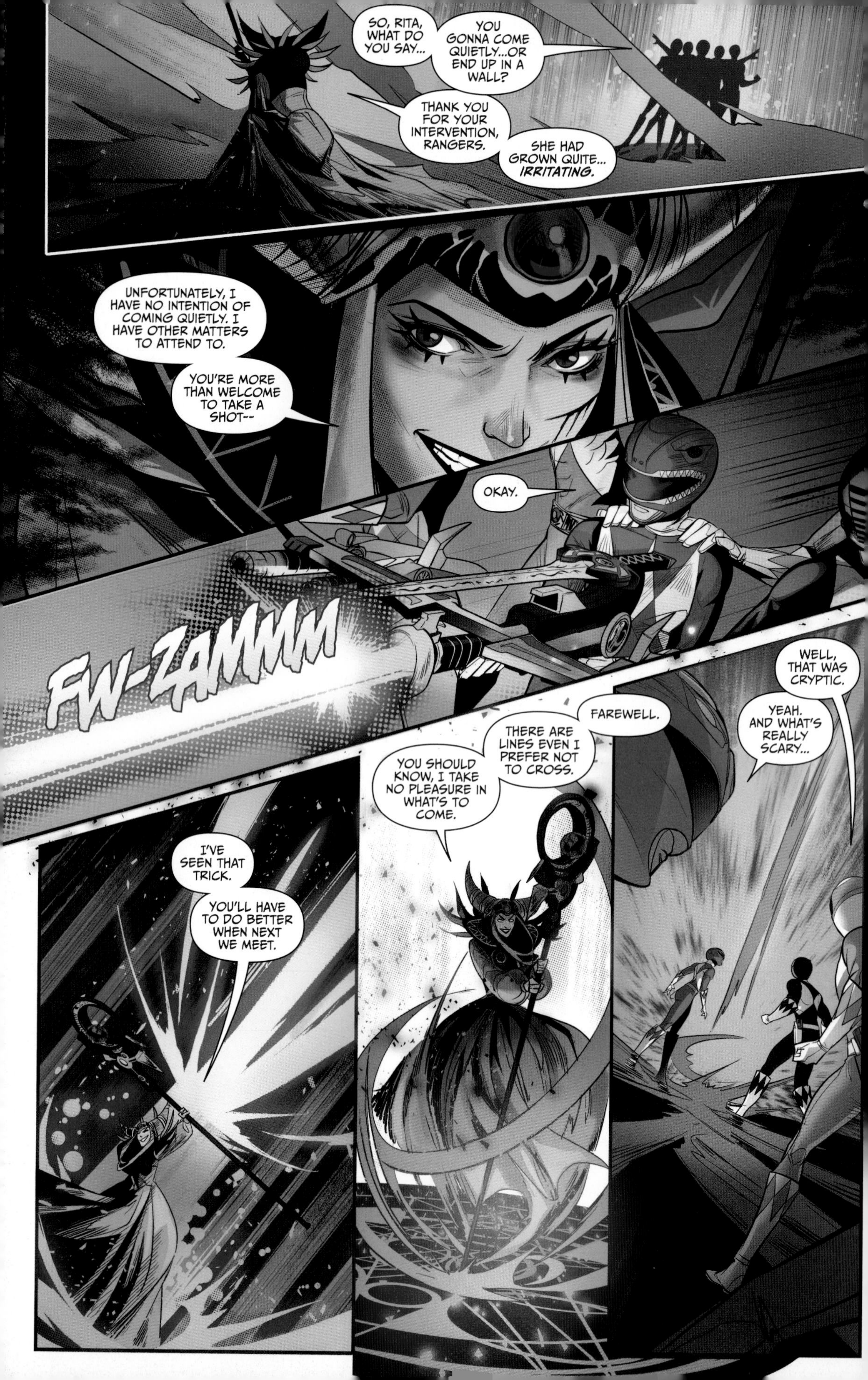
SO, RITA, WHAT DO YOU SAY...
YOU GONNA COME QUIETLY...OR END UP IN A WALL?
THANK YOU FOR YOUR INTERVENTION, RANGERS.
SHE HAD GROWN QUITE... *IRRITATING.*
UNFORTUNATELY, I HAVE NO INTENTION OF COMING QUIETLY. I HAVE OTHER MATTERS TO ATTEND TO.
YOU'RE MORE THAN WELCOME TO TAKE A SHOT--
OKAY.
FW-ZAMMM
I'VE SEEN THAT TRICK.
YOU'LL HAVE TO DO BETTER WHEN NEXT WE MEET.
YOU SHOULD KNOW, I TAKE NO PLEASURE IN WHAT'S TO COME.
THERE ARE LINES EVEN I PREFER NOT TO CROSS.
FAREWELL.
WELL, THAT WAS CRYPTIC.
YEAH. AND WHAT'S REALLY SCARY...

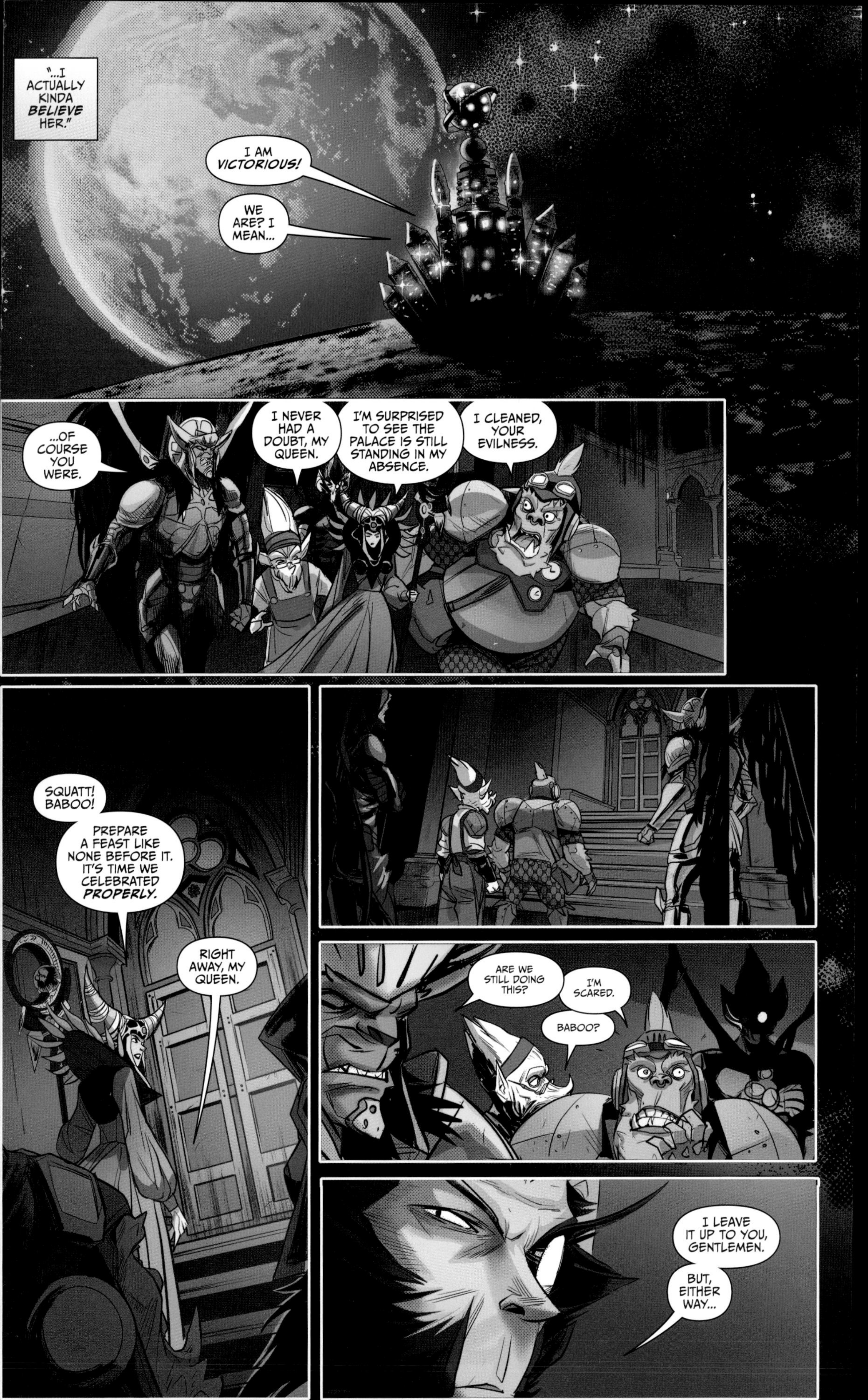
"...I ACTUALLY KINDA BELIEVE HER."
I AM VICTORIOUS!
WE ARE? I MEAN...
...OF COURSE YOU WERE.
I NEVER HAD A DOUBT, MY QUEEN.
I'M SURPRISED TO SEE THE PALACE IS STILL STANDING IN MY ABSENCE.
I CLEANED, YOUR EVILNESS.
SQUATT! BABOO!
PREPARE A FEAST LIKE NONE BEFORE IT. IT'S TIME WE CELEBRATED PROPERLY.
RIGHT AWAY, MY QUEEN.
ARE WE STILL DOING THIS?
I'M SCARED.
BABOO?
I LEAVE IT UP TO YOU, GENTLEMEN.
BUT, EITHER WAY...

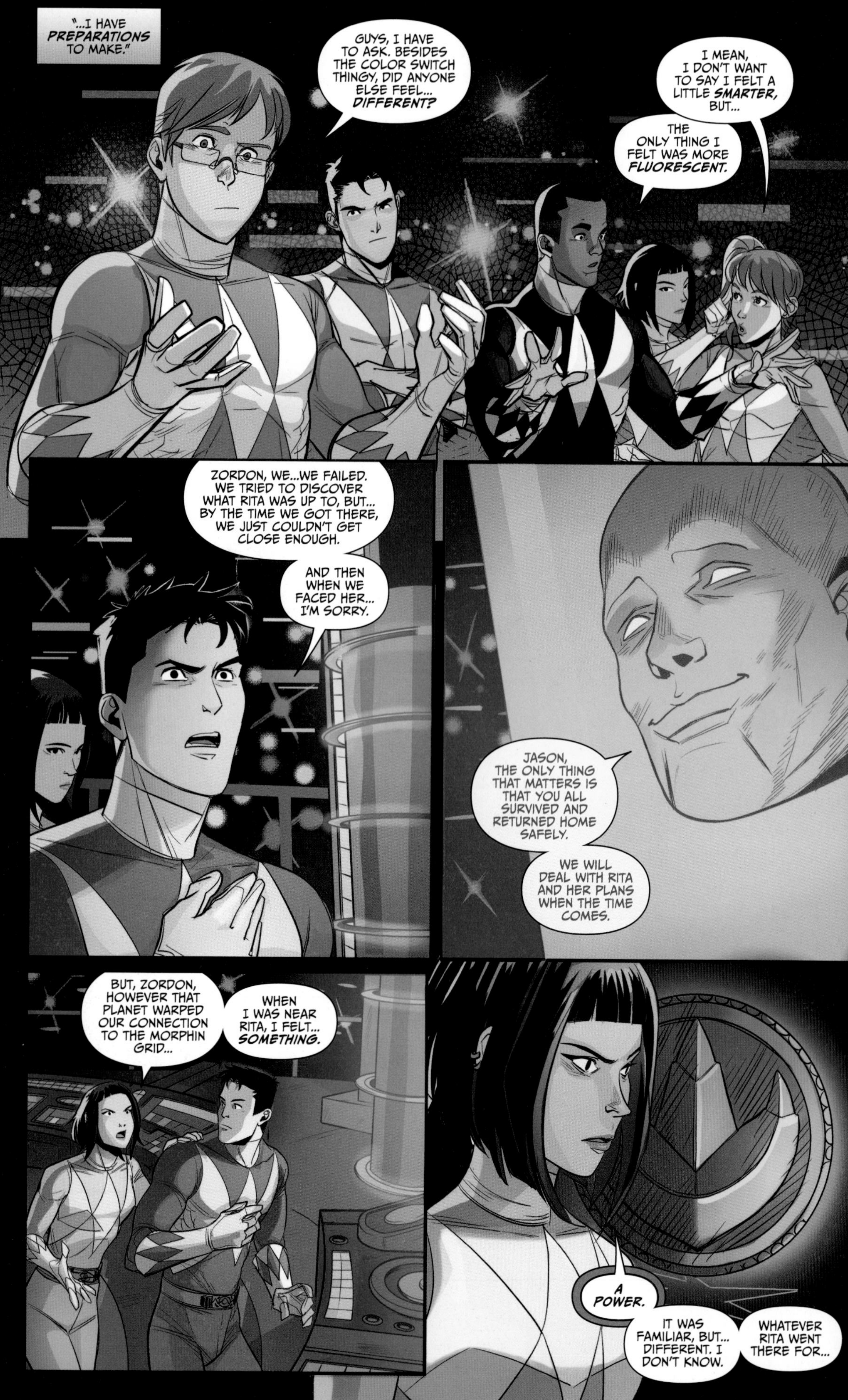

"...I HAVE PREPARATIONS TO MAKE."
GUYS, I HAVE TO ASK. BESIDES THE COLOR SWITCH THINGY, DID ANYONE ELSE FEEL... DIFFERENT?
I MEAN, I DON'T WANT TO SAY I FELT A LITTLE SMARTER, BUT...
THE ONLY THING I FELT WAS MORE FLUORESCENT.
ZORDON, WE...WE FAILED. WE TRIED TO DISCOVER WHAT RITA WAS UP TO, BUT... BY THE TIME WE GOT THERE, WE JUST COULDN'T GET CLOSE ENOUGH.
AND THEN WHEN WE FACED HER... I'M SORRY.
JASON, THE ONLY THING THAT MATTERS IS THAT YOU ALL SURVIVED AND RETURNED HOME SAFELY.
WE WILL DEAL WITH RITA AND HER PLANS WHEN THE TIME COMES.
BUT, ZORDON, HOWEVER THAT PLANET WARPED OUR CONNECTION TO THE MORPHIN GRID...
WHEN I WAS NEAR RITA, I FELT... SOMETHING.
A POWER.
IT WAS FAMILIAR, BUT... DIFFERENT. I DON'T KNOW.
WHATEVER RITA WENT THERE FOR...

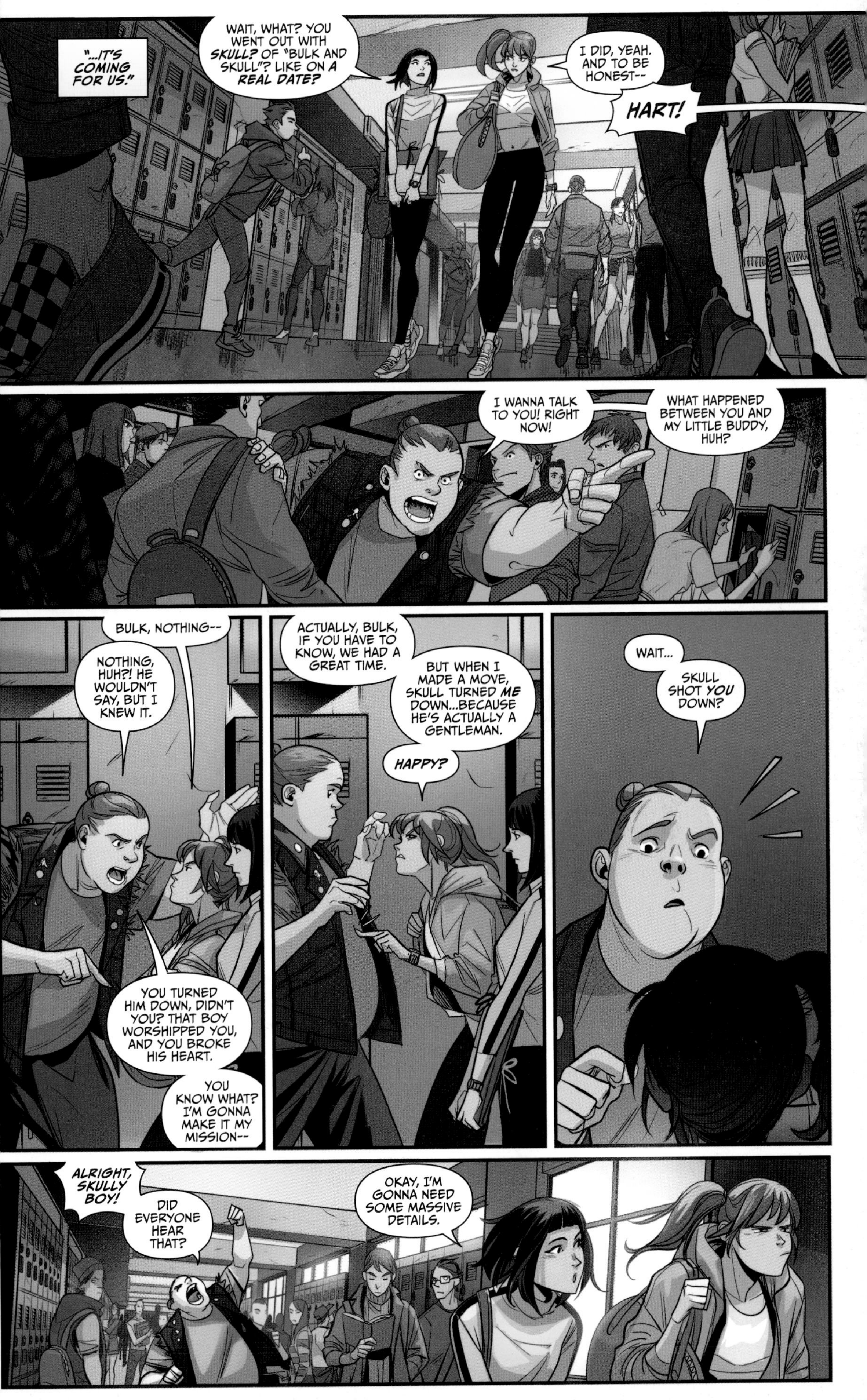
"...IT'S COMING FOR US."
WAIT, WHAT? YOU WENT OUT WITH SKULL? OF "BULK AND SKULL"? LIKE ON A REAL DATE?
I DID, YEAH. AND TO BE HONEST--
HART!
I WANNA TALK TO YOU! RIGHT NOW!
WHAT HAPPENED BETWEEN YOU AND MY LITTLE BUDDY, HUH?
BULK, NOTHING--
NOTHING, HUH?! HE WOULDN'T SAY, BUT I KNEW IT.
YOU TURNED HIM DOWN, DIDN'T YOU? THAT BOY WORSHIPPED YOU, AND YOU BROKE HIS HEART.
YOU KNOW WHAT? I'M GONNA MAKE IT MY MISSION--
ACTUALLY, BULK, IF YOU HAVE TO KNOW, WE HAD A GREAT TIME.
BUT WHEN I MADE A MOVE, SKULL TURNED ME DOWN...BECAUSE HE'S ACTUALLY A GENTLEMAN.
HAPPY?
WAIT...
SKULL SHOT YOU DOWN?
ALRIGHT, SKULLY BOY!
DID EVERYONE HEAR THAT?
OKAY, I'M GONNA NEED SOME MASSIVE DETAILS.

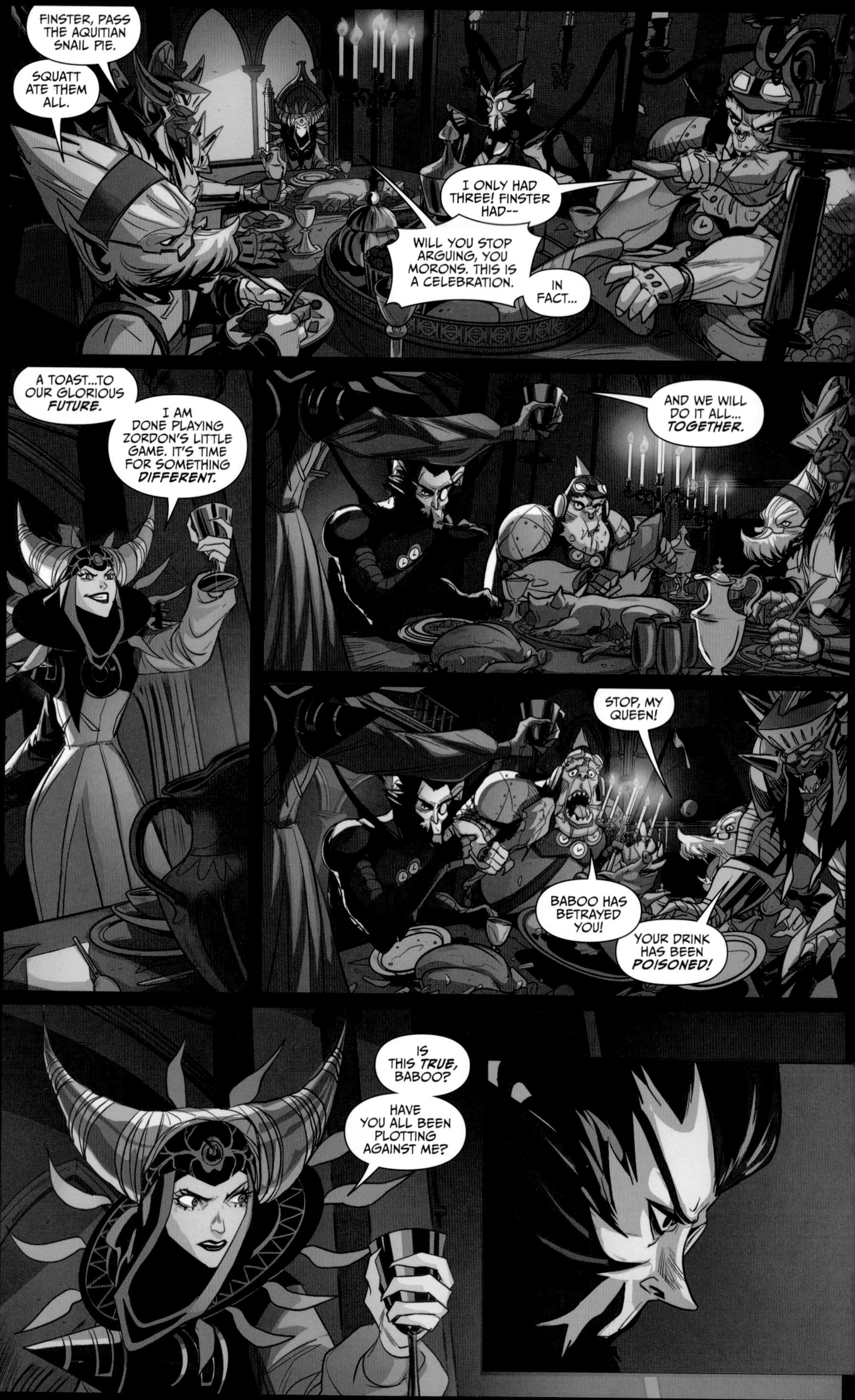
FINSTER, PASS THE AQUITIAN SNAIL PIE.
SQUATT ATE THEM ALL.
I ONLY HAD THREE! FINSTER HAD--
WILL YOU STOP ARGUING, YOU MORONS. THIS IS A CELEBRATION.
IN FACT...
A TOAST...TO OUR GLORIOUS FUTURE.
I AM DONE PLAYING ZORDON'S LITTLE GAME. IT'S TIME FOR SOMETHING DIFFERENT.
AND WE WILL DO IT ALL... TOGETHER.
STOP, MY QUEEN!
BABOO HAS BETRAYED YOU!
YOUR DRINK HAS BEEN POISONED!
IS THIS TRUE, BABOO?
HAVE YOU ALL BEEN PLOTTING AGAINST ME?

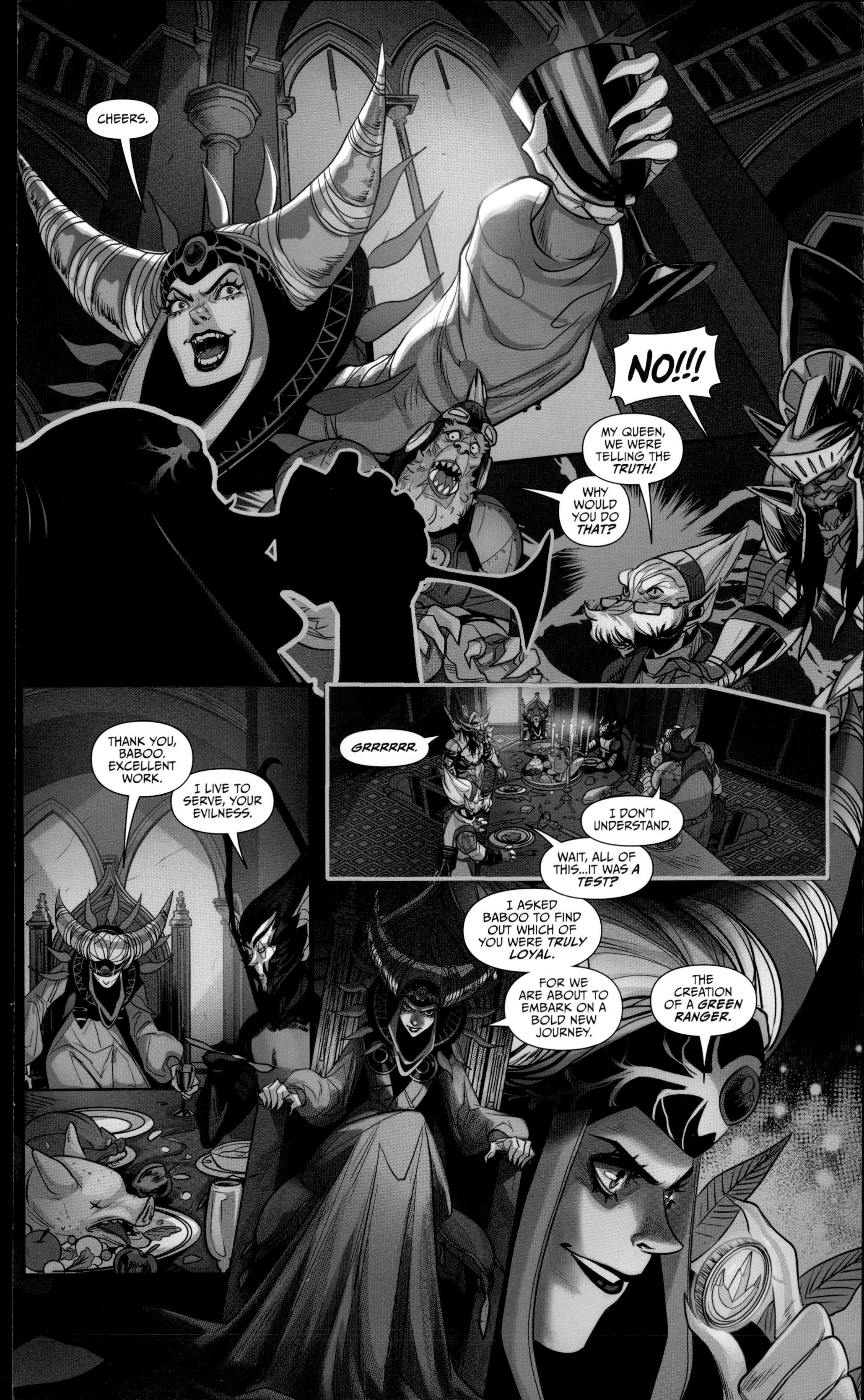
CHEERS.
NO!!!
MY QUEEN, WE WERE TELLING THE TRUTH!
WHY WOULD YOU DO THAT?
THANK YOU, BABOO. EXCELLENT WORK.
I LIVE TO SERVE, YOUR EVILNESS.
GRRRRRR.
I DON'T UNDERSTAND.
WAIT, ALL OF THIS...IT WAS A TEST?
I ASKED BABOO TO FIND OUT WHICH OF YOU WERE TRULY LOYAL.
FOR WE ARE ABOUT TO EMBARK ON A BOLD NEW JOURNEY.
THE CREATION OF A GREEN RANGER.

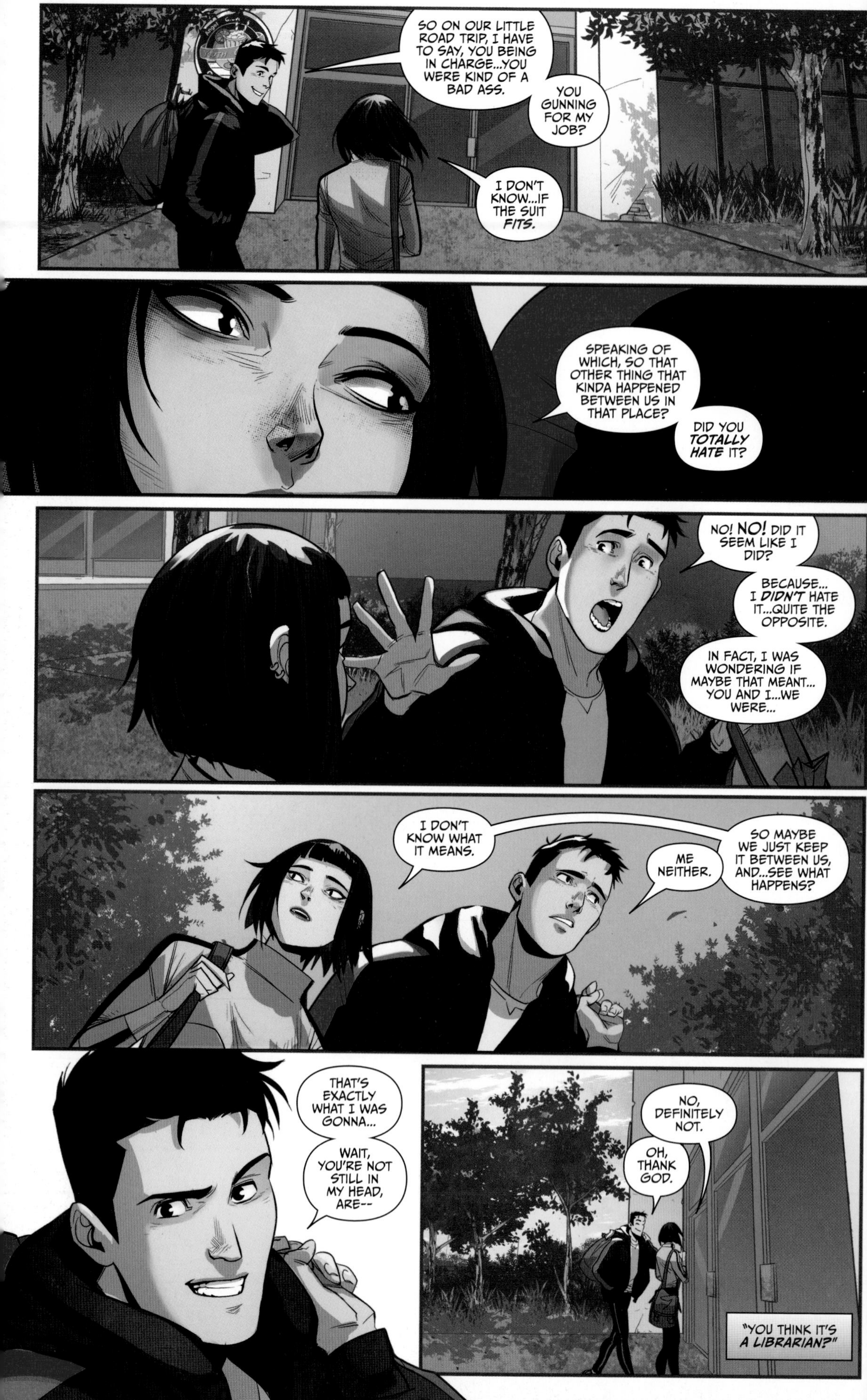
SO ON OUR LITTLE ROAD TRIP, I HAVE TO SAY, YOU BEING IN CHARGE...YOU WERE KIND OF A BAD ASS.
YOU GUNNING FOR MY JOB?
I DON'T KNOW...IF THE SUIT *FITS.*
SPEAKING OF WHICH, SO THAT OTHER THING THAT KINDA HAPPENED BETWEEN US IN THAT PLACE?
DID YOU *TOTALLY HATE* IT?
NO! **NO!** DID IT SEEM LIKE I DID?
BECAUSE... I *DIDN'T* HATE IT...QUITE THE OPPOSITE.
IN FACT, I WAS WONDERING IF MAYBE THAT MEANT... YOU AND I...WE WERE...
I DON'T KNOW WHAT IT MEANS.
ME NEITHER.
SO MAYBE WE JUST KEEP IT BETWEEN US, AND...SEE WHAT HAPPENS?
THAT'S EXACTLY WHAT I WAS GONNA...
WAIT, YOU'RE NOT STILL IN MY HEAD, ARE--
NO, DEFINITELY NOT.
OH, THANK GOD.
"YOU THINK IT'S *A LIBRARIAN?*"

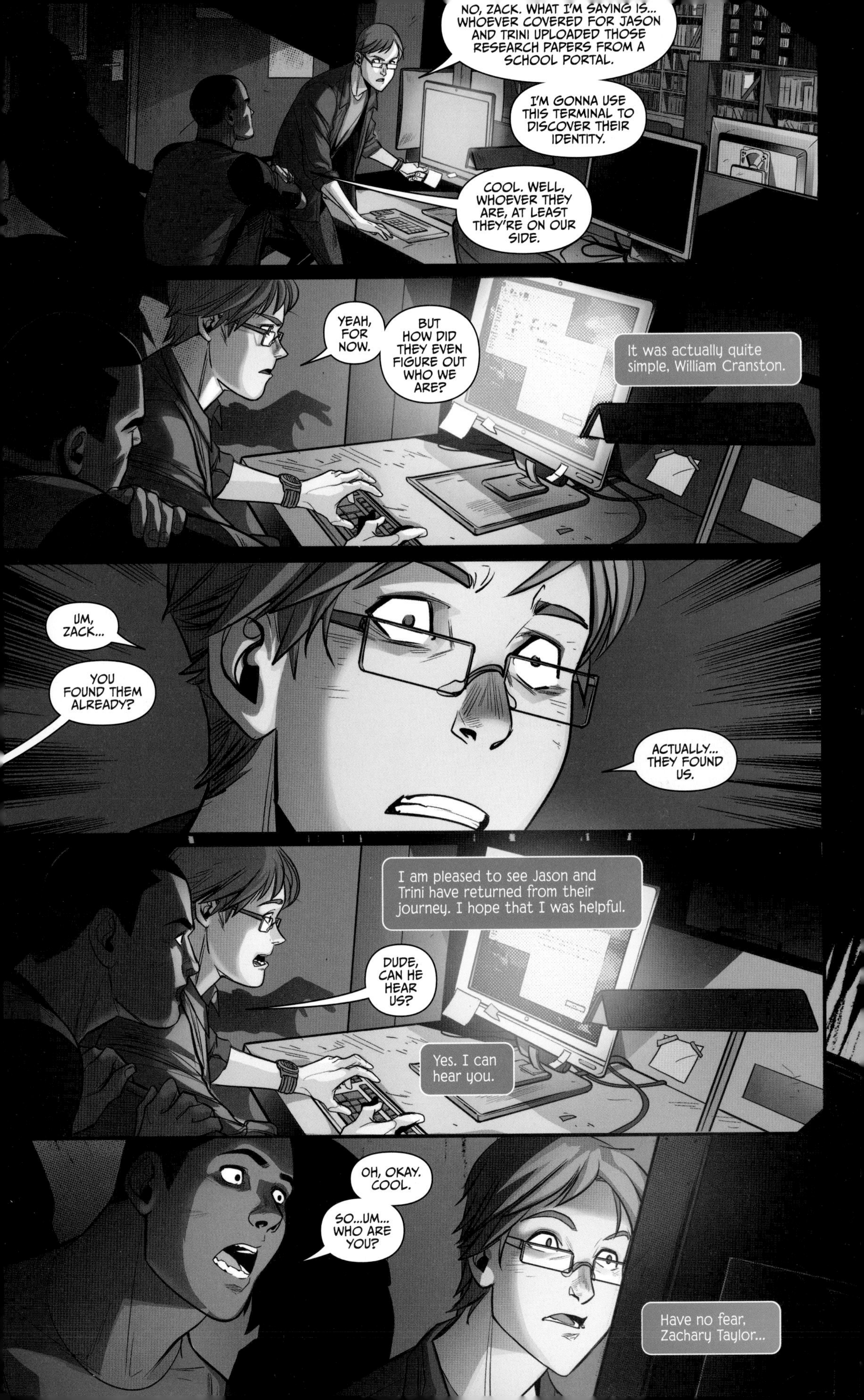
NO, ZACK. WHAT I'M SAYING IS... WHOEVER COVERED FOR JASON AND TRINI UPLOADED THOSE RESEARCH PAPERS FROM A SCHOOL PORTAL.
I'M GONNA USE THIS TERMINAL TO DISCOVER THEIR IDENTITY.
COOL. WELL, WHOEVER THEY ARE, AT LEAST THEY'RE ON OUR SIDE.
YEAH, FOR NOW.
BUT HOW DID THEY EVEN FIGURE OUT WHO WE ARE?
It was actually quite simple, William Cranston.
UM, ZACK...
YOU FOUND THEM ALREADY?
ACTUALLY... THEY FOUND US.
I am pleased to see Jason and Trini have returned from their journey. I hope that I was helpful.
DUDE, CAN HE HEAR US?
Yes. I can hear you.
OH, OKAY. COOL.
SO...UM... WHO ARE YOU?
Have no fear, Zachary Taylor...

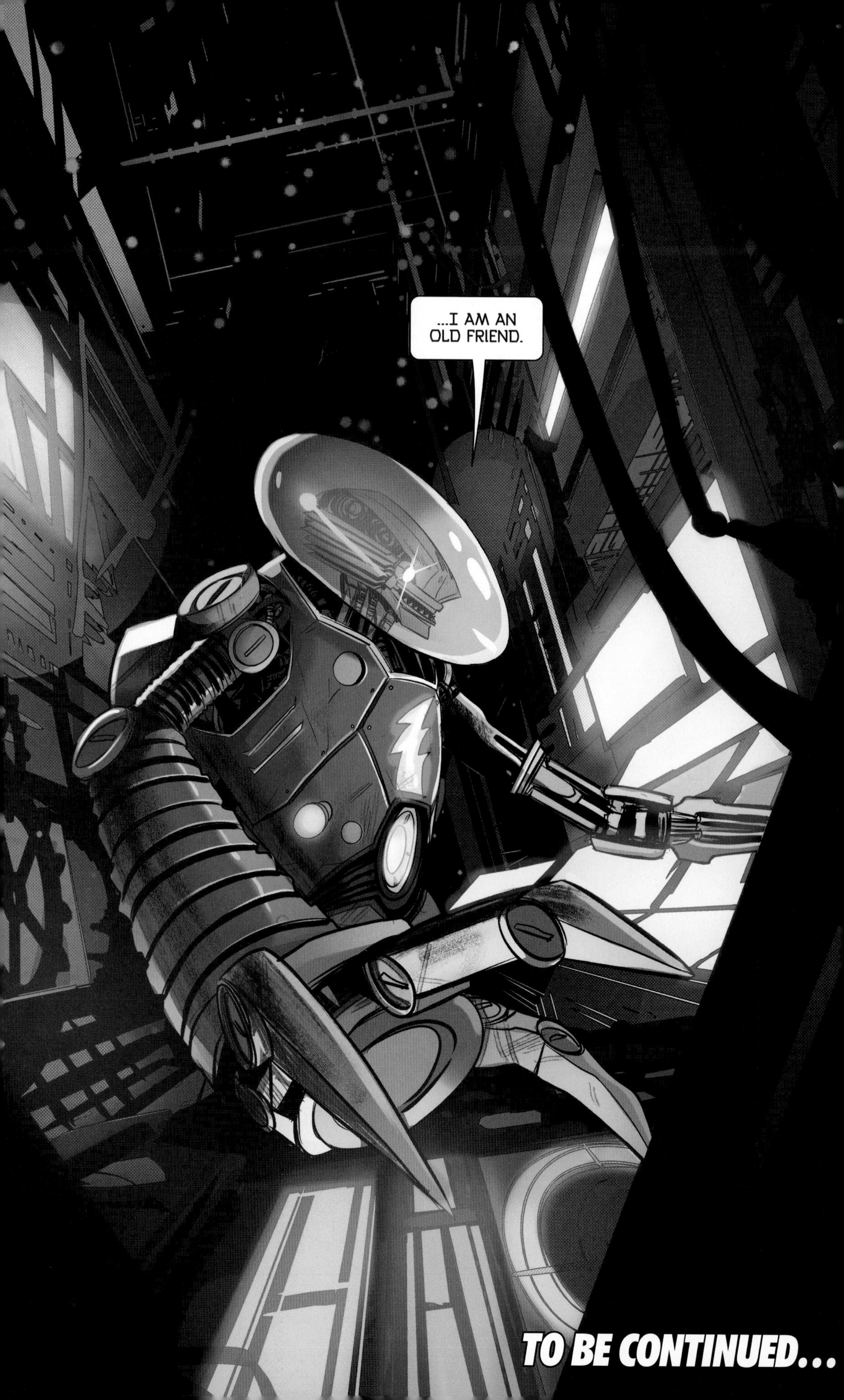
...I AM AN OLD FRIEND.
TO BE CONTINUED...

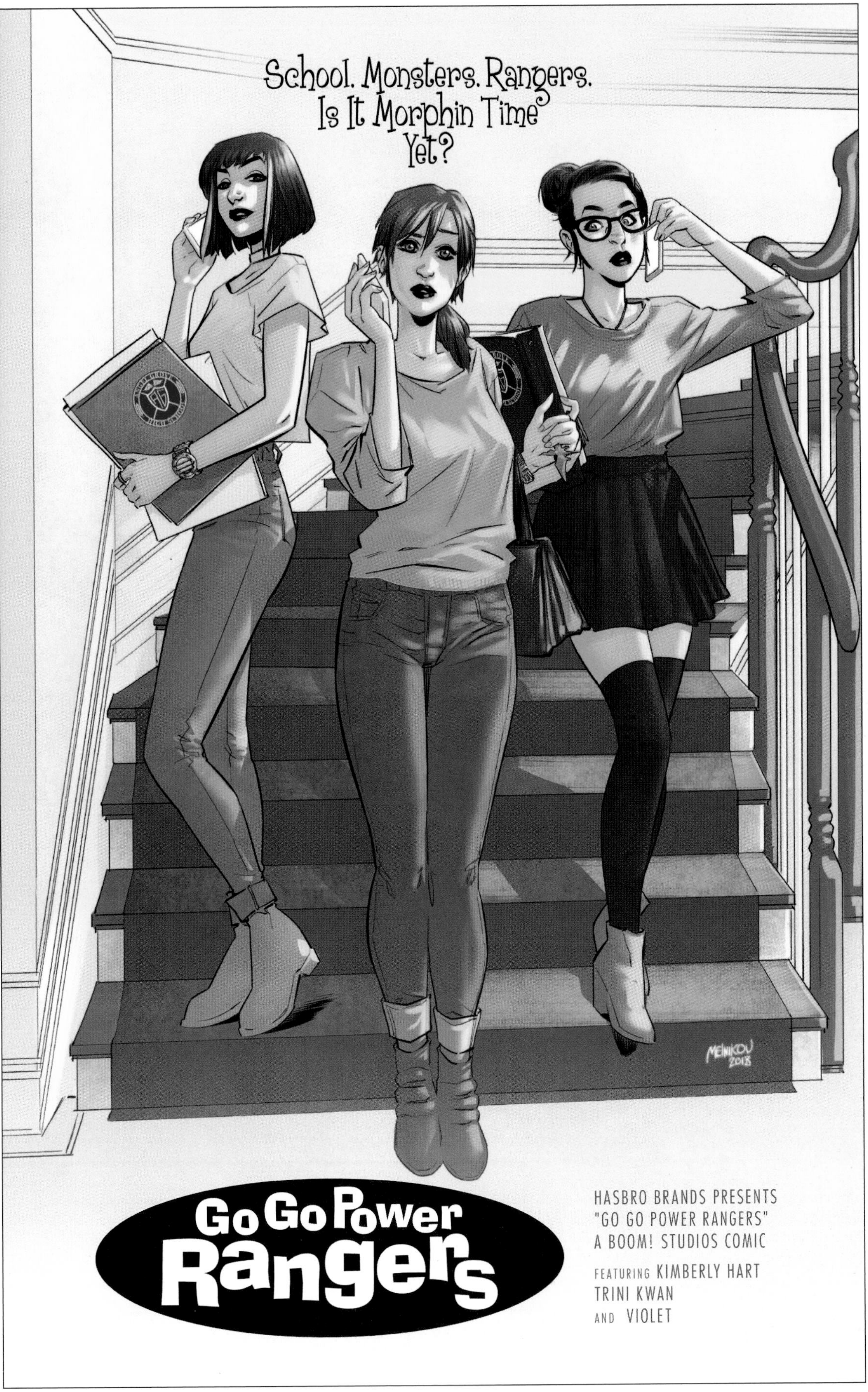
School. Monsters. Rangers.
Is It Morphin Time
Yet?
MELNIKOV 2018
Go Go Power Rangers
HASBRO BRANDS PRESENTS
"GO GO POWER RANGERS"
A BOOM! STUDIOS COMIC
FEATURING KIMBERLY HART
TRINI KWAN
AND VIOLET

GLEB MELNIKOV WITH DESIGN BY **DYLAN TODD** | ISSUE SIXTEEN MOVIE HOMAGE VARIANT

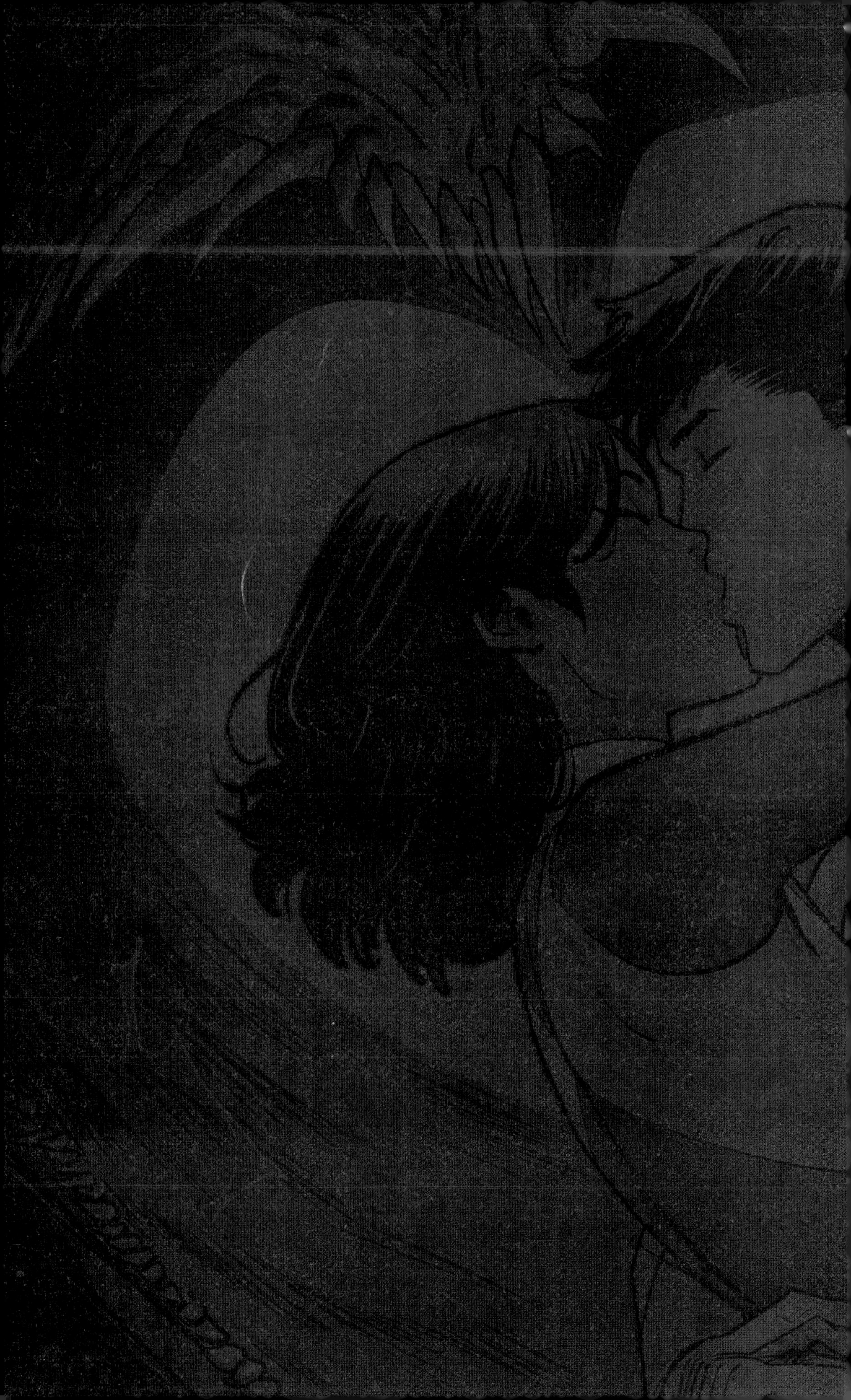

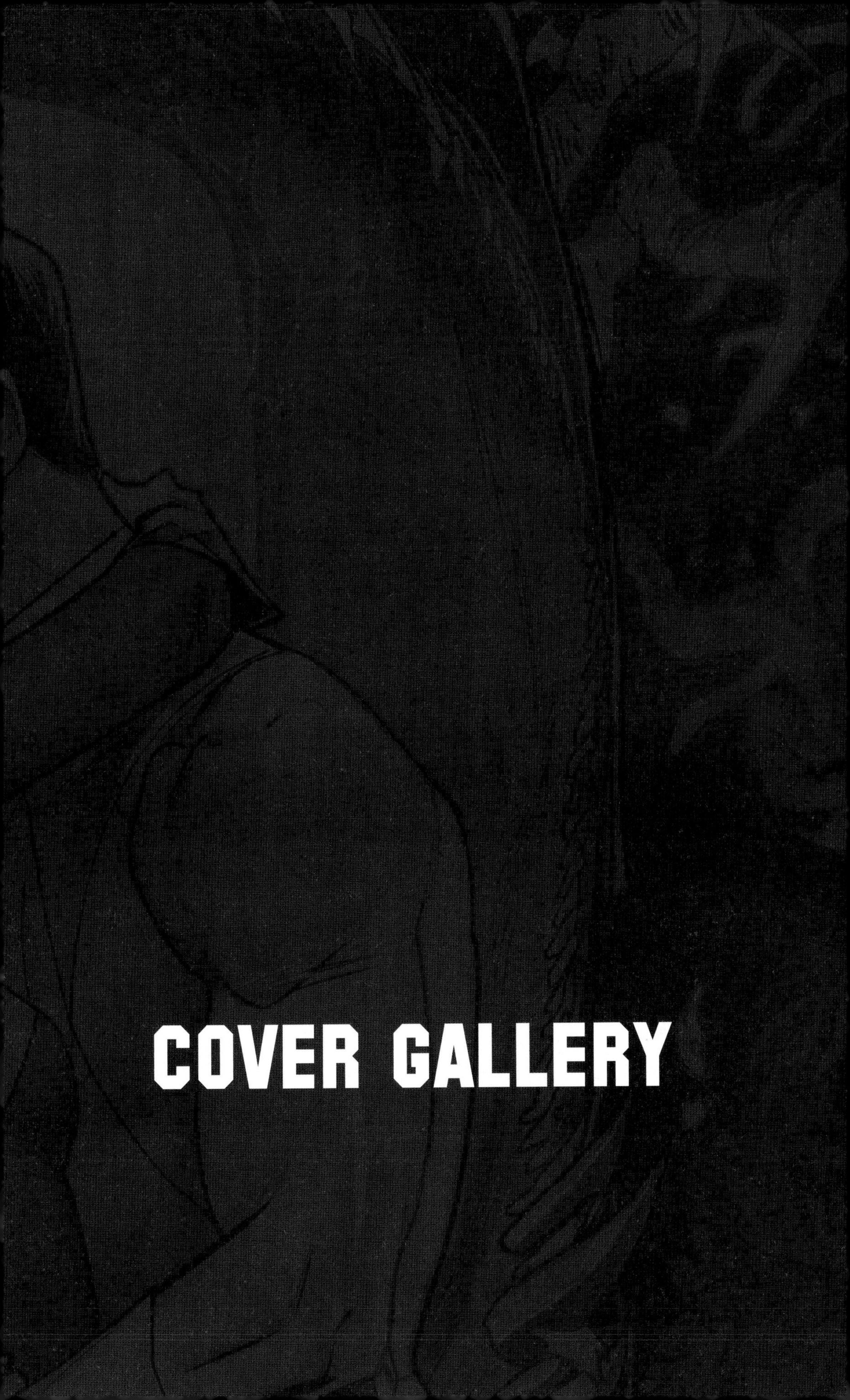

COVER GALLERY

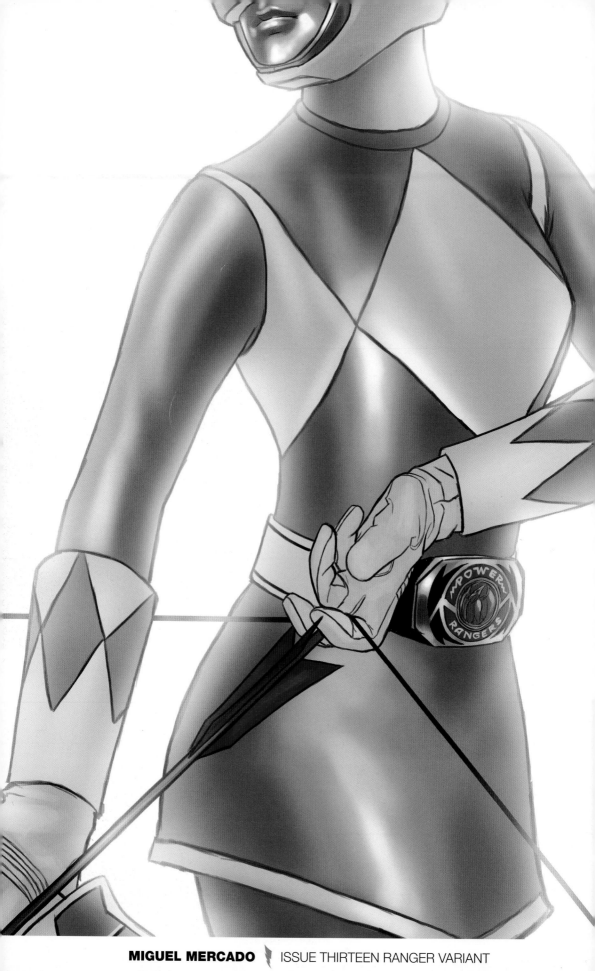

MIGUEL MERCADO ISSUE THIRTEEN RANGER VARIANT

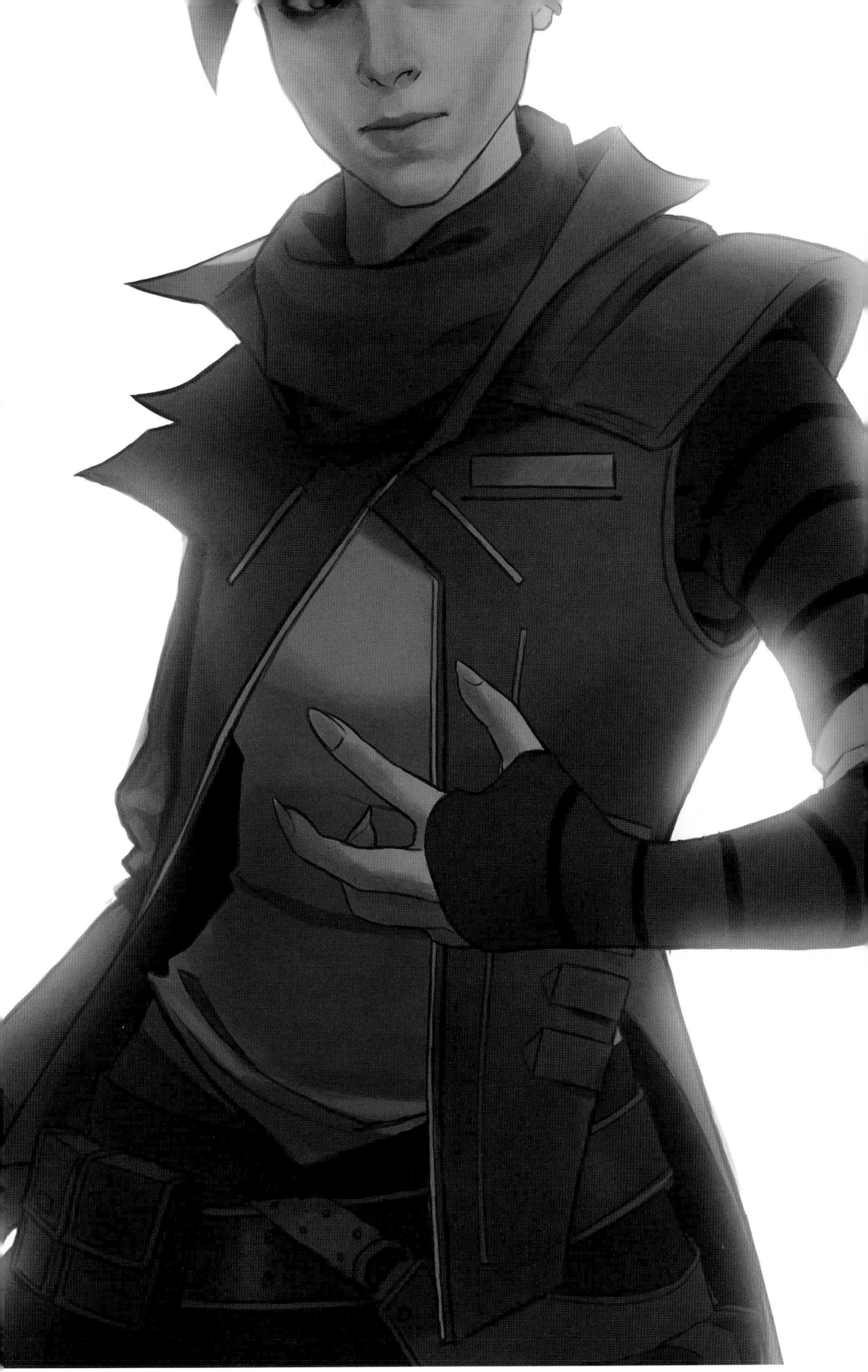

MIGUEL MERCADO ISSUE FOURTEEN RANGER VARIANT

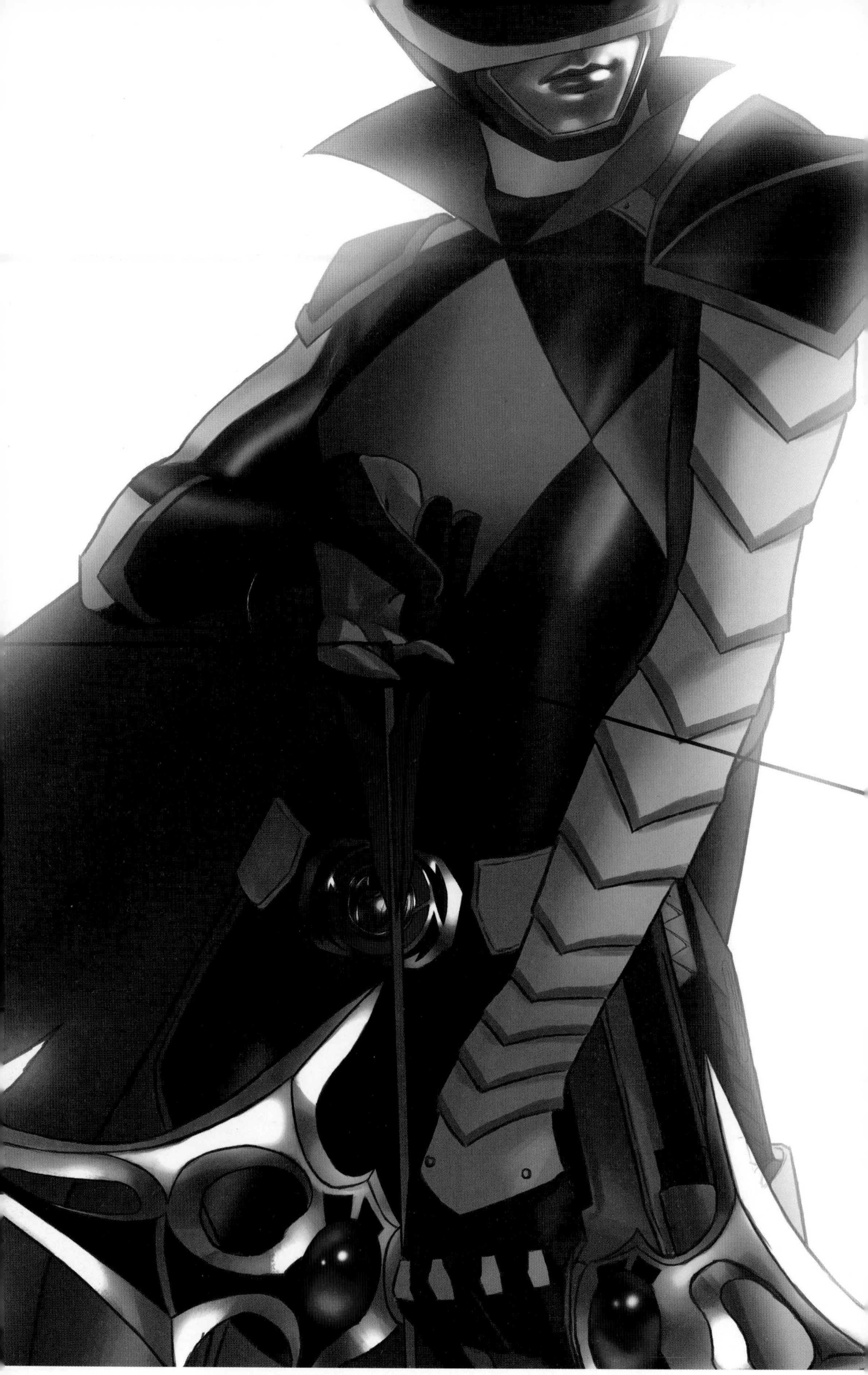

MIGUEL MERCADO ISSUE FIFTEEN RANGER VARIANT

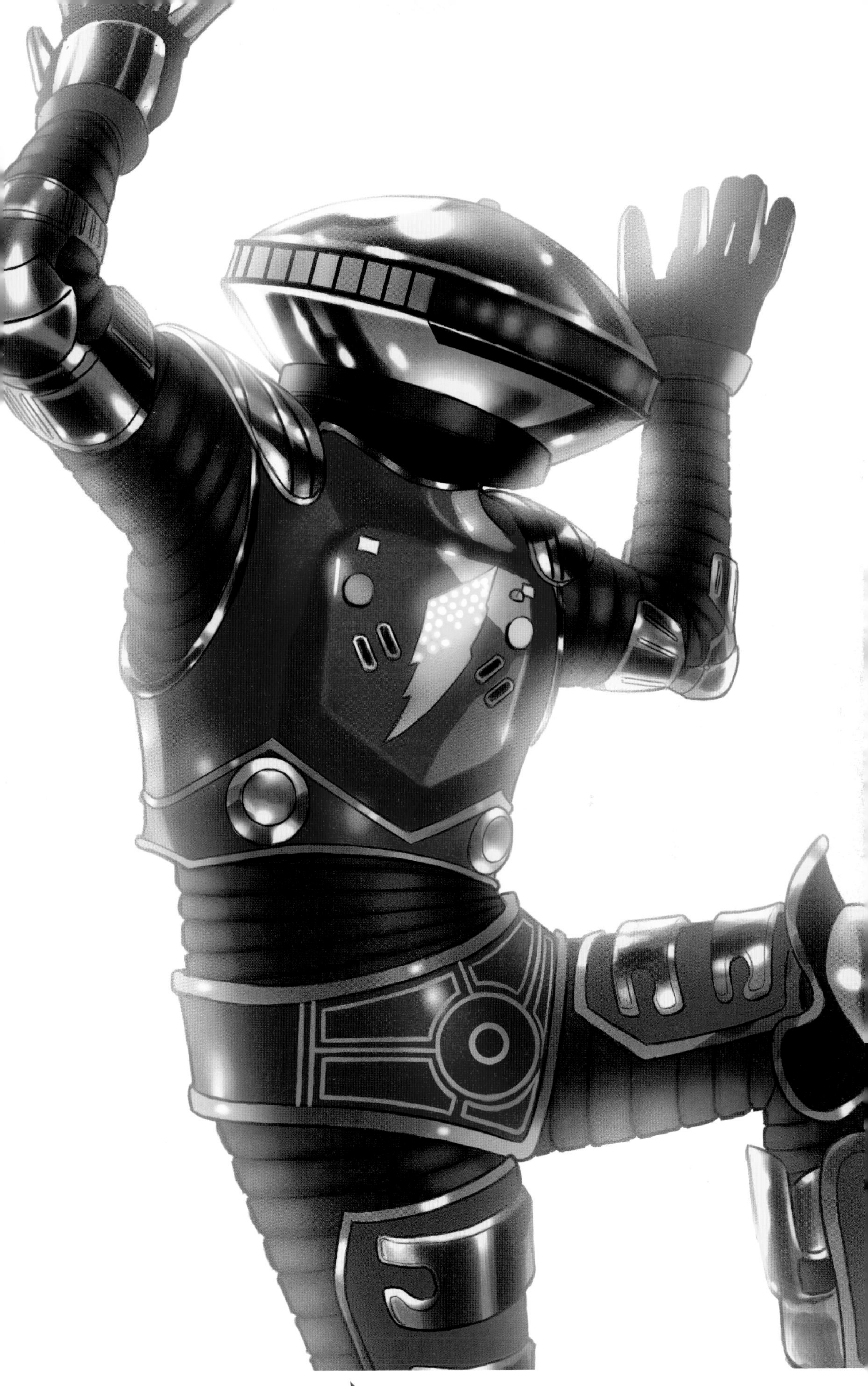

MIGUEL MERCADO ISSUE SIXTEEN CHARACTER VARIANT

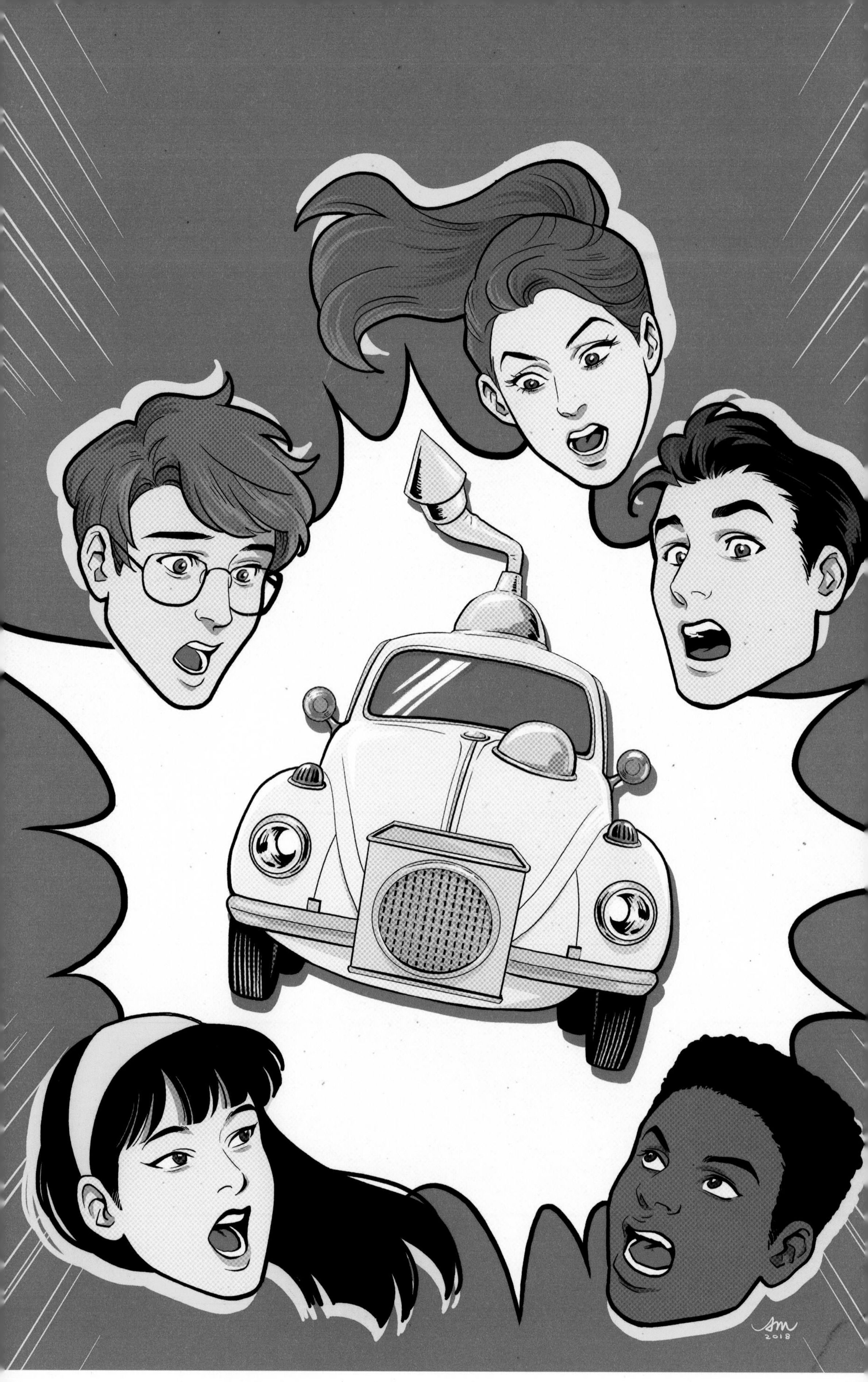
AM
2018

AUDREY MOK | ISSUE THIRTEEN SUBSCRIPTION COVER

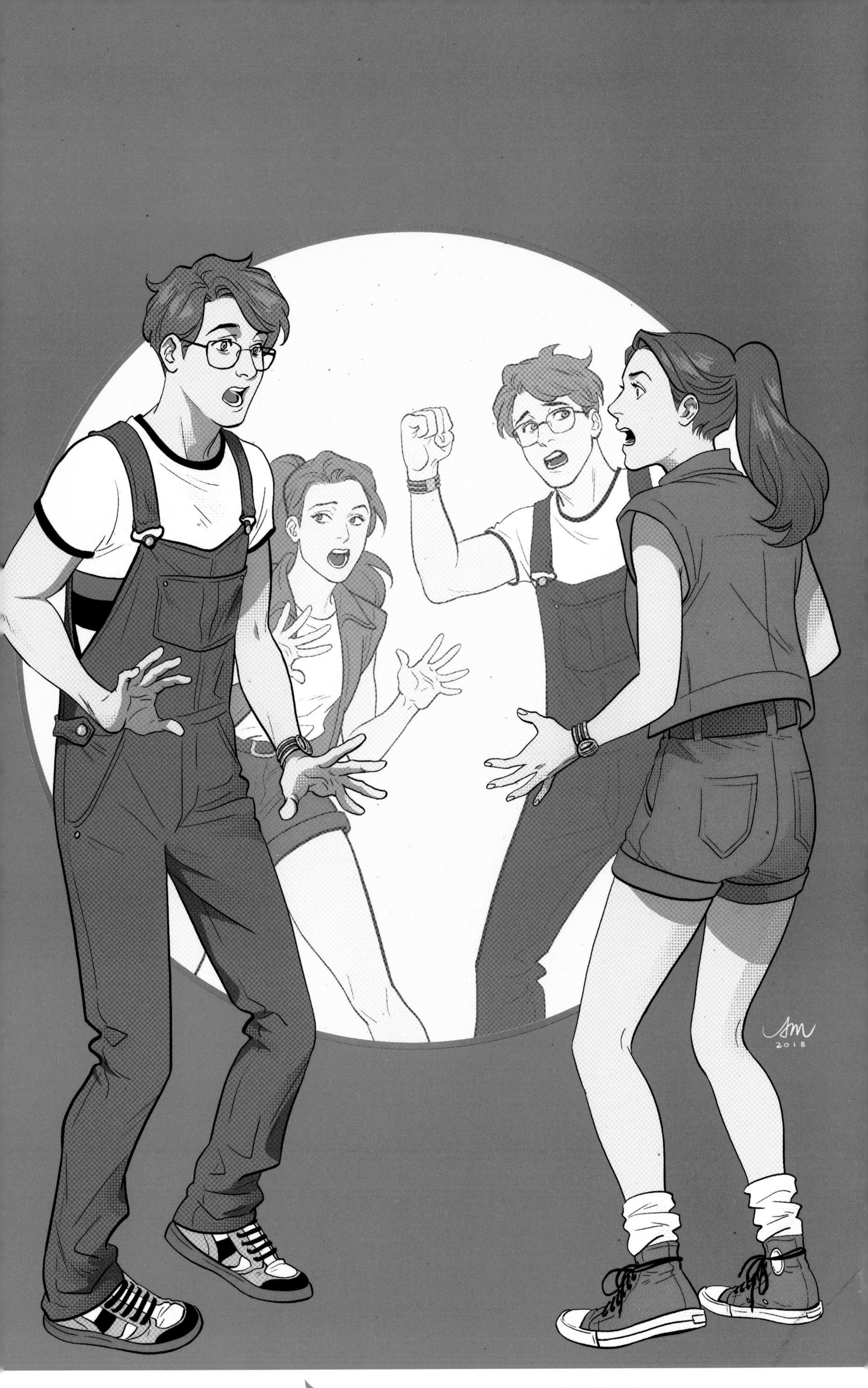

AUDREY MOK ISSUE FOURTEEN SUBSCRIPTION COVER

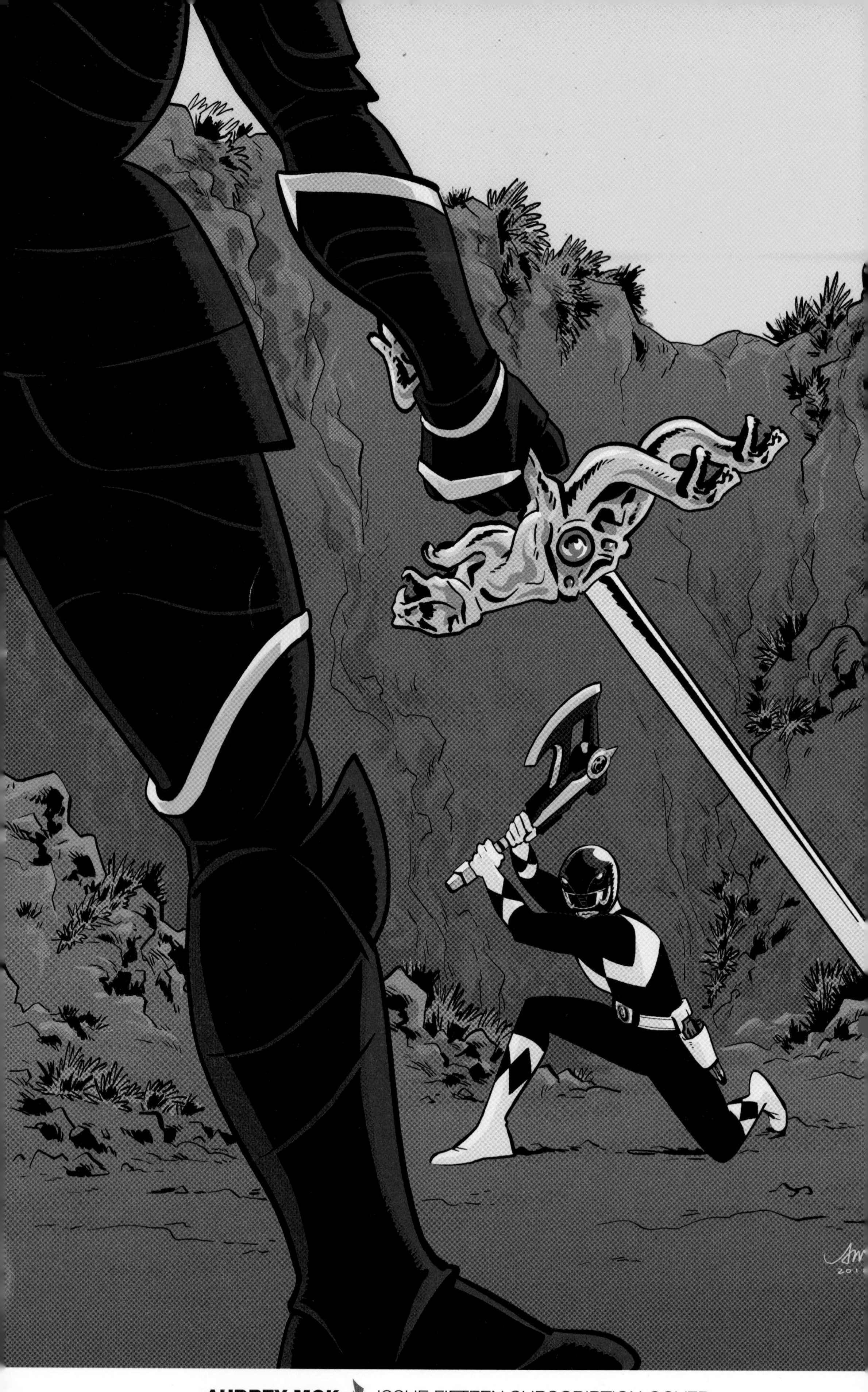

AUDREY MOK ISSUE FIFTEEN SUBSCRIPTION COVER

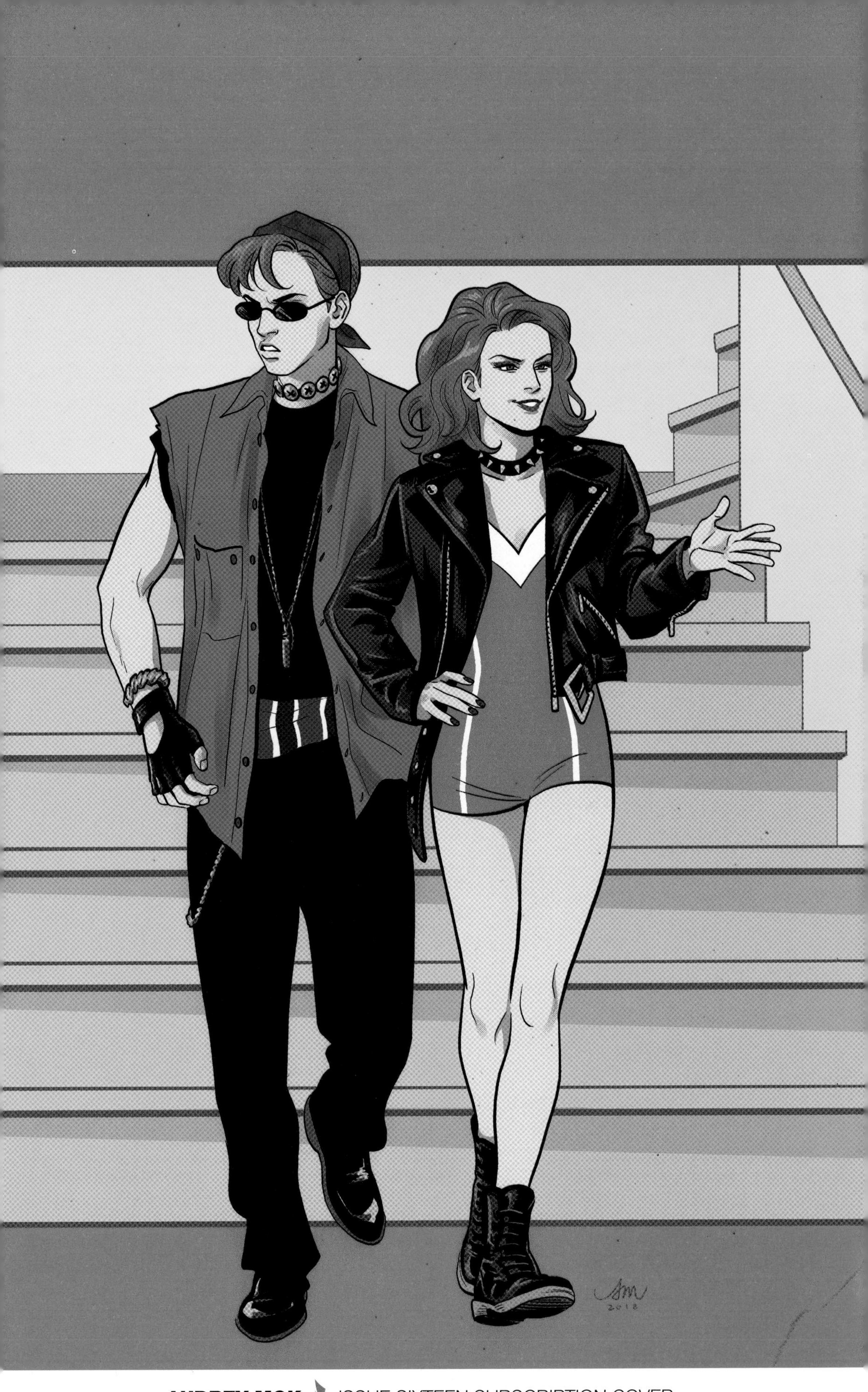

AUDREY MOK ISSUE SIXTEEN SUBSCRIPTION COVER

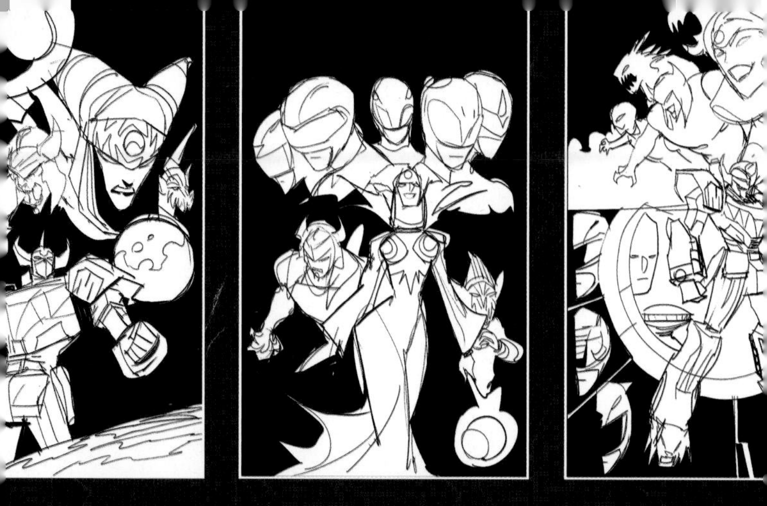

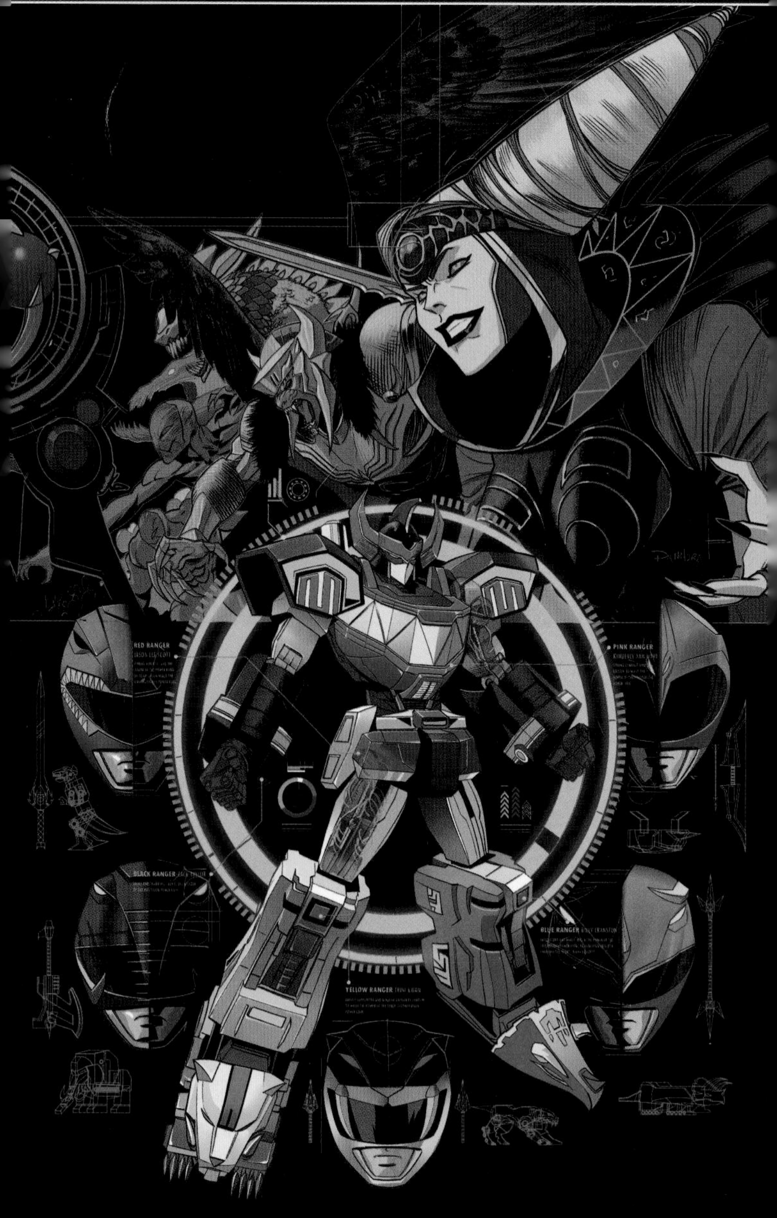
RED RANGER
PINK RANGER
BLACK RANGER
BLUE RANGER
YELLOW RANGER

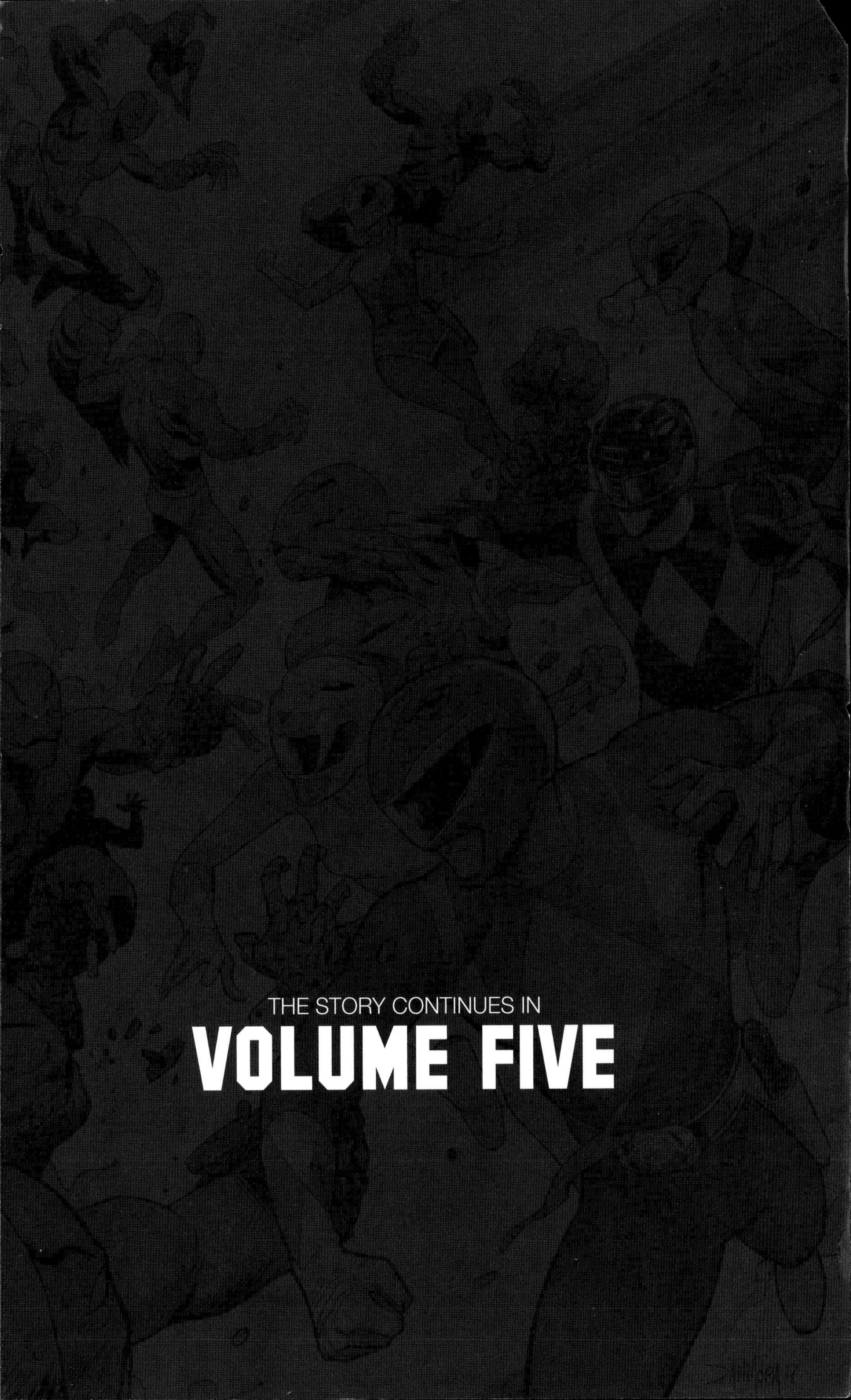
THE STORY CONTINUES IN
VOLUME FIVE

DISCOVER
VISIONARY CREATORS

THE WOODS
JAMES TYNION IV • MICHAEL DIALYNAS
VOL 1 THE ARROW

"The Spire is fantastic! My kind of genre free-for-all." —BRIAN K. VAUGHAN (Saga)
THE SPIRE
SIMON SPURRIER
JEFF STOKELY
ANDRÉ MAY

MARK WAID • PETER KRAUSE
IRREDEEMABLE
AFTERWORD BY GRANT MORRISON

MARK WAID • JEAN DIAZ
INCORRUPTIBLE

MICHAEL ALAN NELSON
DAN MORA
GABRIEL CASSATA
HEXED
THE HARLOT & THE THIEF VOLUME ONE

ABNETT & CULBARD
WILD'S END
FIRST LIGHT
"IT'S REALLY, GREAT!" JEFF LEMIRE

James Tynion IV

The Woods

Volume 1
ISBN: 978-1-60886-454-6 | $9.99 US
Volume 2
ISBN: 978-1-60886-495-9 | $14.99 US
Volume 3
ISBN: 978-1-60886-773-8 | $14.99 US

The Backstagers

Volume 1
ISBN: 978-1-60886-993-0 | $14.99 US

Simon Spurrier

Six-Gun Gorilla

ISBN: 978-1-60886-390-7 | $19.99 US

The Spire

ISBN: 978-1-60886-913-8 | $29.99 US

Weavers

ISBN: 978-1-60886-963-3 | $19.99 US

Mark Waid

Irredeemable

Volume 1
ISBN: 978-1-93450-690-5 | $16.99 US
Volume 2
ISBN: 978-1-60886-000-5 | $16.99 US

Incorruptible

Volume 1
ISBN: 978-1-60886-015-9 | $16.99 US
Volume 2
ISBN: 978-1-60886-028-9 | $16.99 US

Michael Alan Nelson

Hexed The Harlot & The Thief

Volume 1
ISBN: 978-1-60886-718-9 | $14.99 US
Volume 2
ISBN: 978-1-60886-816-2 | $14.99 US

Day Men

Volume 1
ISBN: 978-1-60886-393-8 | $9.99 US
Volume 2
ISBN: 978-1-60886-852-0 | $9.99 US

Dan Abnett

Wild's End

Volume 1: First Light
ISBN: 978-1-60886-735-6 | $19.99 US
Volume 2: The Enemy Within
ISBN: 978-1-60886-877-3 | $19.99 US

Hypernaturals

Volume 1
ISBN: 978-1-60886-298-6 | $16.99 US
Volume 2
ISBN: 978-1-60886-319-8 | $19.99 US

BOOM! STUDIOS™

AVAILABLE AT YOUR LOCAL COMICS SHOP AND BOOKSTORE

To find a comics shop in your area, visit www.comicshoplocator.com

WWW.BOOM-STUDIOS.COM